Tales of
Superhuman
Powers

T0276961

# Tales of Superhuman Powers

## 55 Traditional Stories from Around the World

CSENGE VIRÁG ZALKA

McFarland & Company, Inc., Publishers
*Jefferson, North Carolina, and London*

LIBRARY OF CONGRESS CATALOGUING-IN-PUBLICATION DATA

Zalka, Csenge Virág.
   Tales of superhuman powers : 55 traditional stories from
around the world / Csenge Virág Zalka.
      p.      cm.
   Includes bibliographical references and index.

   **ISBN 978-0-7864-7704-3**
   softcover : acid free paper ∞

   1. Parapsychology.   2. Supernatural.   3. Tales.
I. Title.
BF1031.Z35 2013
398.22—dc23                                    2013029890

BRITISH LIBRARY CATALOGUING DATA ARE AVAILABLE

On the cover: Manuscript illustration from Baysunghur's
*Shahnameh*, "Isfandiyar's first labor: he fights the wolves," 1430
(Gulistan Palace Museum, Tehran, Iran)

Manufactured in the United States of America

*McFarland & Company, Inc., Publishers
   Box 611, Jefferson, North Carolina 28640
   www.mcfarlandpub.com*

# Acknowledgments

It feels like there is at least one person to thank for every single tale included in this collection. It also feels like when it comes to stories that is the way it should be.

First and foremost, I would like to extend my special gratitude to Fulbright Hungary for giving me the opportunity to study storytelling in the United States of America (yes, you can get a master's degree in that) and have a chance to meet so many amazing people involved in this art form.

I would like to thank my mentor and advisor Dr. Joseph Sobol for his help and support in all my academic endeavors. I also owe special thanks to Krisztina Kinga Hoppál for her help with the Chinese sources, Noémi Nagy for the Scandinavian, master storyteller Alton Chung for the Hawaiian, and Lovranits "Rigó" Júlia, storyteller and my long-time writing buddy, for allowing me to tap into her extensive research on the fairy folk. I am eternally grateful for the help with folkloristic details to Veronika Filkó.

Last but not least, I would like to thank my workplace for having their full-time Fulbright scholar storyteller work front desk duty seven hours a day so she could finish her manuscript. I could not have done it without them.

# Contents

## Part II: It's All in Your Head — Mind Games, Mental Prowess, and the Power of Knowledge

## Part III: At the Mercy of the Elements — Powers of Water, Fire, Earth and Weather (and Ice)

## Part IV: Transitional Powers — From One State to Another

# Introduction: Greetings, Dreamer

Let's play a little game.

I'll say: "This book is about folktales with superpowers in them."

And you'll say: "Uh-huh... Wait, what?"

What do comic books, blockbuster movies, and videogames have to do with oral storytelling?

What indeed.

One day at work I was supposed to tell stories to a group of boys between the ages of 6 and 12, hopped up on pre–Halloween candy and instant mischief. Educational purposes thrown out the window, I told them we will be talking about heroes, and asked them to name a few.

No reaction.

I tried again: "Come on guys, you must know at least one!" Someone in the back row said, suddenly very shy: "Um ... like, you mean, like Superman?" They are just not used to Superman being the answer. "Exactly like Superman," I said. The levee broke, and I was flooded with Marvel and DC and the odd Indiana Jones and Assassin's Creed. Suddenly everyone had something to say. When they quieted down I asked them if they have ever heard about a guy named Thor.

For the next five days, I was the coolest person on the planet... Well, the second coolest. After Thor.

Anyway, my point is: these kids live and breathe popular culture. They *are* popular culture. And this is a great help to all of us when we are choosing stories and hoping to capture their attention, imagination, and enthusiasm. All those comics, movies and games are giving us clues to what kids like. Then it is only a matter of a storyteller's creativity to sneak them treats of our own design.

Let's not stop at children, though. When I became a professional storyteller, my mother, who teaches high school English, offered her classes as guinea pigs for my strange ambition of a career. Despite the warnings and the pitiful looks from seasoned teachers, I found teens to be not only responsive to folktales and

1

legends, but also highly creative, fun, and every bit as sensitive and enthusiastic as fifth grade and below. Nobody needs brave heroes, independent heroines and challenging adventures like people on the verge of adult life.

In fact, everyone needs heroes. Stories speak to all ages, and there is no bad audience for a good story. (I am still not sure about middle school though. Those kids eat you alive.)

Most superpowers that keep popping up on the big screen, the television screen and on the brightly colored pages of comic books are not *nearly* new at all. In fact, there are many myths, legends and folktales out there that feature the exact same supernatural abilities, and the heroes that take on the responsibility that comes with them. They are etched into our minds, sometimes in runes, sometimes in color and ink, and they all represent the dreams of humanity. Tales about flight drove us to invent the airplane and make wings for ourselves. Tales about strength continue to inspire people to excel in sports and take good care of their bodies. Tales about great magical powers teach us to keep learning, but also warn us about the consequences of taking our powers lightly. Time and time again, people dream of being special. Unique. Gifted. These dreams and hopes are the seeds that grow into tales all over the world, and even if they put on new names and new costumes, in the end, they have been with us since we first mastered the use of flame.

Let's try that game again.

This book is a collection of folktales with superpowers in them.

Pick your favorite, and let's delve right in.

## Rules That Are Not Rules

In order to make my life easier (or harder, depending on how you want to look at it), I set a few ground rules for selecting stories for this book. None of them are carved in stone anywhere; they merely serve the purpose of keeping me from wandering off the path and getting lost in the endless wilderness of tales. I tend to ... Look, a squirrel! They are also pretty useful for narrowing down the selections in the cases where I had too many stories to choose from.

So, before we get to the tales, here are the

### Unofficial and Thoroughly Subjective Guidelines for Superpowers in Storytelling:

**1. A superpower is a supernatural abnormality in a person**

This means that you ain't special if everyone else has it. Superpowers make people special. That is the general idea. Also, if they are simply a talent that you happen to have, they are not "super." However talented you are at playing the guitar, that will make you a star, not a superhero. It is important to note the difference.

## 2. Stay away from divinity

If you are a god with divine powers ... you are a god with divine powers. Refer to Guideline No. 1. In most cases, if I could find a story with a mortal, or at least half-human, hero in it, that story took precedence over deities of various mythologies. Simply because if you are a god, lifting heavy things is just not that impressive anymore. Superheroes in popular culture cheerfully break this rule left and right, and so will I. But pssst.

## 3. Look for treasure

I made extra effort to choose stories that are less well known to the general public. Nobody likes to hear the same well-worn tales over and over again, and why would you buy a new book anyway if it is full of stories you can easily find elsewhere? Given my own Hungarian heritage and the places I have visited as a storyteller, I gathered stories that are less well known, or not available in English translation, in order to bring in something new. Some of them might be confusing, thought-provoking, or downright weird. You are welcome.

## 4. Do not mess with powers you don't have

Even though the stories in this book are traditional tales retold in my own words and sometimes adjusted to my own style, I have never messed with the powers in them. Sometimes it would have been easy to give supernatural powers to well-known folktale characters, sit back, and watch what happens, but that is not the point of this collection. Simply put, I did not feel the need to do that, when there are so many original tales out there where people have done the creative work for me hundreds of years ago. My goal is not to create new superhero tales (not now, anyway) but to show you what has been out there for a long time, ready to be found and re-told.

## 5. Magic is not a superpower

Being a wizard does not a superhero make. This is another thing that is not a hard-and-fast rule, rather a general guideline, given the number of magical people in folklore (it's a big number). If I started filling this book with wizards and witches, they would soon overpower (pun intended) the general public of single-ability heroes, and then the book would be about something else. Magic, mostly. So *unless* their magic was very well defined and specific, I just put those stories away for another project. Sorry, Dr. Strange.

## 6. A superpower has to be consciously controlled, or at least managed, by the hero

This one rules out stories where the magic simply *happens to* someone. Being turned into stone and back by someone else does not mean you have the *ability* to turn into stone. Being a cursed frog does not make you a frog shifter. Being put together by someone else and revived does not mean you have a healing factor. A hero has to *own* his or her powers and use them at will, or at least manage them in some way, in order to qualify. We like active heroes and heroines. They are much more fun.

### 7. Shifting has to work both ways

Shape-shifting is undoubtedly one of the most common abilities in folktales and legends. People turn into animals, plants, and other people all the time. But when you start looking at the stories more closely, a lot of them are about people being *turned* into things, rather than doing it themselves (see the previous point). Also, if you only change once, even if at free will, and stay like that for the rest of your life, that is not really shape-shifting ... well, technically, it is. It is just not what I had in mind.

### 8. Past and future tales

When looking at the endless list of possible supernatural powers that people have come up with since the beginning of time, my main goal was to find the ones that continue being popular. In order to show what captured the minds of people hundreds of years ago, and still manages to do so in this day and age, I selected powers that show up both in folklore and in popular culture. I also have to admit I have an ulterior motive with this: I want to educate people through these tales, and in my career as a storyteller I have found that stories capture the imagination easier if we have something to relate them to. So the tales you will find in this collection all deal with supernatural abilities that managed to make the transition into the popular stories of our age, including comics, games, and visual media.

### 9. Tellable tales

As a storyteller by profession, I know that written stories always need to be translated back into live telling. For that reason I tried to use the language that I normally use when I tell these tales. This will cut from the fancy language and the dialogues, but in exchange I can guarantee you that all the tales in this book have been told, tried, polished and tested with live audiences. It does not mean, of course, that they will not need your ingenuity and experience to become even better. Quite the opposite. Please play with them all you want.

### 10. No capes, no boots, no gadgets

This one is an "if possible" rule: When it came down to a story where the hero's ability is stored in a magical item (seven league boots) and another one where he/she possesses the power (runs really fast), I always chose the latter. Of course there wasn't always a choice. Then again, if one looks at the crowds of modern superheroes, they are not always "born with it" either.

**+1 "Oh, and if possible, try to do something heroic."**

I believe this goes without saying, but I will write it down anyway: one of the main rules that I set for myself for selecting these tales was that they had to be *fun*, good stories. Heroes have to be heroic, adventures have to be exciting, endings have to be satisfying, and listeners have to be inspired. As I have mentioned before, superpowers make people special. But in the end, it is what you *do* with them that makes the story live on for generations to come.

## Introduction to the Aarne-Thompson numbers

There are two kinds of numbers that will keep making guest appearances throughout this book: One is for folktale types, and the other is for story motifs. They are to folklorists what the periodic table is for chemists, or latitude and longitude for geographers. With a little bit of practice, anyone can use them to track stories across cultures.

Folktale type numbers look like this: AaTh 510A (Cinderella). Sometimes in English publications the letters are AT instead of AaTh, but both abbreviations stand for the same thing: the last names of the two people, Antti Aarne and Stith Thompson, who created this classification system for folktales. Sometimes they are marked ATU, which stands for Aarne-Thompson-Uther and refers to the updated edition by Hans-Jörg Uther in 2004.

If one identifies the number a certain tale belongs to, one can use that number to search for other versions of the same story. Many of them are digitized and available on the Internet, and folktale collections, unless they are written for children or purely for entertainment purposes, usually note the numbers as well. There are publications that specialize in collecting the many versions of one particular folktale type — since folklorists around the world use these numbers, one can track Cinderella (or another hero of choice) around the globe and through the centuries.

Folktale motif numbers look like this: B11 (Dragon). They are a combination of letters and numbers, in which the letter stands for a general category (Animals, Magic, Tests, etc.) and the number for one particular motif. This system was also created by Stith Thompson. Instead of assigning one number to an entire folktale, it breaks stories down into smaller parts. These numbers were incredibly useful during the creation of this book — most of the superhuman powers included have their own motif numbers that can be used for tracking down folktales which include them. Because one particular motif can show up in many different stories in many different contexts, searching by motif yields more (and more diverse) results than searching by folktale type.

Once you get the hang of using the AaTh system, an entire new world opens up for story-hunting. Sometimes during my research I downright felt like Indiana Jones as I followed the mysterious numbers and symbols back in time through library books, online archives, and old copies of folklore journals. I included them in this book in case someone wanted to take a sudden turn and wander off in search of a shiny piece of folklore that caught their eye.

## Character Sheet for a Folktale

Mostly because in my free time I like to play role-playing games, and that is the kind of hobby that seeps into one's view on storytelling, I decided to follow the gamer approach in organizing information for this book. In most role-playing games you work with a character sheet that includes all that people need to know about your character in the story. So, in order to make sure this book is not only entertaining, but also useful and arranged in an at-a-glance format, I came up with my own little system for presenting the tales.

Here is what you need to know about it:

*Similar heroes*: This is the place where I note the contemporary cousins of heroes in the story. Some you might be familiar with, others might be more obscure. Sometimes I also included some well-known villains. All in all, this is where tradition meets popular culture.

*Title*: The title of the story. Folktales usually do not have titles — those were invented by people who wrote them down and needed labels to organize. Titles in this book are no exception.

*Ability*: The supernatural power presented in the story. Might be more than one if it's a good catch — also, the listed powers might belong to several different characters.

For a complete list of tales organized by powers, see Tales by Powers at the end of the book.

*Source of power*: Heroes can receive their powers in many different ways. There will be stories where abilities are bestowed upon someone by a god or goddess (divine); sometimes they come from an enchanted object, other times they are a special gift granted by a helpful animal or edible plant (natural). It is always interesting to note the sources people associated with special powers.

*Origin*: The origin of the story, cultural and geographical, and sometimes even temporal (because you can never have enough fancy words in a publication).

*Teachings*: Also known as "here is what I like about this story." Useful bits and pieces that help convince people that, as Maynard Moose says, stories are not just "mindless entertainment."

*Age group*: The ages the story can be told (or adapted) for. As a storyteller I don't like putting a "maximum" age on stories, but some of them do require a minimum, if not for blood, gore and sex, then because some of these tales are quite complicated and unsupervised young children might get lost in the story-line. Do not let this stop you from adapting the tales, though, if you work with a particularly superhero-savvy group of kindergarteners. It has happened to me before.

*Sources*: The actual sources of the story. Books, websites, manuscripts, inform-ants, treasure chests, and other trustworthy wells of knowledge. I note these for people who would like to read the fabled "Original."

*Variants*: Notes on tale types, motifs, and variants of the tale, in case you want to build your own version from scratch.

*Text*: The actual story. Finally.

*Comments*: My notes and comments on the tale. Might be a very eclectic selec-tion of opinions and side notes and footnotes and margin notes, but I promise one thing: I will let you know what I changed in the story, so you don't confuse my own version with that of "the folk."

# PART I

# Physical Powers — Also Known as the Classics

## SUPERHUMAN STRENGTH

Basic powers are basic.

Strength is one of the most common abilities both in folklore and in popular culture. Who has not wished at one point or another to be able to do more than what our bodies are capable of? Human strength is limited, and that is the exact reason why dreams and stories are not.

This section could overflow in a second with heroes of legendary strength like Hercules or Cú Chulainn, so I had to be extra careful with the selections, to show the range and variety of superhuman physical strength. I wanted to include physically strong female characters as well as male heroes, for example, and show the many different origins of powers.

The Thompson Folktale Motifs for extraordinary physical strength are F610 (Remarkably Strong Man) and F565.2 (Remarkably Strong Woman). They show up in a great number of different folktales all around the world.

*(Some) Similar Heroes with superhuman strength:* Asterix and Obelix, Colossus (Marvel), Hulk (Marvel), Mr. Incredible (*The Incredibles*), Molly Hayes (Marvel), Monet St. Croix (Marvel), Nicki/Jessica Sanders (NBC's *Heroes*), Supergirl (DC), Superman (DC), The Thing (Marvel), Thor (Marvel), Wonder Woman (DC)

### *János and Rózsa*

*Ability:* Superhuman strength, stainless steel protection shell (keep reading), magical healing powers, withering touch

*Source of power:* Unknown

*Origin:* Roma (Gypsy) tradition from Transylvania

*Teachings:* Bravery, friendship and brotherhood, honesty, sacrifice, life is an adventure.

*Age group:* 12+

*Sources:* Nagy, O., and J. Vekerdi (2002). *A gömböcfiú: Edélyi cigány mesék.* Budapest: Terebess Kiadó.

This tale has been collected by Olga Nagy in the 1970s, recorded both in the Romani and Hungarian languages. The storyteller was Gyula Dávid, 52.

*Variants:* This is a piece of a much longer folktale, quilted together from several different story types. In this form I have not encountered it in any other source — the bar fight scene seems quite unique. The main reason why it is included in this section is the piece known as AaTh 519 (Strong Woman as a Bride), where the groom's magically strong helper defeats the bride in a feat of strength before he hands her over. This story exists in many different forms internationally, the most well-known being the story of Brünhilde in *Das Niebelungenlied.*

*Text:* Once upon a time there were two brothers: the older was called Rózsa, the younger János. Their father raised them alone in great poverty, until one day Rózsa decided to go out and seek his fortune. It would take a long time to tell about all the adventures he had in the service of the king, fighting knights and chasing fairy maidens — let us just say he soon became famous for his extraordinary strength and his bravery. With the gold he won for his services, Rózsa did not only make his fortune, but also made sure that his family did not have to live in poverty anymore. Now his younger brother János could afford a sword and a new set of armor, and he could go out to find adventures of his own.

The road János chose to take led him to the kingdom of the Red King, right to the royal city, glowing in all the colors of fire, that was more splendid than any other place he had ever seen. Right by the city gates there was a royal inn for travelers. As soon as János stepped across the threshold twenty-four waiters appeared out of nowhere, all bowing and waiting on his orders. He took a seat by a table, and asked for food and drinks. They roasted an ox just for him, and rolled a barrel of wine up from the cellar; he ate and drank his fill, and when he looked around, he saw that all the other travelers in the inn were avoiding his gaze, and staying respectfully away.

Suddenly, there was a loud bang as the door of the inn burst open, and in walked the Iron Knight, one of the most famous champions of the kingdom. He walked straight to János's table.

"Good day," he said.

"Good day to you too," answered János. "I have been wishing to meet you for a very long time. Come, join me, I still have food left."

They ate, drank, and talked, and by the time the food was all gone, János turned to the Iron Knight. "Let us become sworn brothers, and seek adventures together. What do you say?"

The Iron Knight agreed, and they swore on their swords to become brothers.

Not long after, the door opened once again, and in walked another famous champion: the Son of the Wind. He greeted János and the Iron Knight, and joined them at the table. They ordered more food and drinks, and soon Son of the Wind was accepted into the brotherhood. Next came the Son of the Sun, and then the Golden Prince, both famous champions themselves. By this time empty plates and barrels towered around the table...

... and then some new guests walked in. Three demons from the Kingdom of Darkness, one with seven heads, one with fourteen, one with twenty-seven.

"The three princes of the Kingdom of Darkness," whispered Son of the Sun, and everyone else in the inn looked away.

But even the demons were not the last ones to arrive. This time, the door burst open from a kick, and in marched the three worst troublemakers in the world: the Knight of Bones, the Knight of Wood, and the Knight of Mold. They marched over to a table, demanding food and entertainment. The musicians played for them like the world was ending, until the Knight of Mold slammed his fist on the table for silence, and leaned over to the Knight of Wood: "Brother, look at those demons over there. I dare you to go and slap one in the face."

The Knight of Wood stood, walked over to the demons, and slapped the youngest one in the face ... in that second, the demon collapsed into a pile of ashes and dust. The two others jumped up from their seats, but in the same second the Knight of Mold was by their side, and with a single touch of his hands, he turned both of them to dust. In the frozen silence that followed, the troublemakers walked over to the table where the newly sworn brothers were sitting. János had just left them for a moment before the trouble started, to go relieve himself.

"And who are you, champions?" Knight of Mold demanded to know. "Why did you not introduce yourselves to us?"

"We did not want to get in your way," said the Iron Knight very politely.

The Knight of Mold sneered. "You dare talk back to me?!" And with a touch of his hand, he turned the Iron Knight into a pile of rust. The brothers jumped up, and a fight broke out, but none of them were a match for Mold's powers. The Golden Prince was left last. He tried to run and warn János, but he never made it out the door. Once all the champions were gone, the troublemakers turned to the innkeeper's young daughter.

"Sing for us!" They yelled, dragging her out from behind the bar, "Sing for us, little bird! If you do not sing, we will turn the whole house into dust!"

The girl, terrified as she was, started to sing in a clear, beautiful voice. While the troublemakers were cheering her on, in walked János through the back door, and he knew exactly what had happened. As soon as he appeared the girl jumped off the table they stood her on, and ran over to his side seeking protection.

"Do not worry, little sister," János whispered to her, "Just stay by my side."

With that, he breathed out, and a shell of steel encircled the inn. There was no way in, and no way out.

"You are done," he said to the troublemakers. "You cannot leave this inn anymore. Now you will pay for all the evil you have done, all the people you have hurt, all the sadness you have caused!"

"Is that all you can do?" laughed the Knight of Wood. "I can break through this wall with one punch!"

And as he said that, he punched the wall ... but did not even put a dent in it. The Knight of Bones and the Knight of Mold tried as well, tried hard enough that they almost broke their own hands, but the steel shell held out. They started to realize that János had power that matched their own. They fell to their knees, asking for forgiveness.

"You cannot give back all the people you killed, why should I forgive you?" asked János.

"We can, we can!" They all cried, "Look!"

And, breathing onto the piles of ashes, they brought back to life the Iron Knight, the Son of the Wind, and the rest of the brothers, and even the three demons they had killed. Once that was done, János nodded.

"You have done enough trouble in here. Let us go outside."

With that, he grabbed all three troublemakers with one hand and dragged them outside for everyone to see. While people were gaping at his strength, he grabbed them one by one by their ankles, and threw them across the town back to where they came from. The Knight of Mold landed in his own backyard, on top of a tree, and then fell to the ground, where his mother found him.

"Who has done this to you, my darling?!"

"It was a champion called János, stronger than the three of us together."

"No wonder he is," the mother nodded. "János is your cousin, just like the Knight of Wood and the Knight of Bones. His mother is my sister, the oldest of four. She has always been the strongest. Did I not tell you that you were going to get into trouble one day with someone even you cannot defeat?"

Back at the inn, János decided he had enough adventures for a while. He said goodbye to his brothers. After all the goodbyes, it was only János and the Golden Prince who were left behind.

"Come home with me," the Golden Prince offered, "Be our guest for a couple of days. I am sure my father would like to meet you."

He was right. János's fame walked before him, and as soon as the Golden King saw him he ordered the most splendid feast and the best entertainment his kingdom could provide. He also ordered his two daughters to dress up in their finest garments and put on their finest make-up, hoping that János would fall in love with one of them and decide to stay in the kingdom as his champion. The girls sat by János to the left and to the right, and offered him the best pieces from their own plate, smiling as charming and delightful as princesses will ever be ... but János hardly looked at them at all. He was thinking of adventures, long roads to travel and glory to win, and that was all that was on his mind.

At midnight everyone retired to bed. The king drew his daughters aside: "Go to his room and confess your love to him; maybe he will take a fancy to one of you."

The princesses, obedient as they were, went to János's door ... but that was as far as they could go. A shell of steel encircled the room, and there was no way in, no way out.

"Daddy, daddy, look what happened to the door!"

The king took a look and realized that János was as pure of heart as any champion could dream of. "Do not worry, my darlings. I will keep him here as a guest for a few months, I am sure he will change his mind."

It was a good plan. Still, barely three days passed with feasts and celebrations before János grew bored, and told the king he was ready to go on.

"Are you leaving already, dear brother?" the Golden Prince asked.

"I am. I have to go seek my fortune."

"I have a favor to ask of you," confessed the prince. "I thought I had time, but I cannot wait anymore. There is a girl I love with all my heart, and I know she loves me back, even though we have only seen each other from far away, across the border. She lives in the next kingdom, and I cannot cross over there for her. I tried twice, and both times her mother killed me, tore me to pieces, and sent me home in the saddlebag. Twice did my mother put me back together and she brought me back to life, but the next time I die, it will be final."

"Do not say any more," János nodded. "Let's go and see what we can do."

They rode all the way to the border, and stopped there. The Golden Prince told János that the mother of the princess was an evil witch, and if he crossed the border again, that would be the end of him.

"Do not worry about it," said János. "Just make a fire here and wait till I return." And with that, he crossed the border.

The first person he came across was an old woman, carrying a rake on her shoulder. He asked her politely where the castle was, and she pointed him in the right direction. He followed the road, asking directions from other old women until he finally arrived to the home of the witch.

It was a castle, tall and glowing, made entirely of porcelain, standing on an enormous duck's leg, turning slowly to always follow the sun. János drew his sword and slashed at the duck leg; the castle stopped spinning abruptly, and collapsed to the ground.

He walked in, going from room to room. Behind every door there was an abundance of gold, silver and other treasures. When he arrived to the seventh door, he heard a buzzing sound — the first sound since he had walked into the castle — and a small voice in his ear.

"Careful now, János, if you walk through that door, you might never return!"

"What is in there?" he whispered.

"The princess that you seek. But she is strong, stronger than you can imagine, and she does not take kindly to strangers. She will grab you as you walk in, and smash you into the ground with a force that will break all the bones in your body. Make sure that when you walk in, you grab her first, because if you don't, she will give you no time to explain."

János nodded, and knocked on the door.

"Come in!" called a cheerful voice.

Sure enough, the moment he stepped inside the princess sprang at him, ready to throw him to the ground, but János was quicker and stronger. He grabbed the princess, lifted her up, and threw her into her armchair with a force that made the chair collapse under her.

"I thought you wanted me for yourself" she said, calming down. "But now I know who you are, and who sent you here. The Golden Prince has been pining after me for three years, but my mother, the witch, will not let me leave. Let us hope you can get me away without her killing you and me both."

They left the room and ran downstairs — but the witch was already waiting for them. She had been filing her teeth with twenty-four rasps, and she grinned at the runaways.

"Where are you taking my daughter, János?"

"I am taking her where you do not want her to go," he said. As the witch pounced towards him, fangs ready to bite, he reached out, grabbed her by the hair, and slammed her into the floor so hard that she broke into pieces.

"Run!" the princess yelled. "She will not stay dead for long."

They ran, and they barely ran a hundred yards before the witch was after them again. János once again killed her ... but she came back to life. He killed her twenty-four times by the time they got back to the border.

"She cannot die in her own kingdom!" the princess yelled. "You need to drag her across the border!"

János grabbed the witch one last time, and with a mighty struggle, he dragged her across the border. Once she was there, she fell into pieces and the wind blew her away like dust.

The princess and her lover finally met, and they embraced each other and shared a kiss. All three of them returned to the Golden King's castle, and a wedding was held for the prince and the princess. János celebrated with them until it was all over, and then he said his goodbyes.

"Are you sure you do not want to stay and make this your home?" the Golden Prince asked, wishing he would stay. But János just shook his head and smiled — he had other adventures waiting for him down the road.

*Comments:* Have I mentioned before that this is a part of a longer folktale?

It is really hard to choose from all the heroes in folktales and mythology who have superhuman strength. Especially if you are looking for supernaturally strong female characters. A lot of stories that deal with those are tall tales or nonsense tales, sometimes downright making fun of the image of a woman stronger than any man. I sorted through quite a few AaTh 519 type folktales to find one where the strong bride does not end up being punished for defeating her husband, and doesn't maim everyone else in a jealous rage.

This story captured my attention because of the intriguing characters and imagery. Even though we don't find out a lot about the brotherhood of heroes, they still sound like fascinating characters — not to mention the troublemakers and their supernatural powers. The entire bar fight scene is something out of a *Dungeons & Dragons* (D&D) adventure (or a western movie, take your pick). The steel shell János pulls up for defense sounds a lot like a force field, similar to many seen with modern superheroes, such as the Invisible Woman. And then there are the strong female characters — the witch that keeps coming back to life and the princess who does not sit around waiting to be rescued (rather, she is likely to kill the rescuer out of self-defense).

All in all, I find this folktale unique and interesting. Sadly, I had to cut it down to size to fit into this book. I tried to keep the original flavor of the dialogues in the translation from Hungarian as much as I could, but I tweaked some parts that did not make sense to my audiences. The biggest change was implemented when in the original story, János (pronounced Yah-nosh) watches all his sworn brothers die without lifting a finger, and then goes out to relieve himself, comes back, and punishes the troublemakers. None of my audiences were okay with that, so now I tell it in the version you have read above. The previous part deals with the elder brother Rózsa (Roh-shah, Rose) and his adventures, while the rest of the tale after this episode tells us about János seeking fame and fortune, dying and being revived again, and finally finding happiness and a shape-shifting fairy wife. All is well if it ends well.

## *Alderblock*

*Ability:* Superhuman strength
*Source of power:* Natural / Magic potion
*Origin:* Finland
*Teachings:* Bravery, teamwork, self-sacrifice.
*Age group:* 6+
*Sources:* Fillmore, P. (1922). *Mighty Mikko: Finnish Folk and Fairy Tales.* New York: Harcourt, Brace & Co.
*Variants:* There are many folktales that are collectively referred to as "hero rescuing the sun, moon and stars" or by some other similar description. Sometimes this mission involves killing dragons, sometimes rescuing a magical horse or a couple of princesses. The folktale type is AaTh 300, Dragon Slayer. You will see why.
*Text:* Once upon a time there was a poor couple. They were poorer than anyone else in their village, not because they had less money or food, but because they had no children at all. They wished for a child, a boy or a girl, but their hopes were in vain. Finally, one day the wife said: "If I do not get to have a real child, I will at least have a child of wood."

Going out into the woods, she picked up an alder log, carried it home, wrapped it up in a warm cloth, and laid it in the cradle. She and her husband rocked the cradle and sang lullabies to the log for three whole years.

One afternoon as the couple returned home, they were greeted with the unexpected sound of a baby crying in the cradle. Running over to take a look they saw that their wish came true: instead of a log, there was a real child inside, demanding to be fed. Their happiness knew no bounds. They raised the boy as their own, and he grew stronger day by day. Everyone in the village knew him as Alderblock, and he needed no other name. By the time he reached adulthood there was no one near or far who was stronger than him.

Then, one day people woke up to a great disaster: the Sun, the Moon and the Dawn had gone missing overnight, and the world was wrapped in freezing darkness. The king immediately announced that he was looking for the strongest, bravest champions that would go out and bring back light to the world. But because heroes fit for that task not only had to be valiant and strong, but also had to endure all the hardships of the journey, he also announced that first they all had to take a test. He had vials of magic water that gave extraordinary strength to whoever drank from them. The king decided to send three heroes out on the mission, just to be sure. One had to be able to drink and hold three bottles worth of the magic water, one had to drink six, and the strongest had to drink nine. From all the knights and princes gathered in his court he soon found Three Bottles and Six Bottles, but no one could suffer to drink nine.

Some people from the village saw this and they called out to the king: "Send for Alderblock! He can do it! Send for him!"

The king did, and the young man was brought to the palace where he drank nine bottles of the magic water without any trouble at all. The king announced that he had found the three champions, equipped them with swords and shields, money, food, horses and dogs, and sent them on their way. People huddled in the darkness and waited to see if the Sun, Moon and Dawn would ever return.

The three heroes rode on until they crossed the border of the kingdom, and now they were in a strange land. The darkness was less dense here, more of a constant grey twilight, and soon they could make out the silhouette of a castle, and a small town below. Knocking on the door of the nearest house, they greeted the old woman who lived there, and wished her a good day.

"Good day indeed!" cackled the old woman. "We have not seen any kind of day, let alone a good one, since the Evil One cursed the Sun and the nine-headed dragon took it away God knows where!"

The heroes' eyes lit up. "You can tell us what happened to the light?"

"Who can't? The Evil One snatched down the Sun from the sky because it burnt him with the light. Then he snatched down the Moon because he could not do his evil things at night. Then he cursed down the Dawn for not letting him sleep late. He gave them to the dragons, the evil sons of Suyettar, one with nine heads, one with six, one with three, to guard. We have not seen the light ever since."

"Where can we find these dragons?" asked the heroes, already reaching for their swords.

"They go out to the sea where no one can reach their treasures. The three-headed dragon stays in the water for a day before it has to come out again. The six-headed dragon stays for two days; the nine-headed dragon only comes out every third day."

The heroes thanked the old woman and rode on toward the palace. As they got closer, they noticed a strange sight: half the people in the palace were laughing and cheering, while the other half was weeping bitterly. This sight troubled them so much that they returned to the old woman to ask her what was wrong with all the people.

"They are thinking of the princesses' fate of course," the crone explained. "The dragons demand the three princesses as a sacrifice. Some people think this is the end of it all, and after them they will devour everyone else as well. So they cry. Others think a hero might show up to rescue them, and bring back the light. They are the ones cheering."

That was all the champions needed to hear. While the king in the castle said goodbye to his eldest daughter as they sewed her into a sack, telling her it will all soon be over, the heroes went down to the beach, and Three Bottles drank down the magic water he was named after. When the procession of servants left the sack full of princess on a high rock and retreated to the palace in fear, Three Bottles walked over and cut the sack open. The princess was lying curled up in a ball, waiting for the end ... and when nothing happened she opened her eyes and said, "Oh."

"Don't be afraid, I am here to rescue you," said the hero with a smile. "You can call me Three Bottles. Now go and hide behind that rock while I fight the dragon."

Soon enough, as soon as twilight turned to dark, the three-headed dragon appeared, breaking through the surface of the sea and sliding up onto the beach like a giant, ugly serpent. "I smell flesh!" it roared, swinging its heads around.

"That is my flesh that you smell," answered Three Bottles. "Come and fight me!"

"Make us a platform of copper, pretty boy, and we shall fight," answered the dragon, but the hero shook his head and drew his sword. "You make us a platform of cold iron, and we shall fight!"

And so they did. The battle raged back and forth, coils of scaly serpent tails and heads thrashing around in the sand, the sword of the hero flashing and slicing, until two of the three heads fell to the ground. The third almost succeeded in biting Three Bottles in half ... but from behind the rocks out sprang his dog, and with the help of the faithful animal he managed to kill the last head, and with that, the dragon. By this time he was so exhausted, he needed the help of his companions to return to the old woman's hut to sleep and heal.

Night passed, and in the morning, instead of grey twilight, the real Dawn appeared on the horizon. People cheered and celebrated all across the kingdom. Their joy was even greater when they discovered the carcass of the dragon on the beach, and the oldest princess sitting next to it, alive and unhurt.

The king was happy and sad at the same time. Happy that someone had rescued his eldest daughter and released the Dawn, but sad because that night the six-headed dragon was bound to appear and devour the second princess as a sacrifice.

He didn't know that Six Bottles was already preparing for the fight. As night fell and the servants left another sack on the beach, the second champion sliced it open and rescued the second princess just in time to see the six-headed dragon emerge from the sea. With the strength that the six bottles of magic water gave him, he attacked the monster on a platform of red copper and the battle raged all the way till dawn, five out of six heads rolling one by one onto the sand. The last one almost finished the hero; but his dog joined the fight just in time to tip the scale to his favor, and by the time Dawn appeared, the dragon was dead.

Alderblock barely managed to drag his friend home to the old woman before servants were already on the beach, passing the word of good news along that the princess was alive and the dragon had been slain. But lurking behind the joy was the dreadful truth: the nine-headed serpent was yet to come, the most powerful of the offspring of Suyettar, the guardian of the Sun.

This time, Alderblock waited on the beach, with the power of nine bottles of magic in his veins. The youngest princess was left as a sacrifice, just like the others, and he promptly rescued her from her fate. They waited together as the newly rescued Moon rose to the sky, and when the water began to boil, Alderblock prepared to fight. The nine-headed dragon rose up from the sea and attacked him over a platform of shining silver. He had lost his brothers to the heroes of the land, but no one had ever defeated him in combat. The battle raged back and forth until only three heads remained. Alderblock's strength was waning from exhaustion, so he tried trickery: "Look, look, the Sun is escaping!" As the dragon turned to look, two more heads fell to the ground. The last one almost finished the hero, but his dog ran to his rescue, and as Dawn broke over the horizon, the dragon fell dead to the ground.

Following the Dawn, the Sun came up, and people cheered and celebrated that their hardships were finally over. The king was joyful that all three of his daughters had been rescued, and announced that whoever could bring the heads of the dragons up to the palace and thus prove they had been the ones that killed them will receive a great reward. Alderblock and his two companions did not hesitate long; and when they appeared before the king to claim their reward, they were given the right to marry the princesses they rescued. A triple wedding was celebrated, and the young couples could not have been any merrier.

*Comments:* The end? Not really. The story goes on to tell us about how Suyettar the Witch sets out to take revenge for her dragon-sons, and manages to murder Three Bottles, Six Bottles, and their brides, on the way home. She also puts a curse on Alderblock to make sure he cannot tell anyone about what happened, so eventually rumor starts to spread that he himself killed his companions to take all the glory. When he finally tells the king what happened, the curse takes effect, and he is turned into a blue cross that will stand in the cemetery forever. The king, the bride, and the kingdom weep for Alderblock and remember him forever as a hero; eventually, the king marries the bride. Not the ending one would expect.

I chose this tale of strength partly because of the magnitude of the mission: the existence of the entire world depends on getting the light back, and heroes are carefully selected for the task. "Saving the world" has always been right up the alley of heroes like Alderblock, with his strange origin and early fame. The magic water that gives strength, but only to those who can handle drinking it, calls into mind the super soldier serum that turned Steve Rogers into Captain

America (or, in the world of cartoons, Asterix's potion of strength or Popeye's spinach).

The original text is very repetitive and formulaic. I shortened it by quite a bit, because even though repetition gives rhythm to the live telling, unfortunately many modern audiences above the age of six have no patience for triple repetition of long portions of the story. Still, if you have the time and the right audience, read the original text and give it a try. It is a whole different experience.

# INVULNERABILITY

Contrary to popular belief, invulnerability and strength do not always go together. Invulnerability is the power that prevents someone from being physically harmed, but in itself it does not mean the person also has to be stronger than usual. It is also different from a healing factor: someone with a healing factor can still be harmed, mangled, cut, etc., but they heal instead of dying. Invulnerability comes in a few different forms. Sometimes it is magical and covers all bases, while other times it is limited to one's unbreakable skin.

With that said, strength and invulnerability often go together both in folklore and popular culture. Another term that is frequently used is invincibility, which means a person cannot be defeated. This, however, always comes with a "but" because "buts" make good stories — if someone was really, truly invincible, there would be no story. It would be more accurate to say that most of the heroes in this section are "almost invulnerable."

I gave some thought to what stories to choose. The example that comes to mind first is Achilles and his heel (we all know how that ended). Another fairly well known story is Siegfried from *Das Niebelungenlied* who bathed in dragon blood. However once someone looks into the world of folklore and mythology, there are other, less generally well-known stories that carry the same motif. The motif, by the way, was classified by Stith Tompson as Z311, Invulnerability with an Exception, but is more commonly known as "the Achilles Heel." The fact that it has its own name and number proves that it is much more common than one would think.

Let us explore some of the less well known, but not less tough heroes of the world.

*Invulnerable heroes:* David Dunn (*Unbreakable*), John Hancock (*Hancock*), Luke Cage (Marvel), Monet St. Croix (Marvel), Supergirl (DC), Superman (DC)

# Isfandiyar

*Ability:* Invulnerability, superhuman strength

*Source of power:* Magical Water

*Origin:* Persia

*Teachings:* Destiny, respect, ingenuity. Nobody is invincible. Respect your enemy and avoid violence if you can. For older age groups one can also include some religious history.

*Age group:* 12+

*Sources:* Ferdowsi. *Shahnameh* (*Book of Kings*), chapters 16 and 17.

*Variants:* Both Achilles and Siegfried are pretty closely related to this story — Achilles because of his death by an arrow, and Siegfried because of the dragon blood (Isfandiyar was also known for creating a magical pool of dragon blood by killing a dragon). Another fairly well known tale is "The Death of Baldr," the Norse god who had been made invulnerable by his mother by all things in the world, except for mistletoe, and eventually he is killed by an arrow made of that plant. But enough of the spoilers.

*Text:* A long time ago, in the land of Iran, there lived a shah named Gushtasp. They say he was a good king. They say that during his reign peace ruled the land for many years, and wolves and sheep could drink from the same well.

But that heavenly peace could not last forever.

It was during Gushtasp's time as the shah of Iran that the prophet Zerdusht (also called Zarathustra) arrived in the kingdom and started teaching a new faith. Gushtasp took on this new faith with all the rest of his subjects and followed the word of the prophet — but the neighboring kingdoms did not take to the changes well. One by one they rose up against Iran and attacked the borders. The first to declare war was a king called Arjasp, and when his messengers arrived at the court, Gushtasp assembled his army and charged his oldest son, Isfandiyar, to lead them to war.

Isfandiyar was already a hero despite his young age, and it was said that no one could defeat him in battle. Arrows skidded off his chest, swords slid down his arms without leaving as much as a scratch on his skin. People believed he was invincible.

Isfandiyar led his father's army into battle, and defeated Arjasp. When he returned home, he was full of pride and boasting, and he asked his father to step down from the throne and make him shah. This angered Gushtasp: he remembered all too well the time when he was young and he made the same demand to his own father. He was not ready to give up the throne — not now, not ever. He told his son it was not time yet; he had to prove himself with more heroic battles before he could rule the kingdom.

There was an evil man in Gushtasp's court. After he witnessed this exchange between father and son, he saw a chance to get rid of the prince once and for all. He started whispering into the shah's ear, telling him his son was plotting against him, planning to overthrow his rule and seize the throne. Gushtasp believed the whispers, and ordered the prince to be thrown into the dungeon in chains. It looked like Isfandiyar's sun was about to set.

As soon as the news reached Arjasp, he thought it was his time to take revenge. Now that the hero was in chains, there was no one to stop him. He swept over the land with his entire army, and did not only win the battle, but also took the younger son and daughters of Gushtasp as prisoners of war. When the shah heard the news, he was angry and worried; he knew all too well there was no one in his kingdom who could turn the defeat around ... no one, but Isfandiyar.

He sent people to the dungeon to release him. When Isfandiyar heard what happened, he only shook his head: "My father believed that I could betray him, and he threw me into the dungeon in chains like a criminal. Why would I help him now?" No matter how they tried, they could not convince him to leave his cell ... until he heard that his brother and sisters had been taken. As soon as they told him that, he stood, broke the chains off his arms and feet, and walked out of his prison.

The moment Isfandiyar was back on the battlefield the war turned around. In a few days he rid the kingdom of Arjasp and his army, and returned home victorious. His father was already waiting for him — hoping he could send him away again, and keep his throne for himself. "Your brother and sisters are kept in a fortress of brass," he said. "Arjasp and his men locked themselves up in there, and there is no one who can reach them."

"I will go," said Isfandiyar. "Just show me the way."

"There are three roads you can take," said the shah. "The first one takes three months to travel, but it is safe, and there is plenty of food and water on the way. The second one takes only two moons, but through a desert. The third road will take you to the fortress in a week, but it is full of danger."

"I have no time to waste," said Isfandiyar. "We are taking the shortest road."

The road he set out on took seven days, and each day brought a new danger greater than the one before. The first day Isfandiyar had to fight and defeat two wild wolves. The second day he faced two evil demons disguised as lions. The third day brought a dragon with venomous breath, and the fourth an evil magician that tried to lure the heroes off the path. On the fifth day they were attacked by a giant bird, and Isfandiyar shot it down with an arrow, something no hunter had managed to do before. On the sixth day, the elements turned against them and it started to snow; they all would have frozen to death if Isfandiyar had not been blessed for his bravery, and the snow melted around them. On the last day they had to face a flood, and they barely escaped with their lives.

After the flood, they finally stood before the Brass Fortress, and Isfandiyar sighed. "It was all for nothing. This place cannot be taken."

The fortress did look impregnable. But they had made it this far, and Isfandiyar was not going to turn his back on his brother and sisters. He pondered for a while, and he came up with a plan.

Putting on the robes of a merchant, he loaded a string of camels with whatever merchandise they had been carrying. Then he hid his best men in treasure chests and loaded them onto the camels too. Walking up to the gates of the fortress he pretended to be a wealthy merchant traveling across the land, and Arjasp fell for the trick. He did not only let him and all his camels inside the fortress, but he also arranged a feast in his honor. When the guards were drunk and asleep, Isfandiyar let his men out of the chests, and they took the fortress from within.

Isfandiyar returned home, once again victorious. People rejoiced to see him and everyone celebrated him as a hero and the savior of the kingdom. His father was worried that they would want him to become the new shah now, and sure enough, the prince brought up the question of the throne again. Gushtasp needed another excuse to win some time.

"I cannot give up my throne yet," he said. "There is one more person who does not accept my rule, and never paid his respects to me. If you bring that man to me in chains, I will step down and make you shah, my son."

"Who is that man?" asked Isfandiyar.

"Rustem."

The prince stared in stunned silence. Rustem? Rustem the Mighty? Rustem, the son of Zal, the greatest hero Iran had ever seen? Rustem, the Invincible?

"Father," he said. "There is no man more respected or honored than Rustem. Why would you want to see him in chains?"

"I am the shah, and even heroes should pay respect to me!" roared Gushtasp. "If you want to be shah after me, you *will* bring Rustem to court!"

Isfandiyar was quiet for a while. "If that is what it takes to earn the throne, father," he said finally. "Then I do not desire to be shah anymore. You are still my king, and I have to obey your orders. But know this: I do what I do against my will and with a heavy heart. If I die from Rustem's hand, my blood will be on your head."

With that, Isfandiyar set out to travel to Zaboulistan to meet Rustem. When they were close, he sent out his own son, Bahman, as a messenger to tell Rustem he meant no harm, and that if he came to him he would be willing to discuss the matter. Bahman took the message to Rustem's palace, but he found the hero was out hunting, and only his parents, the famous white-haired Zal and the lovely Rudabeh, were home. When he told them the message was urgent, they pointed him in the right direction, and soon Bahman found a valley where

the next morning off he went to the woods again. He did not get away without a fight either. An older giant with two heads on his shoulders tried to grab him for lunch, but Tom was faster and beat the giant to the ground.

"Spare me! Spare me! I will give you a fife that makes anyone or anything dance!" he yelled, and another deal was made. Tom played the little flute, and the pile of firewood danced all the way home.

There used to be a lot more giants around back in those days — maybe because of lads like Tom, there are barely any of them left today. But back then, on the third day Tom went for firewood, another one was bound to show up, and this one had three heads instead of two! Tom grappled with it for a while before the giant fell to the ground, and offered the most useful deal of all: a vial of green ointment that would render whoever used it invulnerable to any weapons, and impervious to flames. Tom walked home victorious, and no giant ever bothered him again.

Not long after this, a messenger came to Tom's village and announced that the king of Dublin's daughter, the princess, had not shown a smile for seven years. After trying all the cures and all the spells, the king resorted to declaring that whoever could make his daughter laugh three times could have her hand in marriage. Tom thought this sounded worth trying and, kissing his mother goodbye, he set out for Dublin.

However, when he arrived at the city gates, the guards refused to let him in. He was a sorry sight, wearing only a goat's skin around his waist, unshaven, carrying a club. They made fun of him, but Tom did not say a word ... until one of the guards stuck his side with a knife. The stab slid off his skin that had been made invulnerable by the ointment, but it made Tom angry, so he grabbed the soldier by the scruff of his neck and the back of his pants, and tossed him into the canal. Now all the other guards charged at him, but all hits and stabs skidded off his bare skin, and he easily defeated all of them with a swing or two of his club. The last guard standing decided to let him in.

Inside the palace courtyard there was a great gathering of people, and they were all trying to entertain the princess at once. Some of them sang, some of them juggled, or danced, or held duels, or tumbled, or did any number of things — but the princess just stood on her balcony and did not even smile. In fact, she looked terribly bored. When Tom walked in, however, he caught her eyes at once (even ragged and unshaven he was still a handsome lad), and she gave him a look that made the other suitors instantly jealous. One of them, a fellow with flaming red hair, stood in his path, demanding to know his business with the princess.

"I am here to make her laugh," Tom answered very patiently, which just angered Redhead even more.

"You?! You are trying to accomplish something that none of these fine gentlemen here could do in the past seven years?! Who do you think you are, Goat-skins?"

The king heard the yelling and came out onto the balcony to see what was going on. The princess was watching with intense curiosity.

"Sire, this man is challenging your best men!" yelled Redhead, and the king smiled a little.

"Well then, let him try his best."

One of the champions in the courtyard picked up his sword and shield, and charged at Tom. The lad waited patiently until his attacker was close then flicked his club at him, hitting the man square on the elbow of his sword arm. Flying went the sword onto the ground, but the next attacker was already on Tom. One by one they all charged at him, trying to land a hit — but even when they did, their weapons slid off his skin and no one could do him harm. Tom, on the other hand, distributed hits and punches left and right, making sure not to kill anyone, and he did it with such patience and a good-natured smirk that the princess on the balcony started to laugh.

Everyone stopped and stared at the unusual sound, and Tom's smirk grew into a smile.

"Your highness, I believe I have just won one quarter of your daughter."

And so it was. Tom was invited to dine with the royal family that night. Servants scrubbed him and shaved him and dressed him, and he was quite the fetching sight. Redhead was more jealous than ever, and the princess's blood ran from her heart to her cheeks.

The next day, in order to get rid of him, Redhead told Tom about a great wild wolf that had been killing sheep and people outside the city walls for weeks. He suggested that it would be a task fit for a hero to kill the beast. Tom nodded with his usual peaceful smile, and walked out to meet the wolf.

He returned the same afternoon, the wolf walking ahead of him like a cow being herded, and as soon as people in the courtyard saw the beast, they ran for the nearest door or window to get out of the way. Some of them were fast enough, some of them were not. As the wolf started to growl, Tom pulled the fife out of his pocket and started to play. People all around started to dance, and so did the wolf, standing up on his hind legs, and snarling all the way. The flaming red hair of Redhead intrigued him, so wherever Redhead skipped and hopped and danced, the wolf danced after him, and it all made such a comical sight that the princess laughed again, a clear, happy laugh. Tom smiled and bowed.

"Your highness, I believe I just won half of your daughter."

The wolf stopped dancing when the music ended; Tom turned to give him a stern look. "And you. I do not want to see you around Dublin ever again."

The wolf, as if it understood what was being said, ran away with its tail between its legs.

Redhead, on the other hand, had still not given up the hope of getting rid of Tom. His next chance presented itself when news came that the Danes had landed outside Dublin and they were preparing to attack the city.

"There is only one weapon they are afraid of," Redhead whispered to the king. "The flail that hangs on the wall of Hell. Send Tom to fetch it, for there is no better hero for the task than him."

When Tom was told about this, he only had one question: "Sire if I return, will you give me the other half of your daughter?"

But the princess, afraid for his life, refused. "I would rather not be your wife at all than to send you into danger!"

But it was too late. Tom said goodbye and went on his way, straight down to the gates of Hell. He knocked on the great iron doors, and half a dozen tiny imps popped out their heads. "I want to speak to the big devil," Tom announced to them, and they let him in. The Devil himself greeted him with a smile.

"A good day to you, Tom. What can I do for you today?"

"I came to borrow the flail than hangs on your wall."

The Devil grinned, and nodded to the imps. "Give him the flail."

You see, what Redhead did not tell Tom was that the flail was burning as hot as the fires of Hell. He hoped Tom would burn to cinders the moment he took it into his hands. But there was one thing Redhead did not know: Tom's skin was impervious to flames.

"Thank you," he said politely, picking up the flail as the Devil's eyes grew wide. "I will be on my way now."

"Oh, you think walking out is as easy as walking in, do you?" asked the Devil, and with that, all the imps and demons attacked Tom at once. The lad swung the flail around and fought them off, cracking bones and breaking horns all around, until the Devil himself was hit on his elbow.

"Let him out!" he yelled. "Let him go, and make sure no one ever lets him in here again!"

Tom returned from Hell with the flail, and people were stunned and relieved to see him. The royal family greeted him in the castle gates, where he placed the flail at their feet.

Redhead was more than furious. In his anger he ran forward and reached for the flail to put an end to Tom and his glory ... but as soon as his fingers touched the flail, he yelled in pain as his skin started to burn. Tom, seeing this, ran over to his side, took Redhead's hurt hands in his own rough ones, and gently patted them to put out the fire and ease the pain. Redhead, between agony, shame and frustration, made such a pitiful sight between Tom's hands that the princess could not hold back laughter any longer. Soon the royal family and all the servants joined in too, and Tom smiled at the king.

"Your highness, I believe I have just won your daughter."

"Indeed you have," said the king, and he himself put the princess's hand into Tom's.

A wedding was held, everyone celebrated, and Tom became the heir to the throne. While no one was watching, the flail slowly melted itself into the ground, and nothing was left on the steps but a deep, narrow hole that maybe went down all the way to Hell. The Danes heard about Tom and his deeds, and they were so scared they sailed away, and did not bother the Dubliners again for a very, very long time.

*Comments:* Talk about a feel-good folktale. Tom's character is more lovable than your average strong hero's, since he does not even consider revenge against the people who meant him harm. He is kind of a big softy, no wonder he succeeds in making the princess laugh. The strong simpleton is also a character that shows up quite often, one being the unsuspecting Parsifal when he arrived at King Arthur's court.

Invulnerability in this story comes from the use of the magic ointment. It does not only protect the hero from injuries, it also repels heat and flame, very much like the ointment Medea gives Jason to help him win the Golden Fleece. The hero being forbidden to enter Hell is a positive outcome, and also appears in a number of folktales — although sometimes, like in the Appalachian tale of "Wicked John and the Devil," it comes back to bite the hero in his invulnerable behind.

This story is very useful for starting conversations about relationships and the importance of humor. In the age of angsty teenage heroes and love stories, teenagers especially need tales that show that power does go along with kindness and good humor quite well. Instead of simply offering the princess as a prize for missions accomplished, the mission is to win her over. There is more than one important lesson in there, especially for young (and actively dating) audiences.

# FLIGHT

Flight is possibly the most popular superpower humanity has ever dreamed of. Our myth and legends were filled with flight millennia before we first discovered a way to rise into the air. Only a few stories have ever been powerful enough to become reality through hard work, trial and error, and the sheer desire to make them come true. Flying fills our dreams, our nightmares, our folktales and, lately, our everyday life. It is something very elemental to human nature and thus very common in the world of stories.

Whether carried by a magic carpet or granted by a fairy godmother, the ability to fly shows up very frequently in folklore and mythology. When selecting the stories for this collection I had to sort through all the different ways of flying: giant birds, chariots drawn by various species of livestock, floating baskets (possibly the lower part of a hot air balloon), broomsticks, mortars, snakes with wings, horses with wings, sandals with wings, and elephants with double beetle wings. In many stories flight without a mount or vehicle is the privilege of the divine or the supernatural — and following the rules I have set for myself, I had to exclude all of them, gods, fairies and bird people alike. What remained were heroes who have found a way to acquire wings for themselves, or people who have found the secret of simply rising into the air.

The following tales, as well as some others later on in this book, represent different ways of flying, almost as diverse as the early history of airplane models.

*Some (of the many) modern heroes with flight:* Angel (Marvel), Ms. Marvel (Marvel), Nathan Petrelli (NBC's *Heroes*), Pixie (Marvel), Storm (Marvel), Superman (DC), Wasp (Marvel), Wonder Woman (DC)


## The Winged Prince

*Ability:* Flight (wings), technomancy
*Source of power:* Mechanical
*Origin:* Hungary
*Teachings:* Love conquers all (also, the devil is in the details). I have used this story to introduce science classes where students learned about the physics of flight and the anatomy of birds' wings.
*Age group:* 6+
*Sources:* Benedek, E. (1988). *Magyar mese — és mondavilág III.* Budapest: Móra Ferenc Könyvkiadó.
*Variants:* When it comes to man-made wings, there are quite a few more famous characters of mythology out there, such as Daedalus and Icarus and their tragic fate (in the tradition of Greek mythology), or Völundr the Blacksmith and his bloody streak of vengeance (in the tradition of Norse mythology). This story, however, is quite a rare type, and I have never encountered another version (not yet, anyway).
*Text:* Once upon a time, there was a king whose only daughter was as beautiful as the most brilliant star in the sky. When she was old enough to marry dozens of suitors came to ask her, but it was the poorest of the young princes that caught the princess's eye. Naturally the king did not like this at all. He wanted

his daughter to marry the richest of the suitors, for her own good and the kingdom's. When the princess refused, he grew furious and locked her up in a tower, telling her she was not allowed to leave until she had changed her mind.

The king did not know this, but the princess was not alone. Every night her lover visited her in the tower. How? The prince had a servant who could craft marvelous things with his own hands. This servant made the prince a pair of wings. As soon as the sun set, he flew up into the air at the edge of the royal city, and landed on the balcony of the princess's tower, meeting with her in secret behind the king's back.

This went on for a week or two, until one day the king decided to pay his daughter a visit to see if she had changed her mind. He arrived at the worst possible moment: he found the princess and her lover embracing each other ... planning her escape from the tower. The king's fury returned as only a father's can, and he drew his curved sword to kill the prince right then and there. But the young man was faster — with a flap of his wings he threw himself out the window, and flew back to his own castle in the woods.

The king called for his carriage right away, drawn by six black horses, and he rode out to the woods. Now he knew the prince had been hiding out there to be closer to the princess. After the carriage rode an entire contingent of soldiers that surrounded the prince's castle while the king himself marched inside.

The first room of the castle was empty. The second room had two beds, two chairs, and a chest. In the third room he found the prince sitting at a desk, writing a sad poem about his love.

"You, winged prince!" roared the king. "Were you the one visiting my daughter?"

"Yes, your highness. I cannot deny it, and even if I could, I would not."

"Well if it was you, I will strike you down right here and now!"

The prince looked at the king, and spoke very politely. "Your highness, if you wish to punish us for what we have done, at least let us die together. Take me back to your palace, tie me to the princess, and throw us from the tower."

"If that is all you wish for, I am happy to oblige," said the king. "You two shall die together for causing me such grief!"

The soldiers escorted the prince back to the palace. There they tied him together with the princess and pushed them from the tower.

But they did not fall to the ground.

The prince strained his wings once, twice, three times, and the ropes broke — stretching his wings to the sky, he flew away with the princess in his arms, faster than the wind.

The king could yell after them all he wanted, threats or promises, they did not turn around. The prince flew back to the court of his own father, and held the wedding there right away. By the time the princess's father caught up with them, they were already husband and wife, and there was nothing left for him but a handful of morsels from the wedding feast.

And they lived happily ever after.

*Comments:* I only tweaked this one a little bit. When I read this story as a child I was always bothered by the fact that the reason why the lovers got away was that the soldiers *forgot* to tie the *wings* down. I thought (and still think) that no soldier, even in a folktale, can be dumb enough to tie someone up and forget about the huge *wings* on their shoulders.

Other than that, I quite like this story. The father-daughter-boyfriend relationship is something most people encounter in their lives, from one perspective or another. I also like the fact that this one, unlike Daedalus and Icarus or Völundr, has a happy ending.

Finally: technically, flight in this case is not a supernatural ability as much as advanced technology, but I only have two words to say to that: Iron Man. Lovesick puppy that he is, the prince acquires, masters and uses his flying ability, and it becomes part of his identity as the Winged Prince, eventually saving his life multiple times. Rings a bell, anyone?

## People Who Could Fly

*Ability:* Flight

*Source of power:* Natural

*Origin:* African American

*Teachings:* Freedom, the power of human will, pride, and the history of civil rights.

*Age group:* 8+

*Sources:* Bennett, J. (1943). *Doctor to the Dead: Grotesque Legends and Folktales of Old Charleston.* Columbia: University of South Carolina Press.

Cole, J. (1983). *Best-Loved Folktales of the World.* New York: Anchor Books.

Dicker/sun, G. (2008). *African American Theater: A Cultural Companion.* Malden, MA: Polity Press.

Granger, M. (1940). *Drums and Shadows: Survival Studies Among the Georgia Coastal Negroes.* Georgia Writers' Project.

Hamilton, V. (1985). *The People Could Fly: American Black Folktales.* New York: Alfred A. Knopf.

Lester, J. (1991). *Black Folktales.* New York: Grove Press.

McDaniel, L. (1990). "The Flying Africans: Extent and Strength of the Myth in the Americas," *New West Indian Guide* 64 (1990): 28–40.

*Variants:* This tale exists in many versions and variants, representing the belief in the flight to freedom. People talked, sang and whispered about other people who "looked like everyone else" but had the secret ability to fly and be free. McDaniel's article lists a series of examples of these tales, and makes a very interesting, educational read.

*Text:* They say that in the beginning all of God's children could fly. Everyone in Africa had wings, and they could fly like birds, from one place to another, without anything standing in their way. But when strangers came, and captured the children of God, and took them over the ocean away from home, they shed their wings. They had to. In the bellies of slaving ships it was dark, and damp, and crowded, and there was no space for wings. So they shed them, and when they arrived in the Americas, they looked like people without wings or dreams. But secretly, deep inside, they still had the ability to fly.

They say there was a plantation on the Georgia shore where the master was as cruel as a mortal man can be. He drove his slaves to work hard and without a break, he made the women and the children work just as hard as the men. Even if one was old or sick, they still had to bend their back and work on the fields, and if they were not working fast enough, the slave driver would pull out a whip and beat them to do it faster, until they dropped from sheer exhaustion.

One day, the master bought a new group of slaves, straight off the ship from Africa. They were taken to the fields and put to work right away. Among them there was an old man, and a young woman who just had a child. She worked as fast as she could, but the baby started crying, and she could not get it to stop. The slave driver whipped her, and she fell; the old man helped her back to her feet. She asked him something in the language that only they understood, and he shook his head as they both went back to work. But soon the young woman fell again, and the driver raised the whip. She was too exhausted to stand up, and the baby just kept crying and crying, so she looked at the old man and asked the question again. The old man nodded, and said a few strange words, loud and clear, and the young woman stood up, and she rose up into the air, out of the reach of the whip and the slave driver. Holding her baby, she flew over the fields, away from the white man.

The slave driver was scared and confused, so he drove the rest of the slaves even harder to work, angry at himself, and furious at them. Soon after a young man fell and the driver started beating him; the old man spoke the same strange words and the young man rose into the air above their head. One after another, all the slaves started standing up tall, and then flying away. The slave driver knew it was the old man who was responsible for this, and turned against him; but the old man just laughed, spoke the strange words, and joined the rest of the people in the air. When they were all together, they turned, and they flew away back to Africa.

They say that not all the slaves could fly. There were some who had forgotten how to do it; they had forgotten too much to learn again. The old man did not have time to teach them, so they were left behind, grounded, without wings. These were the slaves who told the tale to their children, and to their children's children, and this is how this story was kept alive to this very day.

*Comments:* I realize this story is deeply symbolic, but I decided to include it anyway. Just like many other tales from the slave era, this one speaks in hidden words and images, similar to the words spoken by the old man, only known to those who shared knowledge and faith. Flying in slave songs and tales meant freedom, in many ways — from running away at night all the way to spiritual freedom, or freedom in the afterlife.

This is a very powerful story that became widely known as a tale of the struggle for freedom and of the human spirit that cannot be broken or conquered. Researchers traced the origins of the motif all the way back to Africa; although as I have mentioned before, the dream of flight is universal to humanity. It manifests itself when life is hard, hopes are broken, and it seems like there is no way out. We look up at the birds soaring above us, and we wish to be one of them.

I did not include this story for the superpower of sprouting wings and flying away. I included it for the power of human dreams. The unexplained yet very real power hidden in all of us — that if enough people share the same dream and speak the same words, unimaginable things, like spouting wings, can become reality.

# HEIGHTENED SENSES

As far as our five senses go, humans have never been on top of the world. There are countless species in the animal kingdom that see, hear, smell, taste or otherwise sense better than we do, and we know it. Ever since we started making up stories, we have always wished for the sight of the eagle, the nose of the hound, or the cute floppy ears of the desert fox (no, really). These wishes and dreams are reflected in many stories around the world. Sometimes it is just one sense over the others; sometimes it is all of them at once. In this section I have gathered a few tales from both kinds.

*Examples of heroes with heightened senses:* **Sight:** Superman (DC); **Smell:** Aquaman (DC), Black Panther (Marvel), Daredevil (Marvel), Tigra (Marvel), Wolverine (Marvel), X-23 (Marvel); **Hearing:** Daredevil (Marvel), Power Girl (DC); **Taste:** Daredevil (Marvel), Rachel Pirzad (Syfy's *Alphas*); **Touch:** Toph Bei Fong (*Avatar: The Last Airbender*)

## Green Péter

(Also known in elementary school as "Princess Hide-and-Seek" and in preschool as "Princess Peek-a-Boo")

*Ability:* Enhanced sight / X-ray vision

*Source of power:* Unknown

*Origin:* Hungary

*Teachings:* Sometimes what we are searching for is closer than we think. I have also used this story as an introduction to classes where children learn about the records of nature such as deepest ocean, highest mountain, biggest bird, etc.

*Age group:* 4+

*Sources:* Csorba, K. (1998). *The Princess That Saw Everything: Twenty-four Hungarian Folktales.* Budapest: Windor.

Gyurica, E. (2010). *Az aranyszőrű bárány és más mesék.* Budapest: Alexandra.

Ortutay, Gy. (1955). *Magyar népköltészet: Népmesék.* Budapest: Szépirodalmi Könyvkiadó.

*Variants:* The Grimm's tale known as "The Sea Hare" (KHM 191) is very similar to this one. The story has variants all around Europe. The Thompson motif number for Person with Remarkable Sight is F642.

*Text:* Once upon a time, there was a princess. She had a very special gift: she could see *everything*. Not just things near and far, but also things that were hidden: people in the other rooms of her castle, fish deep in the sea, gold in the belly of the mountains, and ladybugs hiding in the forest half a world away. (Guess what her favorite game was.)

In time the princess grew up, and it was time for her to marry. But there was a little problem with the wedding plans: whoever came to the castle to ask for her hand in marriage was all nice and polite face to face, but when they thought nobody could see them, they all did things that upset the princess. Because she could see through walls, she could see them making faces, stealing small things from the castle, or even wooing other women! Finally, the princess said to her father: "Papa, I am only going to marry a man who can hide from me so I cannot see him!" The challenge was on. Princes, knights, barons and adventurers gathered to try and win the princess; but no matter where they hid, she could see each and every one of them, and they all failed the test.

In the meantime, not too far away from the castle, lived a young boy whose name was Péter. He had bright green eyes and a mischievous smile, and because he spent most of his time wandering in the forest and climbing trees, people called him Zöld Péter (Green Péter). He lived with his mother, his father and his little sister. But one day, when the children were still quite young, their mother fell ill and died. Because their father was a farmer and he spent all his time on the fields, he decided to marry again, to have someone in the house to look after the children.

The new wife, however, could not stand Péter and his sister. She was cruel to them, and when their father was not around, she even beat them sometimes. One day she decided to get rid of them once and for all, and as they sat down for dinner, she slipped poison into their food. This would have been the end of the children (and the story), if not for the white dove that flew in through the open window and pecked at Péter's hand, whispering "Poison! Poison!" until he dropped the spoon, took his sister by the hand, ran out of the house, and never looked back.

Brother and sister traveled for a very long time, wandering on dusty roads and narrow paths. One day, as they were walking along, Péter noticed a young bird on the ground below a tree. It had fallen out of its nest and was too young to fly, so it just hobbled in the grass, crying bitterly. Péter felt sorry for the little bird, so he picked it up, climbed the tree fast as a squirrel, and placed the tiny creature back into its nest.

As the siblings traveled on, they came across a river. On the riverbank there was a tiny fish, stranded in the sand, flopping this way and that, trying to get back into the water. Péter picked it up and threw it back, and the fish was gone in a flash of silver.

They were walking toward the king's city when they stopped to rest on the side of the road. Looking around, Péter saw a large rose bush that was all dried up and withered. "What a pity," he thought to himself, "this bush could be so magnificent if someone watered it; it would be big enough to offer some shade for travelers like us." Péter walked down to the river, brought water in his hat, and watered the bush before they walked on.

They did not have to walk for long before they started meeting people on the road. Everyone they met was talking about one thing, and one thing only: the challenge for the princess. Anyone who could hide from her at least once out of three tries (the king was growing impatient) could marry into the royal family! This chance only comes once in a lifetime! Péter went straight to the castle, and told the king he wanted to try. He was told that he had till the next morning to find himself a hiding place. Or, even better, get permanently lost.

But where does someone hide from a princess who can see a mole digging a tunnel under a mountain? Péter wandered around all day, trying to hide here and there, but nothing felt quite right. Toward the evening, he was getting desperate, and he wandered into the royal gardens. He was about to give up any hope of a better life, and sat down, sighing to himself, when he heard a little chirp above. He looked up, and there was his bird, the one that he rescued, right above him on a branch!

"What's the matter, Péter, why are you so sad?"

Péter, less surprised about a talking bird than he should have been, told the little friend everything that happened.

"Is that all?" chirped the bird. "I can help you with that! Stay right here, and I will bring help."

The bird flew away and sometime later returned—but it was not alone. Following the tiny creature there was a giant eagle, big enough for a man to ride. It landed right in front of Péter and offered its back. Once Péter was sitting comfortably and holding on to the thick feathers, the eagle rose up into the air and flew higher and higher into the sky, until it found a hiding place behind the Sun.

Morning came and the princess walked out into the garden. She rubbed her eyes, spun around on her heel, and looked around. She only searched for a few moments before she called out: "Come out, come out Péter, from behind the Sun, I can see you!"

The eagle flew back down and Péter, disappointed that he was found, walked back to the castle.

There were two more days left for him to hide. He spent several hours searching for a place, but he could find none, so he walked down to the river and dipped his feet in the water, moping about his bad luck. As he was sitting there, a very familiar little fish poked its head out of the waves.

"What's the matter, Péter, why are you so sad?"

Péter told the fish all his sorrows, and the fish chuckled: "Is that all? Stay right here and wait for me."

Sometime later the fish returned, followed by another fish, big enough to swallow a man whole. It opened its mouth, and after some nudging from his little friend, Péter walked into the enormous mouth, and down into an enormous dark stomach. The great fish then swam down, down, down deep into the river, and buried itself in the mud.

The next morning, the princess walked out into the garden, rubbed her eyes, spun around on her heel, and called out at once: "Come out, come out, Péter, from the belly of the fish, from the bottom of the river! I can see you!"

The great fish swam back to the surface, and a very distressed Péter climbed out of its stomach. Now he only had one more chance to try, and he did not have any more ideas. He spent the rest of the day sitting in the garden, thinking about this and that, but no matter how he tried, he could not think of a single place that would have been a better hiding place than the bottom of a river, or the far side of the Sun. As he sat there in the evening shadows, he suddenly heard a voice.

"Péter, what's wrong? Why are you so sad?"

Péter looked around, but he could not see anyone. He could not tell who spoke to him, until the voice asked again.

"Tell me what the matter is, Péter, maybe I can help."

It was the rosebush right next to him. He barely recognized it: it was lush, green, and full of beautiful red flowers. Once he got over his surprise, Péter told the bush all that had happened. "Is that all?" the bush chuckled. "Come here, I will hide you."

Péter walked closer, cautiously since the bush had thorns, not just flowers — but as he stepped up to it the bush opened up, embraced him, and turned him into a fresh red rose.

The next morning the princess walked out into the garden once again. As she walked past the rosebush, the scent of the flowers was so sweet and so strong that she stopped and buried her face in them for a moment. Before she walked on, she picked the most beautiful of the flowers and put it in her hair.

Then, just like every other morning, the princess once again rubbed her eyes, spun around on her heel, and looked ... and looked ... and looked ... but no matter how hard she looked, she could not find Péter. She rubbed her eyes again, spun around again ... but still no sign of Péter. Finally, she started calling: "Péter! Péter! Come out, wherever you are! I can't see you!"

"I am right here, princess," a voice answered, and the flower that was in her hair turned back into a fine young man. "I have been this close to you all along."

Péter had won the challenge, and the princess's hand with it. She didn't mind: she liked the young man with the bright green eyes. Péter brought his little sister to the palace. In time, he became a king, the princess became his queen, and the little sister became a princess.

They all lived happily ever after.

*Comments:* Elementary school kids love this story. For them I usually rename it Princess Hide-and-Seek, and we spend long minutes discussing what her favorite game would be before I reveal her name (even though sometimes she ends up being called Princess I Spy). This folktale type exists in other variants outside Hungary, but this is the one I am most familiar with, courtesy of a colorful little cartoon that I used to watch a lot when I was a child.

The reasoning behind the princess's challenge (and Péter's name) is entirely my creation. Take it or leave it.

---

## The Tale of Sir James Ramsay of Bamff

*Ability:* X-ray vision (quite literally)
*Source of power:* Natural (Snake flesh)

*Origin:* Scotland

*Teachings:* There is a way out even from the direst situation, learning gives you power, learning from past mistakes, honor and forgiveness.

*Age group:* 10+

*Sources:* Chambers, R. (1826). *Popular Rhymes of Scotland.* London: J. Duncan.

Frazer, J.G. (1888). "The Language of Animals." *The Archaeological Review* I No. 2: 81–91.

Scott, R. (1930). *The Thumb of Knowledge in the Legend of Finn, Sigurd and Taliesin: Studies in Celtic and French Literature.* New York: Publications of the Institute of French Studies.

*Variants:* There are many tales about people acquiring powers through getting their hand burned by magical food. The Irish Finn MacCool (later in this book), the Welsh Taliesin, the Icelandic Sigurd, and a number of folktale characters make the same mistake, with various different results. Extraordinary knowledge and the language of animals are among the most common.

For readings on the story and related subjects, see sources.

*Text:* Sir James Ramsay, the Baronet of Bamff, made some mistakes. One of them, probably the worst, was being caught up in a conspiracy against the king. He barely got away with his life — his lands were forfeit to the crown, his home taken from him, and if he ever returned to Scotland from exile, there would be a price on his head.

Sir James fled to France, and then to Spain, and then wandered all over Europe, looking for a new home. As he wandered, feeling homesick and lonely, through the woods, he met an old man who looked as well dressed as Sir James was ragged and hungry. He introduced himself as a doctor, and asked Sir James to tell him his story.

Sir James was not sick, just starved and tired. The doctor offered to take him on as an apprentice; if he helped with work, he would offer him room and board, and teach him all about healing. This was better than Sir James could have expected anywhere else, so he agreed, and became the doctor's apprentice.

Things were easy for a while. Sir James learned to cure illnesses, set broken bones, and mix medicine for various purposes. Then, one day, the old doctor told him a secret. "There is a medicine," he said, "with more healing power than any other in the world." If they could prepare it, they could make their fortune. The only problem was that the ingredients were very specific and hard to come by. "There is a river in Scotland," he said, "that holds the key to the potion." As he described the river, Sir James recognized it in an instant — it flowed through his own estate in Bamff. He volunteered to travel home in disguise, not only for the special ingredient, but also to see his beloved Scotland again.

The doctor gave him specific instructions on what to do. "There is a place," he said, "where the river widens into a deep, clear pool. Go there on the three nights of the full moon. A white snake will slide out of the water and under a great rock. Watch it carefully, and on the way back to the water catch it and kill it, and bring it to me."

Sir James disguised himself as a poor traveler, and returned to Scotland without anyone knowing. He hid himself by the pool on the full moon nights, and watched as the pure white snake appeared from the water. The first two nights he was not fast enough, and the snake slid back into the pool before he could catch it; but on the third night he succeeded. He returned to his master in Spain, who seemed delighted to see the snake, but was not so kind to Sir James. He ordered him to go down into the vault and stew the snake in a pot until it turned to oil. He forbade him to let anyone know about what he was doing, or to taste the oil. One little taste, he warned, would spoil the healing powers, and it would kill any man in an instant if they did not have the proper remedy.

Sir James went down to the vault and cooked the snake till it turned to oil. But when he was pouring the oil into a bottle a few scalding hot drops spilled out onto his hand, and forgetting about his master's advice, he put his hand in his mouth to cool it down.

As soon as he did, something changed. He did not die, like he was told he would. His eyes opened up and he realized he could see through everything. When his master came downstairs to take a look at the oil, Sir James remained silent, and he was glad he did. He could see inside the old doctor now, and he could tell he was not as good as he seemed: he was ready to kill Sir James if he found out he had tasted the medicine. Sir James realized the doctor only took him on as an apprentice because he knew Scotland well.

Sir James said goodbye to his master, and escaped with his life once again. But now he knew enough to become a doctor of his own, and a very good doctor too, since he always saw exactly what was happening inside sick people. He cured many illnesses and saved many lives. But he always longed to return home to Scotland, even after his life took a turn for the better. One day he decided to risk it; nobody knew him as a doctor, he thought he would be safe.

As soon as he arrived, he was greeted with interesting news. The king of Scotland was very sick; he had been sick for a long time. No doctor in Scotland could cure him, and even the ones who arrived from far away failed at even telling what his illness was. Finally he declared that whoever cured him could marry his daughter, the princess, and become heir to the throne. Sir James presented himself at the castle, and as soon as he was led into the king's bedchamber he saw that there was a ball of hair inside the king that could not be moved or reached. He told the king he could put him to sleep, cut him open, and remove the ball of hair, if he had permission. The king, desperate to be healed, consented, and Sir James performed the surgery; by the time the king woke up, he was cured, even though a little weak from the loss of blood.

He was so pleased with his doctor that Sir James decided to take a gamble: falling to his knees he revealed who he really was, and begged for forgiveness. The king was happy to forgive him. He returned the lands around Bamff to Sir James, allowed him to marry the princess, and finally, after so many adventures, the exiled knight could return home.

*Comments:* As I have mentioned before, there are many similar stories in legend and folklore. Sir James's sight, however, makes this one especially interesting. While in Green Peter the princess's sight is part of a cosmic game of hide-and-seek, Sir James puts his to very practical uses.

Sir James is an intriguing character. He is not your young, strong folktale hero; he has made mistakes, seen the darker side of life, and lives in exile. He escapes death more than once, gains supernatural powers, and puts them to good use, together with the knowledge he had learned the hard way. He does not become a miracle doctor overnight. He works for everything he has, until the happy ending.

---

## Finn MacCool and the Giants

*Ability:* Superhuman hearing, superhuman sense of touch, superhuman agility (climbing, aim, sleight of hand), infinite knowledge, immovable object, technomancy (crafting)

*Source of power:* Unknown

*Origin:* Ireland

*Teachings:* Teamwork, bravery, respect for one's given word.

*Age group:* 6+

*Sources:* Campbell, J.F. (1969). *Popular Tales of the West Highlands*. Detroit: Singing Tree Press.

Curtin, J. (1921). *Hero-tales of Ireland*. Boston: Little, Brown & Co.

MacInnes, D. (1973). *Folk and Hero Tales*. New York: AMS Press.

O'Shea, P. (1987). *Finn MacCool and the Small Men of Deeds*. New York: Holiday House.

*Variants:* This tale belongs to the folktale type AaTh 513, the Extraordinary Companions. I am sprinkling the many variants of this type throughout this book based on what abilities they represent. Even just within Ireland and Scotland, Finn MacCool's adventures have several recorded versions (see sources), which are all very similar and entertainingly different at the same time.

*Text:* One day Finn MacCool, the hero of Ireland, was walking along the seashore deep in thought, when something caught his eye. Far off on the horizon he could see a small dot among the waves, and as he watched, the dot grew bigger and bigger, until he could make out a head. Then, as the head approached the shore, shoulders emerged from the water, then a chest and arms, and soon a giant waded out of the sea and stood in front of him.

"Who are you?" asked Finn, craning his neck to look up. "And what brings you to Erin?"

"I come from the Island of the Big Men, and I bring a message to Finn MacCool," boomed the giant's voice.

"Well, you can give your message to me, and I will make sure Finn Mac-Cool hears it straight from my lips." Finn said. He was smarter than to give himself away to a giant before he heard the message.

"Tell Finn that the king of the Big Men needs his help," said the messenger. "Every time a child is born to his wife, someone steals the babe away on the first night. He had already lost two boys, and he is afraid the third will be lost too, unless the hero of Erin can protect him."

Finn nodded. "Go back home and tell your king that Finn MacCool will hear his message and consider it."

The giant waded back into the sea and disappeared, and Finn MacCool, true to his word, spent a few days thinking the matter over. When he finally made up his mind, he went back to the shore to look for a ship that could take him to the Island of the Big Men. Instead of a ship, however, he came across a group of young men playing hurley on the sand. As he walked closer, he changed his mind about them; they did not look so young anymore, but they still looked smaller than grown men. They stopped the game and smiled, waving at him.

"Greetings, King of the Fians," they said in unison. "What brings you here today?"

"How ... how do you know me? Who are you?"

"We know you very well," said the small men. "That is one of our many talents."

"Talents?" asked Finn curiously, and turned to the biggest of the small men. "What is your talent?"

"If I sit down, no one can move me," the man answered proudly. "That is why they call me Lazy Bones."

"Is that so?" Finn smiled. "I would like to see that."

The young man smiled too, and plopped down right there on the sand. Finn grabbed him by the arm and pulled ... but the small man did not move an inch. Finn pulled with both hands and all his might (and he was a very strong fellow) but no matter how hard he tried, he could not move Lazy Bones.

"All right, then," he huffed, letting go, and turned to another small man. "How about you?"

"They call me Far Feeler. I can feel a leaf fall to the ground all the way from the Eastern World, through the soles of my feet."

"That is a useful talent," said Finn, and turned to the next. "What is your name?"

"My name is Hearing Ear," said the young man. "I can hear people whispering to each other on the other side of the world."

"Hearing Ear indeed. How about you there?"

"Knowing Man is my name."

"What do you know?"

"Everything."

"I like the sound of that," nodded Finn, and turned to the next man. "What is your talent?"

"I can climb a tower made of glass faster than a squirrel climbs a tree."

"A good climber is always useful," Finn said to himself. "Who is next?"

"I can shoot a single fly out of a swarm," said a young man who was holding a bow and had a quiver on his back. "They call me the Bowman."

"That's nothing," another one piped up. "I can steal the eggs from a nest while the mother bird is still sitting on them, and the bird doesn't even notice."

"What is your name?"

"Thief."

"Indeed." Finn smiled to himself, and turned to the last man. "How about your talent?"

"They call me Three Sticks." The last man bowed in greeting. "I am a carpenter. I can make anything out of wood, faster than you can blink."

Finn's eyes lit up.

"Can you make a ship?"

"I can."

"How long would it take you to make one?"

"Just turn around on your heel and you'll see."

Finn watched as the small man picked up a chip of wood from the shore, then spun around. By the time he was finished spinning, there was a ship floating on the waves, complete with sails and ropes and everything a ship could need.

"Very well," Finn clapped his hands. "I am going to the Island of the Big Men to help their king. Would you, my friends, be interested in entering my service and joining me for this quest?"

The small men all nodded as one.

"We will serve you, we will guide you, and we will help you!"

"Name your price," said Finn, for he had never let anyone leave his service unpaid.

"Five gold pieces each, and we will serve you for a year and a day."

"Done!"

They loaded the ship with enough provisions for the journey to the Island of the Big Men (Knowing Man knew exactly how long it would take them to get there), and set sail. During the journey they told stories and talked and sang and played games; but as soon as they reached the Island of the Big Men, they pulled the ship high and dry onto shore, and set out to complete their quest. It was not hard to find the king's palace — it was a palace built for giants, after all, bigger than any fortress Finn MacCool had ever seen. When they walked in and introduced themselves to the king of the Big Men, they received a very warm welcome.

"Greetings, Finn MacCool!" boomed the king. "I am ever so grateful that you could come to help me. My third son was born today. The first two had been taken on their first night, so I am sure whoever stole them will come again tonight. Do you think you could save my babe from being taken?"

"I will guard your child," nodded Finn. "And if I cannot keep him safe, I will give you my own head in the morning."

The king was satisfied with the answer. Finn asked for the strongest room of the castle that had no windows and only one door. He locked himself in there with the babe and two nurses, and all of the small men. The door was locked and bolted from the outside ... and from the inside as well. As night fell, Finn and his companions sat and waited.

"Do you know what will happen tonight?" asked Knowing Man.

"I don't," Finn answered. "Do you?"

"Of course. The thief that took the two other babes will take this one too."

"Is that so? Do you also know who the thief is?"

"I do. It is the sister of the king. She is a terrible old witch who used to live on this island until she had an argument with her brother, and he exiled her to the Eastern World. Now she comes every night and takes the newborn babe to leave her brother without an heir. She will come tonight, and when she cannot find a window or a door, she will reach down the chimney and try to take the child."

As soon as Knowing Man said that, Lazy Bones walked over to the fireplace and sat down, waiting.

A little after midnight Hearing Ear spoke up: "I can hear her! She is leaving her castle now. She is telling ... telling the guards to keep an eye on the children while she is gone!"

"That means the two boys are still alive," nodded Finn MacCool.

"I can feel her," said Far Feeler. "She is climbing to the roof of her castle now ... that is the only entrance. The walls are slippery as glass."

"Warn me when she is near," Finn said. Minutes trickled by, and then Hearing Ear spoke again.

"She is here. She is walking around the castle."

"Why do the guards not stop her?"

"She is invisible," said Knowing Man.

"Tell me where she is."

"She is climbing the walls right now," said Far Feeler, with his palm on the wall. "She is up on the roof...."

A few moments later an arm appeared in the chimney; a hag's arm with long gnarly fingers, scaly skin, and long yellow fingernails. As soon as it appeared Lazy Bones grabbed it and held it fast. The witch struggled and pulled and thrashed, but she could not break free ... then Lazy Bones yanked on the arm and tore it off, and it fell down the chimney. Everyone looked at the terrible trophy in amazement, and they all gathered to measure it — and as they did, they forgot to keep an eye on the child. The hag reached down with her other hand, grabbed the babe, and she was gone.

"I promised I would keep the child safe!" Finn held his head in his hands. "What shall we do now?"

"We still have time till the morning," said Knowing Man. "We can bring the child back."

Quietly Three Sticks opened the door and the little group of heroes ran for the ship in the dark, and set sail for the Eastern World. It was closer than they thought, or maybe some enchantment was helping them along; whatever the case was, they made very good time, and reached the shore of the Eastern World. Finn and most of the small men stayed behind to guard the ship while Climber and Thief went to bring the children back.

When they found the witch's castle, it shone like black glass in the moonlight. It was one huge tower with no doors or windows, not even stones jutting out of the wall.

"Climber," said Thief, "take me to the roof."

Climber let Thief climb onto his back, then he started to climb, and he climbed faster than a squirrel, scaling the glass wall in no time at all. They found the door on the roof. Thief opened it, crept down inside the tower, and soon returned with one child in his hand.

"We are in luck — all the servants are busy tending to the hag's wounds. Take this one down, and come back for me."

And so they did it. Thief stole all three of the babies and Climber carried them down to the ship, until everyone was on board safe and sound. As soon as Thief and Climber returned for the last time, they set sail for the Island of the Big Men once again.

"She will come after us," said Knowing Man. "Even with one arm, she can destroy us all."

"She will not," said Bowman, pulling an arrow from his quiver. "Hearing Ear, tell me when she is near."

"I can hear her," said Hearing Ear, "she just found out the children are gone. She is roaring and cursing at the servants ... now she is leaving the castle ... now she is coming after us."

"Tell me when she is near."

"She is coming closer," said Far Feeler. "I can feel the water boil in her wake. She is almost here...."

Bowman put the arrow on the string and pulled it all the way back to his ear; and when he caught the first glimpse of the hag flying after them, he let the arrow fly. It cut through the air like lightning, and hit the hag right on the forehead. She was dead in an instant; she fell to the water, and sank like a stone.

The ship sailed fast, and the heroes made it back to the island an hour before dawn. When the king woke up at sunrise and hurried to the chamber to see what happened during the night, he did not only find Finn and the small men guarding the babe in the cradle, but he also found the two older children playing together on the floor. His joy was endless as he embraced all three of his children.

Over breakfast Finn told the king everything about the hag and their midnight journey.

"It was your sister who stole the babes, your highness. She will not bother you again, but if you have others in your family like her, you should keep an eye on them. Just in case."

The king ordered a feast to celebrate his family, and the feast lasted for seven days and seven nights. When it was finally over, the king sent all his men to carry treasures and riches to Finn's ship, and it took three whole days to load them all, until the ship was only a few inches from sinking from the weight.

"If you ever need my help," said the king, shaking Finn's hand, "all you have to do is send a message."

Once everyone said their goodbyes, Finn and his crew sailed back to Erin. The king of the Fianna did not forget to pay the small men for their service; and on top of the five gold pieces he also divided the treasures up between them.

This was not Finn MacCool's last adventure by far; it wasn't the last of the small men's either. But to the end of their days, they all remembered fondly their amazing adventures on the Island of the Big Men.

*Comments:* I am quite fond of this story. Just like other variations (see Szélike in the next section), it is full of interesting characters, adventure, and superpowers (note that in the original text they call them "virtues"). Finn MacCool, interestingly enough, does not use his own infinite knowledge while he acts as the leader of the group. In other versions there is a mention of that, or he simply takes on the role of Knowing Man. The tale usually does not tell where the "small men" came from, but it is implied that they might be from the fairy world.

Whatever the case is, Finn is certainly no stranger to leading men with extraordinary abilities — many of the Fians, his own band of warriors, also had "virtues."

The interesting point of the story is Far Feeler, who is the main reason why I included this variant here. Primary senses like sight and hearing occur quite often in this story type, but the sense of touch the way this story describes it is unique to this Irish version. The way Far Feeler and Hearing Ear work together to inform the rest of the group about their enemy (and give "eyes" to Bowman for the final shot) would make any modern superhero team proud. This story is a prime example of teamwork, and always sparks intriguing discussions with the audience about special talents and their many creative uses.

## Three Critical Men

*Ability:* Superhuman sense of smell, superhuman sensitivity

*Source of power:* Unknown

*Origin:* India

*Teachings:* Um ... eat healthy? Oh, and don't fight with your siblings, it's not good for anyone.

*Age group:* 16+

*Sources:* This story is part of the *Kathasaritsagara*, known to English-speaking people as *The Ocean of Streams of Stories*, written in Sanskrit in the 11th century.

Mather, R.B. (1976). *Shih-shuo Hsin-yü: A New Account of Tales of the World, by Liu I-ch'ing, with Commentary by Liu Chün.* Minneapolis: University of Minnesota Press.

Tawney, C.H. (1924). *The Ocean of Story VI.* London: Grafton House.

Zong In-sob (1952). *Folk Tales from Korea.* London: Routledge & Paul.

*Variants:* The first thing that comes to mind is Andersen's "Princess and the Pea." Tawney lists a series of variants in his book from India as well as from the *Arabian Nights.* He calls the main motif of the tale "the Quintessence Motif." Zong In-sob has a slightly different but very much entertaining version called "The Two Brothers and the Magistrate." I have also found a variant from 5th century China (Mather 1976) in which Xun Xu (a 3rd century scholar) tells solely by taste where the cook got the wood he used to roast the meat for dinner.

*Text:* Once upon a time, in the country of Anga, there was a very respectable Brahmin who had three sons, one more fastidious than the other (which is an eloquent way of saying they were very picky about certain things). One day the father sent his sons down to the beach to fetch a turtle for a sacrifice he had been preparing. The three brothers walked together and soon found a turtle scuttling along in the sad. They stood around it.

"Well, go on then," said the oldest brother. "Fetch it."

"Why should we fetch it?" the others retorted. "You fetch it!"

"I can't. It's slippery with slime."

"Then why should we carry it?"

"Because if you don't, you have obstructed Father's sacrifice and you will drag him down to hell."

The younger brothers mused about that for a moment.

"Wait, isn't that the same for you yourself?"

"I can't touch disgusting things. I am very critical about what I eat."

"Well, and I am very critical about women," the second brother stated. "More critical than you will ever be about food."

"Well then, it is decided, you have to take the turtle," the oldest brother said to the youngest.

"I beg to differ. You two might be critical about your food and your women, but I am more critical than both of you."

"About what?"

"Beds."

The three brothers kept on quarreling, and the turtle quietly shuffled away. The argument went on and on until they decided that only the king could make a final decision in the case.

The king of Anga was both surprised and amused when the three brothers explained their disagreement, and decided to put their abilities to the test. He invited them to a great feast for dinner. The food was fit for royalty, displaying all of the five flavors (sweet, bitter, salty, sour and pungent), and the plates were buried under all the delicacies.

"This food smells like corpses."

The king dropped his spoon in shock and turned to the oldest brother who sat by the table with his face puckered up in disgust.

"It is made of the whitest rice!" The king smelled the dish himself. "It does not smell like anything but fragrant food!"

"It does too."

The dish was passed around the table, but whoever smelled it could only say that it smelled like rice. Finally the king sent for the servants and the cooks. After questioning everyone in his palace that worked with or around food, he finally found out that the rice had been harvested from fields that were close to a funeral burning place.

"Told you so," the oldest brother sighed, and everyone was amazed at his refined sense of smell, and his critical taste.

"You are truly particular about what you eat," the king had to admit. "Feel free to choose any other dish you like."

Once the feast was over, the three brothers all retired to the bedrooms assigned to them. The king then ordered the most beautiful dancing maiden in his court to adorn herself and visit the second brother in his chambers. He reasoned that no one could be critical enough about women to turn away a beauty like the full moon in a midnight sky, graceful and slender.

He was wrong.

The moment the maiden in her silks and sparkling jewels entered the Brahmin's bedchamber, the young man held his nose and backed away into the farthest corner of the room.

"Take her away!" he begged the guards. "She reeks of goats!"

In the end the guards, who were too bewildered to act, did not have to act at all. The maiden ran out of the room and straight to the king, and told him about the insults the Brahmin threw at her. The king sent for the young man immediately.

"How can you accuse such a lovely maiden of such horrible and untrue things?! She had perfumed herself with sandalwood and camphor and black aloe, and you still dare to say she reeks?!"

But no matter how furious the king was, the Brahmin kept calmly repeating the same thing over and over again. Finally the king pulled the weeping maiden aside and talked to her quietly for long minutes, before he turned back to the rest of the court.

"It seems that the young man was right," he said finally, as if he himself was not quite believing what he was about to say. "This maiden lost her mother when she was born, and was raised on goat's milk."

"Told you so," the Brahmin sighed, and went back to bed without the maiden.

Just as this matter was settled, a loud scream could be heard, coming from the youngest brother's bedroom. The king and the servants rushed into the room, and found the young Brahmin out of bed, his hands pressed to his side, yelling in agony.

"What happened?!" the king demanded, afraid that someone had attacked his guest.

"The bed! There was something horrible in the bed!"

The king looked at the bed. It was built high with seven mattresses and the softest white linen sheets, fit for royalty and the most esteemed guests. It looked very comfortable, like a big white cloud.

"Something horrible? ... But what?"

"I don't know! But look what it did to my side!"

Pulling up his nightshirt, the Brahmin revealed his side that had a large angry red wedge on it as if someone had hit him with an iron rod.

The king ordered his servants to turn the bed over and look through all the sheets and mattresses (even though he could not even imagine what could hurt a man like that). After searching meticulously through the bedding, the servants finally emerged — with a single strand of hair that had been left under the seven mattresses.

When morning came, the king gave three hundred golden pieces to all three of the brothers, and refused to decide their argument. All three of them had amazing abilities, and they were all equally critical about their fields of expertise — food, women, and beds. The three brothers went home, pleased with themselves. And completely forgot about the turtle.

*Comments:* The kingdom of Anga was one of many smaller kingdoms that flourished on the Indian subcontinent in the 6th century BCE. Brahmin, in this case, does not mean priest as much as people belonging to the highest caste of the Indian caste system. Turtles are sacrificed to this very day in great numbers on the festival of Diwali to the goddess Kali, meeting with great international disapproval. At least this one in the story gets away, but the element of sacrifice still needs discussion with audiences to raise cultural awareness.

Although it is not explained in the story, it is interesting to muse about the fact that the two older brothers only display their special sense of smell related to a "field of expertise." The "superhuman sense of smell" in this case is more of an exaggerated depiction of being a connoisseur of a certain thing, rather than an actual supernatural power (similar to how wine experts can taste flavors in wine other people would not notice). Still, for the purpose of this book — close enough.

# Speed

Another ability that humans cannot compete in with other creatures is speed. Speed has been a long time dream of ours: we have repeatedly broken many records both on the physical level at running races and championships, and with our creations that allow us to travel (and transport information) faster and faster. Not so long ago, jumping from Europe to America in less than half a day would have been a story fit for folktales and legends. And before this dream was made into reality, it was guarded and treasured in folktales for centuries, reminding generation after generation of what we had to aspire to.

*Heroes with superhuman speed:* Daphne Millbrook (NBC's *Heroes*), Dash Parr (*The Incredibles*), Flash (DC), Northstar (Marvel), Quicksilver (Marvel)

# Princess Szélike

*Ability:* Superhuman speed, superhuman strength, long-range telepathy, superhuman aim, and impressive lung capacity
*Source of power:* Unknown
*Origin:* Hungary
*Teachings:* Cooperation and teamwork, creative solutions to problems.
*Age group:* 6+
*Sources:* Benedek, E. (1988). *Magyar mese-és mondavilág II.* Budapest: Móra Ferenc Könyvkiadó.
*Variants:* This story type is another type AaTh 513 (Extraordinary Companions). For my thesis in storytelling, I once collected 37 different versions of it, from Mongolia to the Caribbean. This is one of the two Hungarian variants included in my research. Since there is no more fitting folktale type for superpowers than this one, other versions will be included later on in this book.
*Text:* Once upon a time, far far away, beyond the glass mountains and the Óperenciás Sea, lived a king who only had one son. The prince's name was János. When he grew up, his father said to him: "My son, it is time for you to go out into the world, learn what you can learn, and see what you can see. That is how you will become a great man."

He did not have to tell the prince twice. János took his bag and his walking staff, and set out down the road to see the world.

As he walked he met a very curious fellow who was tall and thin as a splinter.

"Who are you, my skinny friend?" János asked curiously. "And what is your trade?"

"My name is Lightning Fast. I can outrun a lightning bolt any time."

"I would like to see that!"

In that moment, a deer sprang up from a nearby bush. Lightning Fast bolted after it, and one stride, two strides, caught up with the running deer, and soon left it behind.

"Now I believe you," said the prince. "Come with me, let's share our bread, you won't regret it."

Lightning Fast agreed, and they walked on together (although he had to make sure he did not walk too fast so the prince could keep up).

As they walked on, they came across a man with broad shoulders and strong arms who was standing at the bottom of a mountain.

"Who are you, my friend, and what is your trade?" asked the prince.

The strong man turned around to look at them.

"My name is Carries Mountains," he said, "and I am strong enough to carry a mountain on my shoulder."

And just to prove his point, he turned back to the mountain, lifted it up, carried it a few steps, and the carefully put it down again.

The prince only had one question. "Would you like to join us?"

The three companions walked on, and the road led them into a forest. After a while, they noticed a strange sound in the distance: it was the whistling of the wind, mixed with the creaking and snapping of trees. The closer they walked, the louder it became. It was clear that a strong wind was sweeping across the land, breaking grown trees in half like twigs. As they climbed up a hill, they found the source of the wind: it was a broad-chested man, blowing wind out of his mouth with the force of a storm.

"Who are you?" yelled Prince János over the noise. "And what are you doing?!"

The man stopped blowing wind, and turned to them.

"My name is Windblower," the fellow answered, "and a sigh from me can break the strongest oak tree in the woods."

"Sounds like you would fit right in," said the prince. "Come, join us!"

The four unlikely companions traveled on. They did not have to go far before they met another traveler on the road, a young man carrying a bow and arrows.

"Good day to you!" the prince greeted him. "Who are you, and what is your trade?"

"My name is Aimwell," the man answered, "and I am an archer. I can hit a pea on someone's palm without even scratching the skin."

"I would like to see that!" said the prince, and the archer, without further ado, handed him a pea, then he walked away several yards, turned around, aimed, and shot the pea right out of the prince's hand. Now that he had proved his skills, János invited him to join the group.

They traveled together for a while, and as they walked down the road, they almost tripped over a short, stout little man lying on the ground.

"Who are you?" asked the prince. "And why are you lying on the ground?"

"I am lying down because if I put my ear on the ground, I can hear everything people think or do all over the world."

"What is your name?"

"Peter."

The six companions traveled on, and after many roads and many days, they arrived at Fairyland.

In those times, a king ruled over Fairyland, and he had a daughter who could run faster than the wind: her name was Szélike, Little Wind. The king had announced that whoever can outrun her in a race has his blessings to marry her — but he also announced that if the suitor failed, his head would adorn the walls of the castle.

Princes, barons and knights tried their luck, but no one could outrun the princess, and head after head piled up on the castle walls, until ninety-nine suitors had ended their lives that way. The moment the companions heard about this, they went up to the castle, asked for an audience with the king, and nudged Lightning Fast forward.

"This fellow would like to try his luck!"

"Well, let's see him try then," answered the king. "If he fails, his head will make one hundred on the castle walls!"

The entire court gathered to see who would prove to be faster: Princess Szélike, or the tall skinny fellow. The princess bolted first, and ran like the wind, but Lightning Fast only took a few long strides, and left her so far behind that the princess just sat down and started crying.

"Something must be wrong with her," the king said. "Maybe she is ill! Let us try again tomorrow."

Ill or not, the next day they raced again, and Lightning Fast proved to be faster. The princess ran back to the castle, crying.

"Third time is the charm," said the king, stretching the rules very thin. "You shall try again tomorrow."

That evening the princess gave Lightning Fast a diamond ring. The poor fellow was very happy — he did not know that the ring had magic in it. Whoever put it on would freeze as if he had sprouted roots, and would stay frozen until the ring is taken off.

Nobody knew about this secret — nobody except for Peter. He had been listening with his ear to the ground, and found out what the princess was planning. He went straight to Aimwell and told him that if he saw a ring on Lightning's finger, shoot the diamond off of it, that would break the curse.

The next morning the court once again gathered to see the race. The princess bolted first, and Lightning Fast was ready to follow ... but he could not even move a finger. People were starting to think he was going to lose the race — and his head! — for sure, when Aimwell put an arrow on the string and shot the diamond right out of the ring. The curse was broken. Lightning Fast bolted after the princess and left her far behind.

Szélike was not pleased at all. She had been defeated for the first time in her life! And by such a skinny, strange fellow! She had her eyes on Prince János, she would not have minded being outrun by him!

The six companions went to the king and Lightning bowed down before him.

"Your highness — I would not like to marry your daughter. I would rather take silver and gold as payment for my victory."

The king gladly agreed to the exchange, but he told the companions they could only take as much gold as the strongest of them could carry. They did not say anything, only had six carts filled with gold and silver. When they were full, Carries Mountains lifted them all up on one shoulder. The king had to order another six carts to be filled ... and Carries Mountains lifted those too, and didn't even break a sweat!

The king did not have any more coins. They had to gather all the treasures in the palace: jewelry, silverware, vases, mirrors, everything they had, and when that was all piled up on his shoulders, Carries Mountains finally said: "That will be enough."

Once the companions were on their way, the king instantly regretted giving them his entire fortune. He decided to send the princess after them. He was going to claim that she had been kidnapped, and send an army after them to bring the treasures (and his daughter) back.

Princes Szélike was very happy with the plan. She bolted right away, and caught up with the companions in no time at all. She stopped by the prince's side and would not have left him for the world.

When they stopped on the road to camp, Peter lay down and put his ear to the ground.

"I hear trouble," he told the others. "The king is sending an army after us to take back the treasures and the princess!"

"Do not worry," said Windblower. "Just leave this to me."

They waited until the army was within sight. Then Windblower took a deep breath ... and blew them all away, soldiers, horses, weapons, everything, straight back to the other end of the kingdom!

The rest of the way was peaceful. When they arrived home, the six companions divided all the treasures, Prince János married Princess Szélike, and they all lived happily ever after.

*Comments:* This is one of my favorite variations of this folktale type, mainly because the princess actually has a personality. A childish and not really likable one, but at least it is there.

This folktale type is the classic original template of many superhero team-ups in popular culture: adventurers of different and unusual skills setting out together to accomplish a quest. Some of the powers represented can still be found in those modern teams. Some researchers have suggested that this folktale type is the descendant of the myth of the Argonauts, based on the fact that many variants all around the world still contain the image of the magical ship. Others suggested that the heroes with different abilities represent different aspects of the main character: senses, thoughts, physical abilities, etc. Whatever the case is, it is fact that superhero team-ups have been popular for a very long time.

This story is a lot of fun to tell to children. All you need to do is whenever a new companion is described, assign him to one of the children and make sure they remember them. Then, when obstacles are presented, you can ask the crowd who remembers someone who could help the group overcome them. The more actively the children participate in this pseudo-roleplaying game, the more awesome the story gets, believe me. This also works with adults, by the way.

## The Giant's Ankle (or, Betcha You Didn't Know This About Achilles)

*Ability:* Superhuman speed, (near) invulnerability, healing
*Source of power:* Magical bone transplant (yup!)
*Origin:* Ancient Greece
*Teachings:* Even when you think you know a story, it can still surprise you.
*Age group:* 10+
*Sources:* Apollodorus, *The Library* III. 13.6.
Photius, *Biblioteca*, 190 (quoting Ptolemy's New History).
*Variants:* The story as it is, is quite unique, however, burning for immortality does appear in other myths in the region. Demeter, goddess of fertility, burns the mortal child Demophon she is nursing, but is interrupted by the worried parents, and does not achieve her goal. Isis, Egyptian goddess of many things, similarly tries to burn the child of Queen Astarte, and fails for the same reasons. Parents' protective nature clashes with the secrets of the gods quite often, it would seem.

*Text:* Greek praise singers through the ages have called Achilles by many epithets: Lion-Hearted, God-like, Breaker of Men, Leader of Men, Son of Peleus, Sacker of Cities ... but the most interesting story of all belongs to another name: Achilles, the Swift-footed.

Most people have heard the story of Achilles and his heel, of how his mother Thetis dipped him into the River Styx to make him invulnerable all over his body — except for his heel, where she held him. Later on, outside the walls of Troy, Achilles fell from an arrow that struck him right in that vulnerable spot.

But that is not the only story about Achilles' heel. According to another, Thetis did not dip him into water at all. She used another element: fire.

Every night while her mortal husband was asleep, the sea-goddess lit the fireplace and burned the mortal parts away piece by piece from all her children. All of them? That's right. Thetis and Peleus had six children before Achilles, and she burned them immortal one after another. But when it was Achilles's turn, Peleus woke up in the middle of the night, wandered out of his bedchamber, and caught Thetis in the act. Thinking that she was trying to kill the child, he cried out in anger and grabbed Achilles away from his mother. Thetis, her feelings hurt, left the palace, and never came back. She returned to the ocean where she came from, and from there she watched over her ill-fated, almost-immortal child.

Peleus rescued Achilles, and only the child's ankle was burnt — the rest had already been purified and made invulnerable by the flames. The father carried the hurt child to Chiron, the wise old centaur who lived in the mountains and trained young heroes. Chiron knew a lot about healing, and for Achilles's ankle, he had a special remedy. He traveled to the place that centuries before had been the battlefield of gods and giants, and unearthed the grave of Damysos, the fastest giant of them all. Cleaning the remains piece by piece, he took out the anklebone, and with special potions and ingredients, he replaced Achilles's burnt ankle with it. Not only did the child learn to walk, he also learned to run, run as fast as the legendary Damysos could, and for his extraordinary speed, they named him Podarkes, Swift-footed.

There is another legend about how Achilles came to be so fast in running. It says that when the gods were fighting their last, life-or-death battle against the titans, there was a pair of twins among them — Iris, goddess of the rainbow, and Arke, her sister. They acted as messengers of the gods, and had wings to carry the news faster. But during the struggle, when the gods seemed to be losing, Arke deserted their camp and sided with the titans. The gods, led by Zeus, won the fight, and exiled all their enemies into Tartaros; before they threw Arke in her eternal prison, they took her wings away from her. A few millennia later, Zeus presented the wings as a wedding gift to Thetis, and when her son, Achilles, was born, she fastened them to his ankles to make him run swift as the wind.

*Comments:* There is more than one way to make a man immortal. Apparently, there is also more than one way to make them run faster (don't we know that from sports news). In this case, both of those include borrowing body parts from deceased superhuman beings. It would have been easy to file Achilles under Invulnerability — but once I came across the interesting tidbit about the giant's ankle, I couldn't resist choosing Speed instead. It is a less well known power of his — although he did get an epithet out of the deal — but no less intriguing.

This story usually works well with audiences who have some previous experience with Greek mythology. Sometimes I use it to make high school mythology lessons more interesting. It fits snugly into the bigger picture with Chiron's successful career as a mentor of heroes, and serves as kind of a prequel to *The Iliad*. It also presents a fitting end to an ill-fated marriage between mortal man and goddess.

# INVISIBILITY

Another classic. Passing unseen through a crowd or staying hidden from the enemy is as useful as it is popular both in folklore and modern media. It is often mentioned together with camouflage, which, while it yields the same results, is based on different mechanics. Still, I am going to mention them together, mostly because I could not find any good folktales that mention camouflage and don't involve a talking chameleon.

The folktale motif numbers for Invisibility are D1361 (Magic Object Renders Invisible) and D1980 (Magic Invisibility). There is a variety of ways it is achieved: magic rings (that motif makes a return in *Lord of the Rings*), magic caps, magic cloaks, magic ointments, magic spells. One thing that is mentioned quite often in folklore all over Europe is the fern flower (or its seed), a plant of rare legendary beauty that, if found and harvested, can make its owner invisible (D1361.5.1). Another famous example is Hades's helmet in Greek mythology that Perseus briefly borrows in order to succeed in defeating Medusa.

Making yourself invisible without all of the above is usually the privilege of the divine or the supernatural. In popular culture invisibility can be mutation-related or genetic, due to scientific experiments gone wrong (or right), or even the result of high tech equipment.

The tales I included in this section were selected not only based on the different methods of becoming invisible, but also for the various creative uses of said power.

*Invisible Heroes:* Cipher (Marvel), Claude Rains (NBC's *Heroes*), Invisible Kid (DC), Invisible Man (*League of Extraordinary Gentlemen*), Invisible Woman (Marvel), Martian Manhunter (DC), Miss Martian (DC), Simon Bellamy (E4's *Misfits*)

## *The Gold-Spitting Prince*

*Ability:* Invisibility, teleportation, shape-shifting, and spitting precious metals

*Source of power:* Magical objects / Magical food

*Origin:* Mongolia

*Teachings:* Friendship and loyalty, respect for others, leadership.

*Age group:* 8+

*Sources:* Milroy, M.E. (1873). *Sagas from the Far East, or, Kalmouk and Mongolian Traditional Tales.* London: Gilbert and Rivington.

*Variants:* The gold-spitting prince and the turquoise-spitting minister in: Warder, A.K. (1992). *Indian Kavya Literature Vol. IV*. Delhi: Motilal Banarsidass.

The story of the orphan girl who marries the prince of Masar — Hausa in: Abramson, G., and H. Kilpatrick (2006). *Religious Perspectives in Modern Jewish and Muslim Literatures*. New York: Routledge.

*Text:* A long, long time ago a great khan ruled over the land. The land was fertile and rich, for there was a river flowing across it — but the richness came with a price. At the source of the river there was a pool, and in the pool two serpent gods who could send floods or dry up the water as they pleased. In exchange for keeping the land watered, they demanded a sacrifice: one grown man every year, chosen by lot from the people of the kingdom.

One year, the lot fell on the khan himself. There was no one of equal rank to take his place — no one, except his son. The prince volunteered at once, but the khan refused: "You are the future of this kingdom, and the heir to the throne. How could I let you die instead of me?"

"You can have other sons, father," the prince insisted. "And how could I become khan if I let my own father die?"

The prince could not be convinced to stay at home. The khan gave in with a heavy heart, and the prince set out to offer himself to the serpent gods. The people followed him for a while, already crying and wailing as if he was dead, but as they got closer to the pool, they fell behind. Only one person kept following him: a poor man's son who had been his friend since they were children. The prince turned around.

"Go home, friend. I am off to become a sacrifice to the serpent gods so the land does not suffer. You do not have to come with me."

"You have been good to me all my life," the poor man's son answered. "If I cannot go instead of you, I will go with you."

As they got closer to the pool, they heard a low, rumbling sound. At first they thought it must be the sound of the waves, but soon they could make out words: the two serpents were talking to each other.

"Here comes the prince to offer himself in his father's place," said the old gold-yellow serpent. "And with him comes the poor man's son to offer himself for the prince. Look at these people. They are so willing to die for each other, but they do not have the courage to fight us."

"They have tried before," said the younger, emerald green serpent. "But they never succeeded. There is no way to kill us."

"There is," said the older serpent in a solemn voice. "If they chopped our heads off with a staff, we would not come back to life. The God of Serpents declared it so."

"But they are carrying sharp, shining swords!" Now the younger serpent started to panic.

"That's just it, son. Sharp weapons can never harm us, so no one suspects that a mere staff would. And they do not know either that if they ate our flesh, they could spit gold and precious stones. Humans are better off not knowing things like that."

What the serpents did not know, however, was that the prince spoke the language of animals — his mother had taught him that skill. He did not miss a word of what the serpents were saying. Sneaking off into the woods he cut two staffs, one for himself, one for his friend. Together they strolled down to the pool, and when the serpents raised their heads from the water, they easily killed them both. Once that was done, they cooked their flesh and ate it. The prince spat, and he discovered he could spit gold; his friend spat too, and he spat emeralds. This amused them for a long time before they decided to do something else.

They decided not to return home. The land was safe now, but people believed they were dead, sacrificing themselves for the good of the kingdom, and it would have been hard to explain how they survived. So instead of going home, they set out on a journey to seek their fortune elsewhere.

As they were crossing a mountain pass, they came across an inn owned by a woman and her daughter. When they saw the travelers were torn and exhausted, they demanded pay up front to make sure they had money. The prince spat a few pieces of gold onto the table, and lo and behold, suddenly the woman and her daughter were as sweet to them as honey, and brought them food and drinks until they were full — and fairly drunk. But once they saw they could not spit up gold and gemstones anymore, they turned them out to sleep in the ditch.

Once the prince and his friend sobered up, they went on with their journey. Soon they came across a palm grove by a river, and a group of young boys fighting loudly under a tree.

"What is going on here?" the prince asked, holding them apart by the scruff of their neck.

"We found a cap on that tree," said one boy, "and we are fighting about who gets to keep it."

"What is so special about this cap?"

"Whoever puts it on becomes invisible to men, gods, and demons."

"I will settle this dispute for you," volunteered the prince. "Go to the other end of the grove, all of you, and then run back to me. Whoever touches the cap in my hand first will get to keep it."

The boys agreed, and left in a hurry. The prince put on the cap, held the hand of his friend, and they both became instantly invisible. The boys searched for them for a while, but could not find them, and they went home disappointed.

Farther down the road they encountered a group of demons quarreling about a pair of boots that could make the owner instantly appear wherever they wanted to go. The same trick that worked on human boys also worked on demons — while they were running a race, the prince put on one boot and his friend the other, and they wished themselves to a land that had no khan.

When they woke up in the morning, they found themselves in a hollow tree. Outside the tree there was a great gathering of people, preparing to elect a new khan. They took a cake out of the straw sacrifice and tossed it up in the air, agreeing that whoever's head it fell on would become the new khan. The cake flew up and up into the air, then it started falling down and down, and fell onto the hollow tree. Walking closer the people discovered the two travelers inside the tree. Although they were surprised, many of them were suspicious.

"How do we know either of them is worth of ruling out kingdom?"

The prince then spat some gold, and his friend spat some emeralds, and there were no more questions. The prince became khan, and his friend the chief minister, and people soon grew to love them both.

The khan married the daughter of the last khan. She was beautiful and kind, but she secretly loved another. The minister soon discovered that every third night she quietly left the palace without anyone accompanying her, and he decided to find out where she went. Wearing the cap of invisibility, he followed her to the edge of the city to a richly furnished house, and watched her as she changed her dress into one more splendid that she ever wore in the presence of the khan. Then through the window came a bird of many colors, and transformed himself into Cuklaketu, the handsome son of the gods. The lovers embraced each other, and started to talk.

"Tell me about your husband," said Cuklaketu. "What is he like?"

"It is too early to say," said the princess. "He is still young, and I do not know him well yet."

The lovers parted at the end of the night. The minister went home, and did not say anything to anyone; he decided to wait and see if the princess continued meeting her lover. Sure enough, three nights later she left the palace again, and the minister followed, listening to the lovers' conversation.

"I want to see your husband for myself," said the son of the gods. "I will visit tomorrow in disguise."

"How will I know you?"

"I will be a swallow, perching upon the throne."

The minister went home and told the khan everything he had seen. He suggested that they set a fire by the throne and when the bird appears, they throw it into the fire, where the khan can kill it, and get rid of the princess's lover once and for all. And so it happened. The minister stood by wearing his invisible cap, and when the swallow perched on the throne he grabbed it by the tail and threw it into the flames. The khan raised his sword to cut the bird in half, but his wife cried out, caught his hand, and the swallow flew away singed by the flames.

The next night the minister followed the princess again as she went to meet her lover. Cuklaketu was burnt and hurt, and the princess cried when she saw him.

"Don't cry for me," said the son of the gods. "Your husband has proven that he is stronger and wiser than me. Now you belong to him. Do not be angry at him, for he is a good man at heart."

That was the last anyone had seen of Cuklaketu, as he flew away on his burnt wings. After that, the princess was faithful to the khan, and she grew to love him.

The minister went on using the magic cap and the boots for many things. He watched over the people of the kingdom, punished thieves and bandits, and reported to the khan everything he needed to know to govern his people in a fair and just manner.

One day he came across a temple, and walked in, invisible, to see who lived inside. He saw a young priest pull out a scroll from a hidden compartment in the wall, and spread it out on the ground. On the scroll was the picture of a donkey. The priest danced around it five times, and as he finished the fifth turn, he transformed into a donkey. Then, he danced around five times the other way, and turned back into a man.

This intrigued the minister. When the priest left, he stole the scroll, and wished himself back to the inn where they had been so badly treated by the woman and her daughter at the beginning of their journey.

"What do you want from us?" they asked as soon as they saw him, afraid that he had come to take revenge.

"I would like to reward you for your hospitality," he answered, and put some gold coins on the table. The woman and her daughter were suddenly as sweet as honey.

"We have seen your friend spit gold," they said. "Do you have the same ability?"

"I do not," admitted the minister. "But I have another way of acquiring as much gold as I want," he leaned closer and whispered. "I have a magic scroll, and if I dance five times around it, it gives me enough gold for whatever I want to buy."

That was all the women needed to hear. They started pouring drinks, one stronger than the other, and when the minister fell asleep, they stole the scroll.

When the minister woke up, slightly hung over but cheerful none the less, he found two donkeys in the room, stomping around in panic. He led them to the khan.

"Sir, these are the two women who make travelers drunk and then rob them blind. What shall we do with them?"

"They shall carry burdens and work on the fields as donkeys for five years," the khan ruled. "After that, they will be forgiven for their crimes."

And so it was.

The khan and his minister ruled over the land for many prosperous years, and they were friends until the end of their lives.

*Comments:* I seriously considered opening up a new category for "turning bodily fluids into precious materials" and filing this story under it, but I decided to go with invisibility instead. One thing for sure, the heroes of the tale put their abilities to good use. They are all acquired skills, even understanding the speech of animals which the khan had learned from his mother. This calls to mind the legends about Olympias, mother of Alexander the Great, and her affinity for serpents.

The cap of invisibility and the boots of teleportation are both common in world folklore, as is the trick by which they are acquired. It is questionable whether or not it just qualifies as theft, though. Actually, quite a few parts of this story are questionable from a moral standpoint, which is why it is important to know one's audience before one decides to tell this tale. The issues of arranged marriage, infidelity and the attempted murder of the lover speak of another time and another world view, as does the (very) corporal punishment for theft and robbery. This folktale is great for starting conversations on moral issues.

## The Tengu's Magic Cloak

*Ability:* Invisibility

*Source of power:* Magical object (cloak)

*Origin:* Japan

*Teachings:* Mischief and the dangers thereof.

*Age group:* 6+

*Sources:* "The Goblin's Invisible Straw Raincoat." (1971). *Japan Report* Vol. 17–18, No. 11: 6.

"Invisible Straw Raincoat of a 'Tengu.'" (1972) *Information Bulletin.* Japan: Ministry of Foreign Affairs. Public Information Bureau.

Manosalva, A. (2004). *Los siete mejores cuentos japoneses.* Bogota: Editorial Norma.

*Variants:* Most versions I have tracked down agree on all the main points of the story. There are many other Japanese tales where tengu display magical powers or carry magical objects.

*Text:* Tengu are well known all over Japan. They are goblins with large noses, wings, and hands like claws; they can fly, they are good fighters, and they possess magical treasures. One of these treasures is known as the *kakure-mino*, the straw cloak of invisibility.

These stories were well known to Hikoichi. One day, maybe out of boredom, or maybe because he had been planning on some new kinds of mischief, the boy decided he was going to find a way to get his hands on one of those magic cloaks. Picking up a piece of bamboo, he walked up the mountain where the tengu lived, and pretended to gaze through the bamboo. When he heard a tengu coming closer, he started saying things like, "Look at that! Amazing! Unbelievable! What a sight!"

This made the tengu curious. "What are you looking at, boy?"

"Oh, nothing, nothing. I am just trying out my new looking glass. It makes you see faraway places, and even places hidden behind walls!"

Now the tengu was really intrigued. "Can I take a look?"

"No! Why would I let you do that? I know that you can fly, and if I give you the looking glass, what would stop you from flying away with it?"

"I will give you my cloak in exchange," offered the tengu, "and once I am done looking, I will take it back."

"Deal," agreed Hikoichi. And while the tengu was gazing through the piece of bamboo, he put the cloak around his shoulders, and vanished.

"I can't see anything!" complained the tengu ... but when he looked around, the boy was long gone.

Hikoichi went straight into town, and walked up and down the street until he was sure the cloak worked: no one could see him; no one even suspected he was close. Cheerful with his new abilities, he went straight to a sake shop, and started drinking in the cellar. He drank and he drank, and when he was quite drunk, he tottered home, threw off the cloak, and fell into bed.

The next morning he woke up late, but with new plans for mischief already on his mind. He looked around for the cloak ... but it was gone! So he did what every boy child does when something is lost:

"MOTHER! Have you seen my cloak?"

"Oh, that dirty old thing you dragged home yesterday? It was so filthy I just burned it in the fireplace."

Hikoichi yelled out in despair and ran to the fireplace. There was nothing in there but ashes. Falling to his knees, he buried his face in his hands, mourning the loss of his magical cape ... but suddenly, he had an idea. The ashes were the ashes of a magic cloak. Maybe they still worked? Reaching into the fireplace he picked up a handful ... and his hands disappeared before his eyes. Cheerful with his discovery, he covered his entire body with the ashes, and, invisible once again, he left the house to find something to eat.

He did not walk far when he came across a rich man's house. They were holding a banquet inside. Sneaking in he started to steal food from the guests' plates, and drink from their cups. Some didn't even notice, but others did, and they thought there was a ghost playing tricks on them. They watched in alarm as cups floated and food disappeared ... but then, gradually, they noticed that a mouth appeared floating in mid-air, and then a nose, a chin, and a palm. Hikoichi, while gorging himself on food and drinks, did not notice that some of the ashes were rubbing off. He went on drinking and eating while the guests gathered around him, watching silently ... then at the host's sign they all pounced on Hikoichi as one, and poured water over his head. There he was, completely visible once again ... and completely naked. The guests chased him out of the house and down the street ... and all the while he was still wondering how they found out he was there.

*Comments:* Once again, invisibility is not a natural power. The hero (or rogue) of this story plots to acquire the object that makes him invisible, and he uses his skills of deception for mischief. An interesting detail in the story is the fact that the coat, even when reduced to ashes, still retains its magical powers. It also works in a very physical way: it has to cover every inch of the person's body, and it rubs off just like make-up would if one is careless. This is a very technical way of achieving invisibility, only magical in origin.

Audiences often raise very valid questions about the technicalities in this story: if any part not covered by the ashes is visible, how do they not see Hikoichi's eyes? Did he rub the ashes in his eyes? And if the ashes had retained the magic powers of the cloak, why did the water that washed them off not turn the floor invisible?

Try to answer at your own risk.

Hikoichi would hardly qualify as a hero (although we do not get to find out what he would have done if he had the chance to become one), but he is a classic trickster character. Telling this story can be very entertaining and also sparks interesting conversations about what people would use the cloak for if they could have one. No one is a saint.

---

## King Laurin's Rose Garden

*Ability:* Invisibility, superhuman strength, fire breathing
*Source of power:* Magical objects (cloak, belt) / Natural
*Origin:* Tyrol
*Teachings:* Honesty, keeping one's word, respect for other cultures, generosity, the importance of beauty, violence is not the answer, think before you act.
*Age group:* 12+
*Sources:* Gunther, M.A. (1874). *Tales and Legends of the Tyrol.* London:

Chapman and Hall. (1870). "King Laurin's Rose-garden." *The Cornhill Magazine* XXI: 717–730.

*Heldenbuch (Book of Heroes)* — English translation in: Weber, H.W., R. Jamieson, and W. Scott (1814). *Illustrations of Northern Antiquities*. Edinburgh: J. Ballantyne & Co.

Sandbach, F.E. (1906). *The Heroic Saga-cycle of Dietrich of Bern*. London: Sign of the Phoenix.

Stoddard, S.W. (1912). *Tramps Through Tyrol: Life, Sport, and Legend*. Boston: Little, Brown and Co.

*Variants:* King Laurin lives in the imagination of the Tyrolean people in many forms, especially around the mountain range still known as the Rosengarten. Local folktales and legends tell about him in many different ways (see sources).

*Text:*

"It should be known for what reason God created the great giants and the little dwarfs, and subsequently the heroes. First, he produced the dwarfs, because the mountains lay waste and useless, and valuable stores of silver and gold, with gems and pearls, were concealed in them. Therefore God made the dwarfs right wise and crafty, that they could distinguish good and bad, and to what use all things should be applied. They knew the use of gems — that some gave strength to the wearer, others made them invisible, which they called fog-caps. Therefore God gave art and wisdom to them, that they built them hollow hills; he gave them nobility, so that they, as well as the heroes, were kings and lords; and he gave them great riches. And the reason why God created the giants, was that they should slay the wild beasts and worms (dragons, serpents) and thus enable the dwarfs to cultivate the mountains in safety. But after some time it happened that the giants became wicked and unfaithful, and did much harm to the dwarfs. Then God created the heroes, who were a middle rank between the dwarfs and giants. And it should be known that the heroes were worthy and faithful for many years, and that they were created to come to the assistance of the dwarfs, against the unfaithful giants, the beasts, and the worms.... Among the dwarfs were many kings, who had giants for their servants; for they possessed rough countries, waste forests, and mountains near their dwellings." — from the *Heldenbuch* [*Book of Heroes*]

The king of the dwarfs was called Laurin. Some legends say he was a wise and just king; other legends say he was mean and cruel. Human travelers all around the mountains claimed that they had been led astray by the sound of dwarven hammers on precious ore. Some said they had been attacked by giants on the dwarf king's command, or that they barely escaped boulders that rolled down the mountainside and across the path.

Then again, people tend to justify things to someone else's expense.

King Laurin ruled over a vast and rich underground kingdom. His halls were filled with gold and silver, and his chests overflowed with treasure. And even though one piece of that treasure, one single gemstone from those chests was worth more than human kings could dream of, his most valued possession was something else: his garden of roses. It was the only thing he owned on the surface, hidden in a deep valley between two mountains. It was filled with the most beautiful roses of exquisite colors, and surrounded by a thin silver web that made a sound if someone snapped it walking into the garden.

Legend also says that one day King Laurin happened to walk in the woods when he came across the lovely princess Similt and her company of ladies. He fell in love with the princess at first sight and, using his cloak of invisibility, he spirited her away to his own kingdom. Similt at first was frightened and distressed, but the dwarf king was so kind to her, and his underground kingdom so full of wonder and beauty, that she soon grew to love him and his people, and most of all, love the garden of roses.

In the meantime, Similt's brother Dietlieb was leaving no stone unturned, looking for the princess. Suspecting that she had been kidnapped, he traveled to Bern to meet King Dietrich and ask for his help in this quest. On his way to Bern, accompanied by an old knight called Hildebrand, he met a forester, who told them about the dwarf king Laurin.

"For thirty-two years he has ruled his kingdom," the old man said, "and no one is allowed to enter. Whoever disturbs his rose garden has to fight him, and even though he is shorter than a man, he is much, much stronger."

Dietlieb knew immediately that his sister must have been taken by the dwarf king — and now it was all about revenge. "We have to protect our people from this tyrant!" he declared. "We must stop him from scaring travelers and taking whatever he wants!"

Arriving in Bern, he managed to convince King Dietrich and his best knight, Wittich, to accompany him on his mission. King Dietrich, hearing the stories about the evil deeds of the dwarf king, decided it was his responsibility to protect the kingdom of humans, and set out at once with his companions, looking for the rose garden in the mountains.

They traveled about thirty miles in the deep, dark forests of Tyrol until suddenly the sight of the rose garden burst upon them from the shadow of the cliffs. King Dietrich was so taken by the beauty and the wonder of the place that he stopped, and refused to go on. "Whoever can create such delicate beauty," he said, "cannot be a bad person."

But Wittich, his knight, did not agree. Yelling that the dwarf king deserved to be punished for his crimes he charged into the garden, snapping the silver thread, turning his horse around and slashing with his sword until all the roses were torn and trampled. As soon as his terrible work was done, King Laurin appeared riding a small horse and wearing splendid silver-and-gold armor the like of which the human knights had never seen before.

"You are trespassing on my land." He pointed accusingly at Wittich, "and you have destroyed my garden. According to the law of my kingdom, the punishment for your crime is the loss of your right hand and your left foot."

Wittich just laughed at the little man ... but he did not laugh for long. Laurin charged at him, and Wittich was out of the saddle and on the ground before he knew what hit him. King Laurin raised his sword to carry out the sentence ... which is when King Dietrich interfered. Even though he did not believe Wittich had been innocent, he felt responsible for his people, so he challenged Laurin to a duel.

"Be careful my king," Hildebrand advised him. "Challenge him to combat on foot. If you lose a fight to a dwarf your knights will never follow you again. Try to hit him on the head."

King Dietrich and King Laurin started to fight among the remains of the rose garden. Laurin was strong and fast, but Dietrich had a longer reach, and he hit the dwarf king on the helmet with a force that made him fall to his knees. Seeing that he needed an advantage, Laurin pulled out his cloak of invisibility and threw it around his shoulders ... forcing King Dietrich to fight blind.

Dancing around the human king he wounded him in many places, while Hildebrand was shouting advice from the sidelines. Finally Dietrich looked down: on the ground among the grass and the rose petals he could see the footprints of the invisible dwarf. He grabbed for him and they both tumbled to the ground, wrestling to come out on top. Dietrich reached for the belt that gave Laurin his extraordinary strength, and when his hands found it, he ripped it off, together with the cape. Suddenly, King Laurin was not only visible, but also weaker. He yielded.

King Dietrich was furious about what he considered cheating: the use of the belt and the cape. "You were ready to carry out the sentence of your own law on my knight, so I will carry out mine — and the sentence is death."

King Laurin knew he could not defeat the human knights alone, so he resorted to the last straw: he called upon Dietlieb, who was now, for all intents and purposes, his brother-in-law. He asked Dietlieb to fight for him.

Even though the request made Dietlieb angry, he could not refuse it for the sake of his sister. Family was sacred to the heroes, so he turned against King Dietrich and challenged him to a duel. The two knights, now truly angry at each other, charged into the fight, but wise old Hildebrand pried them apart, and tried to negotiate a truce that was in everyone's best interest. Finally they all agreed to the following terms: King Dietrich will make peace with Dietlieb and accept him as his first knight. King Laurin will take all the knights as guests to his underground kingdom, so Dietlieb can see with his own eyes that his sister is safe and happy, and he can give her away as a bride. Laurin also offered a generous gift of his treasure in exchange for making peace with King Dietrich.

After agreeing on the truce, the knights followed Laurin into the forest. They rode fifteen miles as the mountains were getting darker and the woods were getting deeper around them, until they came to a fountain in the mountainside, and next to it, a golden bell. As soon as King Laurin rang the bell hidden gates opened up, and the knights caught their breath at the wonderful sight that greeted them.

In the great caverns of the dwarf kingdom gemstones glowed on every wall, filling the darkness with colorful lights. The hidden gates were made of gold, and behind them was another set of gates, made of solid steel. Thousands of dwarfs greeted them, their knights wearing armor and belts set with gemstones and their ladies dressed in the finest silk and velvet. King Laurin ordered a feast for his guests, and Similt, who was now a queen, greeted her brother with great joy.

However friendly the host was, though, and however splendid the entertainment, the knights still felt uneasy, and Dietlieb plotted to rescue his sister from the underground kingdom. King Laurin knew this all too well. When Similt retired to her rooms Laurin talked to her in private, telling her all the wrongs the knights did to him — the reasons why he could not let them go unpunished. Similt, being a kind and gentle soul, convinced her husband to let them live, and begged him to treat her brother well. King Laurin then drew Dietlieb away from the others and asked him if he would side with the dwarfs in this matter, for his sister's sake; but Dietlieb, being a proud knight, refused to turn on his comrades ever again.

With that said, Laurin ordered his magician to put a spell on the knights: at first, they all turned blind so they could not see each other anymore, and then a deadly deep sleep fell on them. King Laurin ordered them tied and chained, and a giant carried them down into the deepest dungeons of the mountain.

When King Dietrich woke up, he was alarmed to discover that he was bound and chained, and in prison. Feeling around in the darkness he knew his companions were with him, and he also knew he needed a way out.

Dietrich had an ability not many people knew about: when he was upset, or angered, he could breathe fire. There is nothing better to upset a king than throwing him in prison. King Dietrich took a deep breath, and breathed fire on the ropes and chains that held them, freeing the knights from their bonds, but not from their cell. Three days and three nights the blind knights sat in the dungeon while Similt was looking for a way to rescue them. Finally she managed to open the cell of Dietlieb, who was kept separate from the others and free of the spell, and he in turn opened the prison of the others.

This was the last act that broke the hard-earned peace between Laurin and his guests. King Dietrich and his knights, even though still blind, charged out of the dungeons and attacked the army of dwarfs that was sent against them. Similt stole rings of power for them that did not only lift the spell of blindness but also gave them each the strength of twelve men. Once they reached her chambers and received the rings, no dwarf could stand against them.

King Laurin, when he saw he was losing the battle, blew a horn and summoned five giants that were in his service. The heroes, although frightened by the thunder of the giants' footsteps and their size, valiantly stood against them and cut their way through to the gates.

King Laurin's kingdom fell with him. Some legends say he was dragged to Bern and forced to live as a juggler in Dietrich's court for the rest of his life.

Legend also says that he put a spell on his rose garden and his crystal palace, declaring that no man will ever set eyes on them by day or by night. However, he forgot about the time between night and day: to this very day, when the sun comes up, or when the sun goes down, the mountains glow with the color of pink quartz and roses, and where once King Laurin's kingdom used to be, people still call the Alps Rosengarten — the Garden of Roses.

*Comments:* Tolkien's got nothing on this story.

I have been working really hard to boil down the legend known as "The Small Rose Garden" (as opposed to "The Greater Rose Garden" which is a completely different story) to fit the limits of this book. It could be a book all by itself, and a good one at that too.

One really interesting aspect of this legend is that there are no clear heroes. For the Medieval mind King Dietrich and his companions were in the right when subduing Laurin's "pagan kingdom" — but I gave up telling it that way. What we see here, whatever the historical heart of the story might be, is a clash of cultures and traditions. The opening about the origin of dwarfs and giants especially fascinates me, since it places the dwarf kings above the human heroes in God's plan. This story can lead to a whole series of discussions on what is right and wrong, and how conflicts can or could have been resolved by diplomacy instead of violence. Stories like this are important, especially in our time.

As for powers, I filed this story under invisibility for the intriguing duel scene between the human knights and the invisible dwarf king. With that said, there is also the "by-the-way" mentioned ability of Dietrich to breathe fire that seemingly comes out of nowhere at the most convenient time. It echoes Sir Kay, King Arthur's knight, who in the Welsh legends had the power to keep men warm and dry by the extreme heat radiating from his body.

# COLOR CHANGING

When one thinks of shifting colors in nature, one usually thinks of a chameleon (or squids, if one is versed in marine biology). I was originally looking for camouflage, the ability to blend into one's surroundings by changing colors, but after a lot of searching and a great deal of animal tales, "color changing" was as close as I could get. On the plus side, we can just pretend that a person who has such a great variety of skin colors as the lady below could easily blend in if she wanted to.

*Color-changing characters:* Martian Manhunter (DC), Mystique (Marvel), Sylar (NBC's *Heroes*)

## The Queen of Many Colors

*Ability:* Changing skin color
*Source of power:* Unknown
*Origin:* Hungary
*Teachings:* Be kind to others and your kindness will be repaid. Don't stop looking for that special someone your mother wanted you to marry (just kidding).
*Age group:* 10+
*Sources:* Benedek, E. (1987). *Magyar mese- és mondavilág III.* Budapest: Móra Ferenc Könyvkiadó.

Dégh, L. (1996). *Hungarian Folktales: The Art of Zsuzsanna Palkó.* Jackson: University Press of Mississippi.

*Variants:* The two main versions I know are listed above. Palkó's story, titled "Blackmantle," has a decidedly darker ending than the other. The story type is called the Grateful Dead (AaTh 505).

*Text:* Once upon a time there was a queen known as the Queen of Many Colors, because she could change the color of her face to seventy-seven different shades. She was a widow, and she had only one son, the heir to the throne. When the prince grew to adulthood, he announced his intentions to get married.

"Go with my blessings my son," the queen said to him. "But remember this: I will not allow you to marry any woman unless they have the same power I do. If you bring a bride home, you'd better make sure she can change herself to seventy-seven different colors, otherwise she will be no daughter-in-law of mine."

The prince set out with an army of soldiers and a dozen carriages packed with gold — unusually well prepared for methodically searching for a gifted bride. But no matter how many people he paid, and how far he traveled, he ran out of money before he found a girl who could change her colors, and had to return home poor as a beggar.

"I couldn't find a bride that you would accept," he admitted to his mother.

"You shall try again. My word is final: either you marry a princess of many colors, or you do not marry at all."

The prince set out again with twice as many soldiers and twenty-four carts of gold. Not far from the royal city they passed by a cemetery. The prince was shocked to see four men with sticks beating the corpse of an old man on the ground.

"Why are you people beating that old man?"

"He owes us a lot of money!"

"But he is dead!"

"It doesn't matter! He did not pay us when he was alive. Beating him makes us feel better."

"Stop it!" the prince ordered in a stern voice. "I'll pay his debt."

"With all due respect, your highness ... you don't have the money for that."

"I have twenty-four carts of gold!"

"Not enough."

By the time the debt was paid the prince was out of all the gold, and the horses of all the soldiers. He sent his army home, and continued his journey alone.

A little ways down the road an old man caught up to him.

"Stop, your highness! Hire me to be your servant. You won't regret it."

"How could I hire you? I don't have a single copper piece left."

"Hire me on good will anyway. I will serve you well, I promise."

The prince agreed, and continued his journey with the mysterious old man. As evening fell they came near an old watchtower.

"Stay here for a moment," the old man said. "I will go ahead and prepare a place for you to sleep."

The tower, as it turned out, was not empty: it was inhabited by a nest of demons, looking forward to the next traveler to eat. That is, until the old man marched in.

"Now, all of you, go into the back room and lock the door. The prince staying here tonight is a legendary hunter of demons and other nasty creatures, so if you value your miserable lives, you will stay in there and not make a sound until dawn. Is that clear?"

"Clear, clear," whined the demons, and huddled in the back room without a sound. The prince slept like a baby till the morning.

They traveled on for a while, but the prince was losing faith every minute that he would ever find a color-changing bride.

"Don't worry, your highness," the old man said finally. "We are here."

"We are where?"

"This is the city where your bride lives."

"My bride?"

"The maiden of many colors. Her father is a sorcerer trained in the dark arts. He will put you to all kinds of tests. But don't worry, I will help you along the way."

The prince was happy, nervous and excited at the same time. He went straight to the sorcerer and announced his intentions to marry his daughter.

"I will give you three tasks," said the father, who was well prepared for suitors. "If you succeed in all three, you can have my daughter. But if you fail, I will put your head on a spike."

The prince agreed. There was no turning back.

"I will send these golden slippers somewhere," said the sorcerer. "You have one day to bring them back."

As he said that, the golden slippers disappeared into thin air — and so did the old man. Before the prince could blink, he as back again, handing the lost-and-found over to him.

"How did you do that?"

"I have a mantle that makes me invisible," the old man shrugged. "The sorcerer sent seven devils to carry the slippers to an island out on the sea. I picked them up before they ever got there."

For the second task, the sorcerer sent a golden knife away — but only a few moments later the old man brought it back, from the far side of the Glass Mountains. For the last task a golden ring was hidden. The old man snatched it up just as the devils dropped it into the gaping mouth of a great fish.

"You know magic better than I do," admitted the sorcerer. "Take my daughter if you please."

The girl of many colors was happy to join the prince, and they held a wedding right then and there. Once they were married they sat in a carriage and started on the way back home.

As they came near the prince's home they passed by the cemetery again. The old man stopped the carriage.

"I only go this far," he said. "But before I go we have to split what we earned: I did half of the work, half of the bride is mine."

"What do you...." But before the prince could shout, the old man grabbed the princess and tore her in half. A snake and a frog jumped out of the wound. Once they were gone, the old man put the girl back together, and she came back to life, a thousand times more beautiful than she had been before.

"And that was the last of the sorcerer's evil spells," said the old man. "You can go on your way now."

"And where will you go?"

"Back to my grave to rest in peace." The old man smiled. "You paid my debts, and I paid for my sins. Go, be happy, and pray for my soul."

The prince returned home and introduced his wife to his mother. The queen was delighted with her new daughter-in-law who could change into as many colors as she did. They celebrated a second wedding, and lived happily ever after.

*Comments:* If you are interested in the darker version of the same tale, read the one published by Linda Dégh. The main story is the same, except the old man goes "Corpse Bride" on the bride, and it all ends in repeated corpse mutilation and exorcism. Good story for Halloween.

Even though neither the queen or the princess ever use their ability, it is obviously important enough to feature into family planning. Dégh suggested that "like mother-in-law like daughter-in-law" implies incest between the prince and his mother. Everyone can make up their own mind about that.

I considered including invisibility on the power list. In the original tale the old man uses a "black mantle" to make himself invisible, but it is also implied that only the prince can see him to begin with. He is obviously a ghost, and as such, in my opinion, he doesn't really need a cloak of invisibility.

# HEALING FACTOR, HEALING OTHERS, OR NOT HEALING AT ALL

First, about the definitions. The term "healing factor" is used in modern media to designate the body's ability to heal itself (usually much faster than normal, see Wolverine). The ability to heal others is simply called ... healing. Most of the time.

Healing in traditional stories is very common, yet not easily defined in terms of "superpowers." Many times it is not even explained (see the story of János and Rózsa where the queen just happens to piece her dead son together and bring him back to life, no muss no fuss). Folklore and medicine is a whole branch of ethnographic study, whether healing work is done by magic (F950), by Helpful Animals (B510), by Potions and Herbs (D1500), by Divine Intervention (V221), or by the Water of Life (E80).

"The hands of a king are the hands of a healer," writes Tolkien in *The Lord of the Rings.* This belief goes back to Medieval Europe where it was believed that saintly kings, being chosen by some higher power, had the ability to heal various illnesses just by the touch of their hands (known as the Royal Touch). We have already seen examples of healing earlier in this chapter in Achilles' bone transplant and Sir James Ramsay's hard-earned medical training. Besides the two folktales that follow, there will be other examples later on. For the most spectacular demonstration of a "healing factor" see "The Daughter of the Sun," under Fire Manipulation.

*Healing heroes:* Adam Monroe (NBC's *Heroes*), Claire Bennett (NBC's *Heroes*), Daniel Linderman (NBC's *Heroes*), Elixir (Marvel), Shawn Farrell (CBS's *The 4400*), Wolverine (Marvel)

## The Prince with the Two Hearts

*Ability:* Healing (organ transplant and behavioral modification)
*Source of power:* Unknown
*Origin:* Hungary
*Teachings:* Emotions are not a weakness. Accept yourself and others as they are instead of trying to change them. Kindness is a virtue.
*Age group:* 12+
*Sources:* Benedek, E. (1987). *Magyar mese- és mondavilág I.* Budapest: Móra Ferenc Könyvkiadó.
*Variants:* This is another one of those strange folktales I have not found many versions of. It reminds me of the "heart outside the body" type folktales (AaTh 302, e.g. Koschei the Deathless) where someone hides his heart where nothing can hurt it. Falling into extremes to prevent being emotionally hurt is very much human behavior.
*Text:* The Black King only had one son. Many kings would have been happy with that, because it meant they had an heir to the throne — but still, the Black King was worried. Not because his son was too sick, or too young to rule; he was just too ... sensitive. His heart was so kind that he could not look at a hungry animal or an old beggar without breaking down in tears, and he spent his days in great sadness and weeping for all the bad things in the world. If a servant broke his leg, if a pig was killed for the feast, he cried and he cried, and that was making his father increasingly annoyed.

"How can I leave my kingdom to this child?!" He shook his head, "I did not build an army for him to waste! The first time he sees a dead soldier or a drop of blood, he will run, and the kingdom will fall!"

One day, a servant brought good news to the king: a famous doctor arrived at court and he was willing to heal the prince from his great sadness. The king was happy beyond measure. He promised that if the doctor managed to heal the prince and turn him into a real man, he could have whatever he wished for.

"I can heal him in a year's time," said the doctor, "but let me take him with me."

The king agreed, and the doctor left with the prince, he went back to Bergengócia, his homeland. A year passed. The prince received a new heart: the doctor took out the soft, kind one, and put another, harder one in its place. The prince seemed to be happy with the change, and grateful to the doctor.

"What would you like for your services?" he asked.

"Nothing right now, your highness. Just promise me that you will give me a bag of gold every time you make someone cry."

The prince made the promise, and started on his way home. He did not go far before he came across a pitiful sight: a big sheepdog was lying on the road, both of its hind legs broken. A year before the prince would have picked the dog up, took it home and nursed it back to health; but now he just kicked it to the side of the road and walked on. As he neared his home, he met a blind beggar on the side of the road; instead of giving him alms like a year before, he just pushed him out of the way with his walking stick, and never looked back.

When he arrived home the king and the queen embraced him with joy, and asked what his year had been like — but he pushed them away and told them their questions were useless and annoying.

The king and the queen realized what had happened: their dear son's kind heart was gone. Now he was cold and cruel, and not a day went by without him making someone cry. And every day the doctor showed up on the doorstep, asking for his bag of gold.

Gold was running out fast, and this worried the king more than his own son's kindness ever had. The prince thought it was too much of an expense, and the next day, he yelled at the doctor.

"I am done paying you, old fool! You are asking too much. You will see no more gold from me. Just give me back my old heart and be done with it!"

The doctor smiled a sad smile, and shook his head.

"I cannot do that, your highness. This is one thing you have to know: you can put a new heart in the place of the old one — but you can never get the old one back."

*Comments:* A short tale with a harsh moral. Hungarian writer Antal Szerb wrote a short story called "Love in a Bottle" in 1935 (published in a collection with the same title, also available in an English translation) that has a similar idea, but a different ending. In his story, Sir Lancelot decides that he has had enough of loving Guinevere, and asks a wizard to take Love out of his heart. Without the emotions making him sigh and cry he is content for a while but he soon realizes that not feeling anything makes him more miserable than suffering from unrequited love ever did — and he asks for his Love back. The doctor did not really heal the Prince — he just gave him a lesson. You can't be free of all emotions if you want to be happy.

Side note: Bergengócia is an imaginary land that is mentioned often in Hungarian folktales as some place very far away.

## *Anne Jefferies and the Fairies*

*Ability:* Healing, invisibility, second sight
*Source of power:* Fairy
*Origin:* Cornwall, England
*Teachings:* Wonder, selflessness, humility, follow your dreams but be cautious.
*Age group:* 8+
*Sources (and further reading):* Hunt, R. (1903). *Popular Romances of the West of England.* London: Chatto and Windus.

Lenihan, E. (1987). *In Search of Biddy Early.* Cork: Mercier Press.

Lenihan, E., and C.E. Green (2004). *Meeting the Other Crowd: The Fairy Stories of Hidden Ireland.* New York: Tarcher.

*Variants:* The story of Anne has a lot in common with another famous fairy healer, Biddy Early. You can read more about her in Eddie Lenihan's book (see sources). Being spirited away by the fairies is also very common in Scotland and Ireland; once again, refer to Eddie's wisdom.

*Text:* There are many tales about people visiting the world of the fairies. Some of them stumble upon the crossings by accident, many are spirited away, and a precious few are invited. There are not many stories that tell about people who wanted to go there, found a way, and then returned. Anne Jeffries was one of these few.

She was born in Cornwall in 1626. She was known as a girl who was braver than most boys. Not because she did reckless things like boys do, like climb trees or hunt in the woods — it was because she did things that not even adults would have tried. She tempted the fairies.

Ever since she was a little girl, Anne had wanted to meet the fairy folk. She walked around on moonlit nights, singing songs and poking around in the fern and the foxglove, calling them to her. She wandered in the woods for hours, hoping she could catch a glimpse of the Good People, but no matter how hard she looked and how long she searched, the fairies seemed to escape her.

She was nineteen years old when her dream finally came true. She was serving as a maid to the family of a Moses Pitt, who later described the events of her life in a letter, leaving us this story.

One afternoon Anne was sitting in the garden, knitting. Suddenly she heard a soft laugh, then the gate of the garden opened and closed again, but she did not look up. For a while, nothing happened.

"You can stand there till the moss grows on the gate, if you are waiting for me to go to you," she called out, eyes still on her knitting. After so many years of chasing, she was determined to play hard to get.

Soft footsteps came closer, and when she heard the laugh again, Anne finally looked up. Or, rather, down. In front of her were six little elfin men, dressed in green. They all bowed and greeted her as if they had been old friends, then one, the most handsome of the six, jumped onto her extended palm, and she lifted him up to her face. The fairy kissed her. They all laughed, and then the other five clambered up her skirt and her bodice and they all started kissing her, on the face and on the lips, until one pricked her eyes with a finger — and Anne went blind.

The next thing she knew she was being carried, spun through the air, surrounded by the shouting of the little men, and after a long time she was set down on soft grass. Someone pricked her eyes again and her vision returned. The sight that greeted her was more wonderful than words can describe — and Anne had not talked about it for a very, very long time. It was a land full of flowers and colors and the song of birds, clear lakes full of fish, temples and castles built of gold and silver, and hundreds of lords and ladies walking merrily around, singing songs and playing games. They were not tiny people anymore. They were the size of humans, and Anne was delighted to see her own six little companions grown into real men.

Anne spent a long time in the fairy kingdom. She loved being there, and she loved her fairy lover even more. They often stole away from the others to spend time together ... and that eventually made the other five men jealous. One day when Anne and her lover were sitting in one of the wonderful gardens, the other five showed up and attacked them. Her love drew his sword to protect her, but he was wounded, and fell to the ground. This was the last thing Anne knew before her vision left her again, and she was hurled through the air for a long time. When she opened her eyes, she was lying in her own garden, with people all around her.

Mr. Pitt concluded that Anne had some kind of a convulsive fit that caused delusions. But there were things about her he could not explain, and he put those in his letter many years later.

Even though Anne could not read or write, she developed a miraculous healing ability — she used no potions or herbs, but still she cured so many people around the village from their illnesses and injuries that she soon became famous.

She never took any money from her patients, even though many rich men came to see her from as far away as London — and still, she never seemed to want for anything. Mr. Pitt said that there were rumors that the fairies kept her fed. They were always watching out for her, even if they never showed themselves to anyone else. In fact, people whispered that Anne could turn herself invisible.

Not all people were pleased with Anne's work. She was dragged to jail and kept there for a while, accused of witchcraft just for being a healer that conversed with the Good Folk. But they still cared for her there, and eventually she was set free. She married a man called William Warren, and she lived to see her 70th birthday.

When Anne was in her sixties, a doctor was called to examine her, to find out how she was healing her patients. Even though the doctor spent a whole day with her, she never told him anything, neither about the healing, nor about the fairies.

"I asked her why she would not tell of these things. She said that if she did, people would make books and ballads out of it, and she would not want her name to be spread around the country in books and ballads, even if someone paid her five hundred pounds."

*Comments:* Whether she wanted it or not, Anne Jeffries's name lived on in tales and legends. Whoever comes in contact with the fairy folk tends to become famous (or infamous) — and she did it on purpose, spending years looking for an opportunity. The fairies, even if they eventually cast her out of their world, never abandoned the girl who loved them. She gained her special healing ability from them, and put it to good use. She did not care for fame or riches in the mundane sense of the world — which is something one would learn from the Good Folk.

This story is a fascinating mix of folklore and history. Anne is a real historical person, but the stories that surround her come from a much older time. I set the age limit on this story knowing that it needs discussion about truth, folklore, history and witches. Proceed with caution with certain audiences.

# GROWTH, ELASTICITY AND BODY SHAPING

This ability might not be as popular as super strength or invulnerability, but it is present in folklore and popular culture none the less. The character that pops into most people's minds is Mr. Fantastic, but he is by far not the first.

Some people in real life are just naturally double-jointed and can bend themselves into shapes others could not even make out of spaghetti during a boring family lunch. It is no wonder that abilities like that would be talked about. People are fascinated by rare skills, and flexibility is one very physical skill that is easy to show off and admire. Think "circus."

One folktale motif related to body stretching is D55.1 (Person Becomes Magically Larger). Although it technically could qualify as elasticity, it is not the most spectacular use of that power. In the folktale below, as well as other similar tales, we see the use of elasticity not only to grow but also to stretch, reach (think of the hag in the story of Finn MacCool earlier), wrap, guard, and even travel faster.

*Similar heroes:* Elastigirl (*The Incredibles*), Mr. Fantastic (Marvel), Monkey D. Luffy (*One Piece*), Plastic Man (DC)

## Longshanks, Girth and Keen

*Ability:* Body shaping / Eye beams / Superhuman vision
*Source of power:* Unknown
*Origin:* Czech Republic
*Teachings:* Creativity and teamwork, friendship. Nothing is impossible. Women should be won, not kidnapped. Don't fall asleep on a date.
*Age group:* 6+
*Sources:* Fillmore, P. (1919). *Czechoslovak Fairy Tales.* New York: Harcourt, Brace and Company.
   Wratislaw, A.H. (1890). *Sixty Folk-Tales from Exclusively Slavonic Sources.* Boston: Houghton, Mifflin and Co.
*Variants:* This is another version of Extraordinary Helpers (AaTh 513), a story type that is responsible for most of the superpowers in the world of folktales.
*Text:* Once upon a time, there was an old king who only had one son. When he felt his death creeping closer, he said to him: "The old fruit must fall to give way to the new. But before I leave my crown to you, I wish to see you happily married."

"I would like that too, father," said the prince, "but I have not found anyone yet that I would wish to marry."

The king gave a small golden key to his son. "Go, take a look around at the top of the highest tower, and let me know if you have seen anything you like."

The prince climbed the stairs to the tower, and opened a small iron door with the golden key. On the topmost floor he found a wonderful room: the ceiling was blue like the sky, the floor was covered in a lush green carpet, and all around him were stained glass windows, showing pictures of the most beautiful royal princesses he had ever seen. There were twelve of them, and all the pictures smiled and waved at the prince, each one lovelier than the other. The prince turned all the way around, and he noticed that one of the windows was covered with a white curtain. Drawing the curtain aside, his eyes fell on the most beautiful princess of all: she was dressed in white, with a crown of pearls, and her face was pale and sad.

"You are the one I want for my bride," he said aloud, marveling at the picture. The princess seemed to blush for a moment ... and then all the pictures disappeared.

When the prince told his father about his choice, the old king was greatly troubled.

"You have chosen danger, my son," he said. "That princess has been kidnapped by a black magician, and he holds her captive in an iron castle. No one who tried to rescue her has ever returned. But you have made your choice, and you have to keep your word."

The prince said farewell to his father, rode out to seek the princess in the iron castle ... and promptly got lost in the woods. As he wandered around, suddenly he heard a voice: "Master! Hey, master, wait up!"

He turned, and saw a very tall, thin man, running to catch up with him.

"I was wondering if you were looking for a servant," the man said. "If you would take me, you wouldn't regret it."

"What is your name, and what can you do for me?" asked the prince.

"My came is Longshanks," the stranger answered, "and as for what I can do ... watch."

And as he said that, his body started to stretch, up and up, until he reached the top of the highest tree. Reaching out the picked a branch, then he shrank back down, and handed it to the astonished prince.

"That seems useful enough," he said, "but I still need to find a way out of the forest."

"That is easy," said Longshanks, and he stretched up, up, up again until he could see over the top of the trees. He found the way out, and the prince and his new companion soon emerged from the forest to a plain.

"There goes a friend of mine!" said Longshanks, and, picking up the prince, he stretched his legs to go faster. In a few gigantic strides they caught up to a man who was as round as a barrel. He introduced himself as Girth: just like Longshanks could change his height, Girth could change his ... girth. He could become as wide and heavy as a mountain. The prince thought this was a very useful ability, so he hired Girth as well.

Walking on the companions came across another traveler: a man with his eyes bandaged.

"Who are you?" asked the prince. "And what happened to your eyes?"

"My eyesight is so good, your highness," said the man, "that I can see like normal people see, with my eyes bandaged. If I take the bandage off, my eyes burn through anything I look at. People call me Keen."

To prove his words, Keen took the bandage off, and looked at a nearby rock. The rock started to crumble, and soon it was reduced to dust, with a piece of gold shining in the middle.

"That looks useful!" said the prince. "You are hired. Tell me, can you see the iron castle from here?"

"I can," said Keen. "We will get there today if we help you. The magician already knows we are on our way, and is preparing for us. The princess is locked in the tower."

The prince and his companions set out at once. Longshanks carried them with long steps, and Keen destroyed everything that stood in their way. When they crossed the last mountain and emerged from the last forest, they could finally see the iron castle looming on the horizon.

The gates were open, and there were no guards in sight — but as they walked in, the gates clanged shut. All around there were people, guards, ladies, lords and servants, all turned to stone. The banquet hall was open, and the table set for four ... but there was not a single living soul in sight.

The prince and his companions were too hungry for caution. They sat down and ate. Just as they finished their dinner the doors burst open and in walked the black magician, a wizened old man in a robe with three iron chains around his waist, and with him, the white princess.

"I know who you are," he said before the prince could speak. "I know why you are here. You can take the princess if you want, but first you have to guard her for three nights. If she does not escape you, she is yours. But if you lose her, you will be turned to stone, just like the others."

The princess, never smiling or saying a word, sat down by the table, and the magician left the hall. The prince sat beside her, swearing he would watch over her all night, and trying to make her smile, or speak. Meanwhile, Longshanks stretched himself around the entire room like a belt; Girth puffed himself up and blocked the door; and Keen took watch by one of the pillars. But as midnight approached, they all started to feel drowsy, and then, one by one, they fell asleep.

The prince awoke at dawn, and looking around he realized the princess was gone. He woke his companions in panic.

"Don't worry, master," said Keen. "I can see her. A hundred miles from here there is a forest, in the forest an oak tree, on the oak tree an acorn. That acorn is the princess. Let Longshanks take me there and I will bring her back."

Longshanks took Keen and they returned in no time at all. Keen handed the acorn to the prince, who dropped it; and as soon as he dropped it, the acorn bounced up and turned back into a princess.

A moment later the black magician burst into the room, already grinning in victory. When he saw the princess, he howled in rage, and one of the iron chains around his waist snapped apart. Grabbing the princess, he dragged her out of the room.

The prince spent the entire day wandering around the castle. It was a strange, strange place. The trees had no leaves, the water did not flow, and there were no birds or insects of any kind. Every room and courtyard was filled with people turned to stone.

In the evening the prince and his companions returned to the dining hall and waited for the magician to appear. Once again they were left alone with the princess; once again they took their positions; and once again, they all fell asleep. The prince woke up first, and shook the others awake:

"Where is the princess? Where did she go?!"

"I can see her," Keen said, blinking the sleep away. "Two hundred miles from here there is a mountain, on the mountain a rock, and in the rock a precious stone — that is your princess. If Longshanks can take me there, I can break the rock and bring her back."

Once again, Longshanks and Keen had just arrived with the precious stone moments before the magician. The princess was returned safe and sound; anger snapped another chain on the magician's belt.

"This time, you will not succeed!" he threatened them before he left.

That evening the companions tried more than ever to stay awake — but with no more success than the nights before.

"Keen, wake up!" the prince yelled before dawn. "We need to find the princess!"

Keen looked, and he frowned.

"She is far away this time," he said. "Three hundred miles from here there is a black sea, on the bottom of the sea a shell, and in the shell a golden ring. We will need to take Girth with us this time."

Longshanks carried Girth and Keen to the black sea. Longshanks tried to stretch his hand down to the bottom, but it was too deep.

"Wait a minute," said Girth, and he leaned down, drinking up some of the ocean. As the water disappeared, Longshanks finally reached the shell, and soon they were on their way home. However, Girth was so heavy full of water that they had to stop and turn him upside down to spill the water. There was so much of it that it became a lake, and it is still out there somewhere to this very day.

As the sun appeared on the horizon, the doors of the dining hall burst open and in walked the magician, already grinning in triumph. There was no princess and no companions to be seen, and the prince braced himself for being turned into stone … but in that moment there was the sound of shattering glass, and through the window flew the golden ring, bounced off the floor, and turned into the princess. Keen knew they had run out of time, and had Longshanks throw the ring through the window.

The magician roared in anger, and the last iron chain snapped. The robe collapsed to the floor as the man turned into a crow, flew out the window, and was never seen again.

The spell was broken. The princess blushed, and finally smiled, and she thanked the prince and his companions for saving her. The castle instantly came to life: all the stone people started moving again, the trees burst into flowers, water started to flow, and birdsong filled the air.

The prince traveled home with his bride and his companions. The old king was overjoyed to see his son safe, happy and finally married.

Once the wedding was over, the three companions said goodbye to the prince. He tried to convince them to stay, but they refused; there were still many adventures in the world, waiting for them just outside the door.

*Comments:* It takes a team to rescue a princess.

While in some other versions of the same folktale type, there is a man for all the different tasks, this tale combines some of the powers into three characters. Longshanks is not only tall, but also fast; Girth is not only heavy, but can also drink up the ocean; and Keen does not only see far, but he also doubles as the team's marksman. The powers are paired in a very logical way.

Guarding the princess is one of the tasks heroes usually have to complete in these folktales (others, as we have seen, include racing the princess, delivering a flying ship, or rescuing giant babies). I decided to include this particular tale because it demonstrates great teamwork — instead of one person doing one task through the story, the three companions invent new and useful ways of applying their powers to help the prince. And in the end, after their mission is accomplished, they move on to future adventures. They are not only convenient helpers to the prince; they have their own life.

Interestingly, some audiences jump into the conclusion that the princess has been changing her *own* shape all along. It is implied in the tale that the magician has been hiding her, but it never said outright. Storyteller's choice.

Wratislaw suggested that this story was originally a "nature myth," in which "Long" symbolized the rainbow, "Broad" the clouds, and "Sharpsight" the lightning. It is not the purpose of this book to contemplate that, but when one thinks about it in pictures, from a storyteller's point of view, it can be an interesting visual addition to the tale.

# A Is for Agility and Archers

You can't really have a good epic (or a superhero team, for that matter) without a good archer, or marksman of any kind, really. The past years have seen an increased interest in archery through movies and media phenomena such as *The Lord of the Rings*, *Avatar*, *The Hunger Games*, *Brave*, *Hanna*, and *The Avengers*. Bows and arrows are cool (again).

The folktale motif for a skilled marksman is F661. But why stop at archery? What happens if a hero prefers another way of fighting, and instead of being physically stronger, he or she is more skilled? Well, that is what this category has been invented for. Not for people with extraordinary supernatural powers, but people with skills, talent and determination that make them heroes (and maybe some powers on the side). For illustration, I selected two very old traditional tales. There could have been many, many more.

*Similar heroes:* Deadpool (Marvel), Green Arrow (DC), Hawkeye (Marvel), Katniss Everdeen (*The Hunger Games*), Legolas (*The Lord of the Rings*), Merida (*Brave*), River Tam (Fox's *Firefly*)

## Ekalavya, the Archer

*Ability:* Incredible skills in archery

*Source of power:* 100 percent self-taught

*Origin:* India

*Teachings:* Dedication, humility, self-sacrifice. You can be anything if you do not give up your dreams. If you are knocked down, get back up. What is your excuse?

*Age group:* 8+

*Sources:* This story is from the Sanskrit epic known as the *Mahabharata*. It is included in Book 1, Section CXXXIV, 31–58.

*Variants:* This story, even though a small part of the *Mahabharata*, is very popular in Indian literature. Ekalavya is a role model and a legendary archer figure, much like legendary archers from other cultures such as the Chinese Houyi, the Norse Egill, or even the British Robin Hood.

*Text:* Ekalavya was sort of a prince. He was the son of the chief of the Nishadas, a hunting and fishing tribe that lived in the forest. But ever since he was a boy, Ekalavya wished for more: he wanted to learn the martial arts, he wanted to study archery just like the princes of the Kshatriya caste. He heard stories about the great teacher Drona who lived in Hastinapura, teaching the five royal brothers known as the Pandavas and their one hundred cousins called the Kauravas to the arts of war. Ekalavya decided to travel to the city and become one of the great master's students. Leaving his home, the forest, behind he walked and walked for a long time before he finally arrived to Hastinapura. He found Drona among his pupils; he greeted him politely and asked if he would be allowed to study with him. Drona was pleased with the strong young man, his politeness and the way he held himself. He asked Ekalavya what his caste was.

"I belong to no caste," the young man answered truthfully. "My father is the chief of the Nishadas. I come from the forest."

"What?!" Drona was not pleased anymore. He was angry. He was the best teacher in the kingdom, and he only taught Kshatriya princes. What was this forest boy thinking, daring to wish to become his pupil?!

Drona chased Ekalavya away with bitter words and contempt. The young man returned the forest, deeply hurt — but he did not give up on his dreams. Finding himself a clearing and building a little hut, he decided he was going to learn archery anyway. He made a statue of Drona out of clay, and day after day he meditated in front of it, pretending it was the real teacher. Even though Drona treated him like dirt, he still looked up to him as his master, and that was his inspiration to keep training. He practiced alone, setting targets for himself, shooting arrow after arrow from morning till night.

One day Drona took his royal students to the woods to teach them hunting. As one of the dogs started to bark, an arrow hissed from among the leaves, closely followed by two others — and they all struck the dog right in the mouth. The old teacher was astonished. He knew that whoever shot those arrows must have been an archer like no other, hitting the target from a distance with nothing but the sound to guide him. Going the direction where the arrows came from, he soon came across the clearing where Ekalavya was waiting, his bow drawn. As soon as the young man saw the teacher he dropped to his knees and greeted him as his guru.

Drona was even more surprised now. He did not remember ever meeting the boy, let alone teaching him — and yet, there was his clay statue, and here was the talented young archer. Pride battled inside his heart with jealousy. Ekalavya proved to be a far better archer than any of his pupils after meticulous training. He needed to do something about that before his reputation as a teacher was ruined forever, and the heroes he trained were surpassed by a casteless boy from the woods.

"If I am truly your guru as you say," he said finally, "then you owe me payment for teaching you."

"Anything!" the young man smiled, happy that he was finally acknowledged as a student. "Tell me what you wish for!"

"I want your right thumb," said Drona, with a face like stone.

Ekalavya started in shock. The right thumb is a vital part of an archer's hand: he cannot draw properly without it. But without a word, always obedient Ekalavya drew his sword, cut off his thumb, and handed it to Drona.

The old master and his pupils walked away, confident that now there was no one who could surpass them in the field of archery.

They were right; without his thumb Ekalavya could not compete with master archers anymore. But he kept practicing anyway, starting again from nothing, training himself painfully slow to use his left hand instead of his right. In time, he became good at archery again; even left-handed and self-taught, he is still remembered as one of the greatest heroes of his time.

*Comments:* First of all, a note on archery. There are many different ways of drawing an arrow, depending on time, culture, and the bow and arrows used. Some people, especially in European countries, draw with the four fingers on their right hand, holding the nock of the arrow between the index and the middle finger. In many Asian cultures such as India and Mongolia, they pinch the nock between the thumb and the first finger, or hook the thumb under the nock and around the string. This latter way (called thumb draw) explains why it is such a disaster for Ekalavya to lose his thumb. Even if he learns to hold the bow with his maimed right hand, it will still lose some of its balance and stability.

If one researches Ekalavya's story, a few different endings can be found. For some reason I have read many times on the Internet that "he became better than the other heroes, even left-handed," a notion which does not appear in the original story. Still, people seem to want a happy ending for the hard-working boy from the woods, and even without a source, the story catches like wildfire.

Ekavalya's is a tale of devotion and commitment. It reflects the strict caste system of the *Mahabharata*: the only reason why the talented youth is not accepted among the greatest heroes of Indian mythology is because he belongs to the lowest level of society. He wishes for something he is not destined to achieve, and he makes it come true through his own hard work and determination. Ekalavya does not have special superhuman powers (I do realize this goes against the guidelines I set at the beginning). However, he bears certain resemblances to the great archer heroes in popular culture such as Hawkeye or Green Arrow. Part of the identity of those heroes is that they stand apart from the superhuman crowd: they earn their skills through training and learning, and work hard for their place on such prestigious teams as the Avengers or the Justice League, standing side by side with gods and heroes. There is a lot of inspiration to be found in these tales; I believe that Ekalavya the archer earned his place in this book.

# Camilla

*Ability:* Superhuman speed and agility
*Source of power:* Divine
*Origin:* Ancient Rome
*Teachings:* Girl power, and some Roman history.
*Age group:* 10+
*Sources:* Virgil, *Aeneid*, Book VII, 1094–1103 and Book X, 1121–1256.
*Variants:* The legend of Camilla must have lived in oral tradition long before Virgil wrote it down, since the events took place centuries before his time. Yet he is our main source of the story that bears similarities with Greek myths about the Amazons, both in terms of fierceness and in sisterhood.

*Text:* When Camilla was just a child, her father, King Metabus of the Volscii tribe, was betrayed by his people. His wife died; he had to flee for dear life, pursued by armed warriors who intended to kill him, to make sure he never returned to the throne. Metabus carried his only daughter, Camilla, but he was not fast enough to outrun the enemy, and to make things even worse, a river blocked his path to freedom. He could not swim with a child in his hands, and he was running out of time. Finally he tied Camilla to his spear, and as he raised it above his head he prayed to Diana, goddess of the hunt. He offered the goddess Camilla as a maid and a servant if she helped them to escape.

The goddess smiled on the king in need.

The spear flew straight and true, and landed safely on the other side of the river. King Metabus swam after it, and soon king and daughter were both hidden from their pursuers, lost in the forest.

In the following years, Diana did not abandon the girl. Camilla grew up to be a huntress, swift and strong, and never interested in men. She was beautiful like a true queen, with long dark hair and a noble figure. The goddess gave her a special blessing: she could run as fast as the wind and as light as a feather, over cornfields without the wheat being bent, and across water without her feet getting wet. She was a huntress, a true follower of Diana, and roamed the hills and the woods with the nymphs who were attendants of the goddess.

Then, one day, news came from the tribes around the river Tiber: a group of strangers landed on the shore, led by a man named Aeneas. They were looking for a new home, land to build a city, and alliances to make. Their leader proposed to marry Lavinia, the princess of the Latins — but there was a problem. Lavinia already had a suitor, King Turnus of the Rutuli, and he was not going to give her up to some wanderer and a handful of ragged soldiers. King Turnus prepared to fight. Camilla, when she heard the news, decided to join Turnus's army.

Aeneas and his Trojan warriors were not used to the sight of a warrior woman.

Camilla was in the center of the fight wherever she went, throwing her javelin with deadly aim, brandishing a battle axe, or shooting people down with her bow and arrows. She fought shoulder to shoulder with other Italian maidens from the goddess's following. It was as if Diana herself had descended on the battlefield, and no man could stand against her. Some tried to flee when they saw her, but she was faster than their horses, and she caught up with everyone that dared to taunt her.

One of the Trojans, a young man called Arrus, decided that he was going to be the one that slayed Camilla. He took his time. He followed her around the battlefield wherever she went, but instead of confronting her, he stayed always at her back, waiting for an opportunity to catch her off guard. Finally, as she was fighting someone else, Arrus raised his spear, and stabbed her in the back.

As Camilla fell to the ground, her friends caught her and raised a cry of grief. One of the nymphs of the goddess, Opis, who had been watching the fight from a distance, saw Arrus fleeing from the field, scared by the voices of the warrior maidens. Drawing her bow, Opis aimed carefully, and killed the cowardly man with a single shot.

Eventually Aeneas did win the fight, and many other fights after. The Trojans settled down and founded their city; the descendants of Aeneas became the Romans, the most powerful empire the land had ever seen.

People did not forget about Camilla. Even the Romans, who had been her enemies, admired her for her skill and her bravery, and they told her story over and over again to teach their children what a true warrior is like. This way, Camilla's name lived on, and lives on to this very day.

*Comments:* The legend of Camilla is one of the most well-known stories from the early days of Rome. Even though they regarded her as a hero, she was not Roman; she belonged to one of the many tribes that inhabited Italy before the rise of Rome. She was also a huntress and a virgin warrior, much like the Amazons of ancient Greek mythology. She was surrounded by other female warriors who fought by her side, mourned her when she died, and avenged her death. Her legend, all in all, is a classic hero story, with royal origins, troubled childhood, superhuman powers, great fame, and a battle to the death.

I initially considered filing Camilla under superhuman speed, but decided she had a better place in this category instead. Her fighting skills seemed to include a lot more than mere speed.

I find this story works especially well with girls (no wonder) 12 and older. They need strong female role models, and even if they don't go on to being archery champions or soldiers, they can still benefit from hearing stories about women who were celebrated as heroes along with the men.

# EYE BEAMS (YES, REALLY)

Does shooting laser beams from your eyes really need an introduction?

The modern superheroes most well-known for this trick (also known as "optic blasts") are probably Cyclops from *X-men* (who, contrary to his name and popular belief, actually has two eyes, not one) and Superman. We have already seen an example for the ability generally called sharp sight (F541.1) in the tale of Longshanks, Girth, and Keen. Cyclops's ability resembles the folktale motif in the sense that it cannot be turned off without covering the eyes, or keeping them shut. In the following folktale another example can be found, from another corner of the world.

*Heroes that shoot beams from their eyes:* Cyclops (Marvel), Superman (DC)

## The Unfinished Story of Princess Greenleaf

*Ability:* Body shaping (stretch and widen), eye beams, superhuman sight and hearing

*Source of power:* Unknown

*Origin:* Andros Island, Bahamas

*Teachings:* Do not be afraid, hold on to your dreams, pay attention to the people you meet, looks are not everything.

*Age group:* 6+

*Sources:* Parsons, E.W.C. (1918). *Folk-Tales of Andros Island, Bahamas.* Lancaster: American Folk-lore Society, 32–35.

*Variants:* This is another AaTh 513 type tale. You have seen enough of these by now (or if not, keep reading).

*Text:* The king of the North had a daughter, and her name was Greenleaf. She was her father's pride and joy, and he raised her in such care that she never even saw the sun until she was fourteen. When the princess grew up, she said to her father: "Daddy, I would like to get married." The king, happy to oblige his daughter's wishes, wrote a letter to all eligible young princes, and gave it to a messenger. The messenger had a horse's body and a man's head, and had wings so he could fly all around the world and deliver the letter to every kingdom.

The prince of the South received the letter, and instantly fell in love without ever meeting the princess. He asked his father's permission to go and ask for her hand in marriage—but the king of the South refused. The prince, as young people tend to do, especially if they are royalty, fell ill with love, and he did not get better for seven years. All the ships and armies of the South stood idle for there was no one to lead them. Finally the king said to his son: "If I let you go see the princess, will you feel better?"

The prince was out of bed and ready to leave in two days. He was followed by an army of soldiers dressed for parade, and a band of musicians; one had to wear dark glasses to look at his shining armor. When he was ready to leave, his father pulled him aside: "Son, I have one piece of advice for you: whatever you meet on your journey, do not be afraid."

The prince left. As he traveled along the countryside he met a man as huge as a mountain. He was quite a frightening sight, but the prince, remembering his father's advice, did not show fear.

"Who are you my friend? And what made you so big?"

"This is nothing," the big man shrugged. "I can make myself twice bigger."

The prince hired the man, thinking he could be of service. Riding on they met a man who was so tall his head was above the clouds; he claimed he could stretch twice as high. The prince hired that man too, and rode on.

The next traveler they encountered was a man with a bandage over his eyes. He claimed that if he took the bandage off, whatever he looked at would catch on fire. The prince hired him too, and as they traveled on, they came across another man, gazing out into the distance.

"What are you looking at?"

"I am taking a look at what people are up to in New York."

"You can see that far?"

"Even farther."

Walking on with his ever growing entourage, the prince had to stop: the road was blocked by a tall may who lay on the ground listening for something.

"What do you hear?" the prince asked.

"I can hear the grass grow," the man answered; and the prince hired him too.

*Comments:* Unfortunately, the story was interrupted at this point, and the second half was never collected. Fortunately for us, it exists in many different versions, and bears resemblance to other stories in this collection ("Longshanks, Girth, and Keen"; "Finn MacCool and the Giants"; "Princess Szélike"). A storyteller with a little bit of imagination can reconstruct how the story was supposed to end. Actually with many audiences it is great fun to try and piece the rest together — it seems that all the heroes are already on the team.

I included this story partly for the eye beams, even though the same power can already be found in Longshanks, Girth and Keen. I also wanted to include it for the messenger (is it just me, or is the flying centaur just kind of dropped in the middle of this?), and the father's advice. Starting out a journey is a crucial point in a hero's life, and conquering fear is an important step for moving forward.

# SONIC BLAST

To be honest, I was surprised that I found a folktale for this one — but it looks like it is less novel an idea than I thought. Sonic screams or blasts are a form of sound manipulation (often mentioned in comics and film together with several other forms like sound distortion or projection) that allow the person to emit a powerful burst of sound that is painful at best, and deadly at the worst. They can appear in the form of a scream, an energy blast, or even a whistle.

*Similar heroes:* Banshee (Marvel), Black Canary (DC), Echo DeMille (NBC's *Heroes*), Hale Santiago (Showcase's *Lost Girl*), Siryn (Marvel)

## *The Robber Called Nightingale*

*Ability:* Sonic blast (whistle), superhuman strength
*Source of power:* Unknown
*Origin:* Russia
*Teachings:* Bravery, think before you act, never too late to become a hero.
*Age group:* 12+
*Sources:* Afanasev, A.H., and L.A. Magnus (1916). *Russian Folk-Tales.* New York: E.P. Dutton & Co.

Bailey, J., and T. Ivanova (1998). *An Anthology of Russian Folk Epics.* Armonk, NY: M.E. Sharpe.

Wratislaw, A.H. (1890). *Sixty Folk-Tales from Exclusively Slavonic Sources.* Boston: Houghton, Mifflin and Co.

*Variants:* Most versions of this tale agree on all the major points; to read them, see sources.

*Text:* Ilya Muromets did not do anything until he was thirty years old. Then, one day he stood up, saddled a horse, donned armor and took up arms, asked for his parents' blessing, and set out to travel to Kiev to meet the prince. (Not all heroes start early.)

His father and his mother blessed him, and warned him not to shed Christian blood carelessly. Ilya was going to travel through dangerous land to Chernigov, and then from there straight through the woods and marshlands to Kiev.

He did not travel far before he ran into a band of robbers. They were ready to attack him for his armor and his horse; but, remembering his parents' warning, Ilya drew his bow and shot an arrow several meters into the ground — as a warning. The robbers all fell to their knees and offered him their arms and saddles. Ilya shrugged, "There is nowhere I could put them," and warned them to give up their wicked ways, or else he would have to come back and fight them.

Traveling on, our hero arrived at Chernigov just in time to see the city besieged by a pagan army. Drawing his sword, he spurred his horse into the fight, and it was not long before the enemy was running from him as if they had seen the devil himself. The people of Chernigov celebrated Ilya as a hero, and treated him as a beloved guest for days before he decided to continue his journey.

The shortest road between Chernigov and Kiev cut through endless forests and marshlands. Nobody ever traveled that road. People talked in hushed voices about a robber called Nightingale who could kill travelers by whistling at them. Still, Ilya was anxious to reach Kiev, and he was not afraid of danger.

Nightingale watched the road from his perch — a giant, elaborate nest built among the branches of twelve oaks. When he saw an armored knight riding towards him, he let out a low whistle. Ilya Muromets did not even slow down. Nightingale whistled louder and louder, and Ilya's horse staggered under him, neighing in pain. Ilya urged it to go on. Nightingale whistled even louder until trees started to bend and all around them the grass lay low on the ground — but Ilya still kept coming and when his horse could not carry him anymore, he drew a rosewood arrow, aimed carefully at the source of the sound, and shot Nightingale straight through the eye.

The robber fell from the tree, bleeding, but alive. Ilya picked him up, tied him to the saddle, and continued his journey. On the way he passed a castle where Nightingale's three daughters lived with their husbands. The youngest girl looked out the window and laughed: "Here comes father with another man tied up, and all the things he took from them!"

But then the oldest daughter looked out too, and she started to cry. "Here comes a stranger with our father tied to the saddle!"

The three husbands rode out to fight Ilya, but Nightingale called out to them from the saddle: "Do not attack this man if you want to live! He is a mighty hero. Let us treat him as a guest, and offer him green wine in our home!"

As Ilya was about to ride through the gates of the castle, he noticed one of the daughters holding a rope. Above the gates was an iron slab; she was preparing to drop it on Ilya's head as he rode through. Ilya threw his javelin into the gates instead, and as the daughter fell down dead, he rode away.

Finally, our hero made his way to Kiev, and presented himself at the prince's court.

"Who are you, and where do you come from?" asked the prince, looking at the strange hero and his armor.

"They call me Ilya Ivanov from the city of Murom," he answered, "and I came here on the road through Chernigov. I helped the city lift a siege, and on my way here I defeated the robber called Nightingale."

"Are you telling lies to me?!" snapped the prince; but his knights took a look at the prisoner and they confirmed it was indeed Nightingale. The prince was intrigued now.

"I want to hear that famous whistle of yours," he commanded the robber. Even though Ilya warned him, the prince insisted, so the hero gathered the prince and the princess under his arms and covered their ears, before ordering Nightingale to whistle with half his strength. The robber, however, seeing a chance for an escape, whistled with all his might, and all the guards and knights fell to the floor in agony. Ilya, drawing his sword, struck Nightingale, and that was the end of the robber's terror on the Chernigov road.

Ilya stayed in the court of the prince, and become one of the greatest Russian heroes that ever lived. This is just the beginning of his story; but let it be enough for now.

*Comments:* Both in effect and in visual description, Nightingale's whistle fulfills the criteria of being included under "sonic blast." The power of the blast is matched by Ilya's extraordinary strength and stamina. Nightingale is a villain with a supernatural power, who can only be defeated by a hero with a power of his own. An unlikely one, too, for Ilya is not one of the young, bright eyed and bushy tailed lads who set out to seek their fortune; he is kind of a late bloomer, and he sets out on his journey with a well-defined goal in mind. Later on he becomes the hero of the Kievan Rus, and the central figure of folk epics and tales.

I am starting to realize at this point that a distressing amount of people are getting shot in the eye in this book. Fair warning, some parents and teachers are not fans of graphic bloodshed. Hence the age limit, and the warning.

# POISON SECRETION

Yes, I included this category for one story (type) only: that of the infamous Poison Maiden. Beauty and deadly danger combined have always intrigued people's imagination. Nature herself warns of danger with brilliant colors and shapes. People just don't always listen.

*Similar heroes (and villains):* Maya Herrera (NBC's *Heroes*), Poison Ivy (DC)

## *The Poison Maiden*

*Ability:* Poison touch
*Source of power:* Natural
*Origin:* India, Greece and Medieval Europe
*Teachings:* Not all that glitters is safe to touch.
*Age group:* 16+
*Sources: Gesta Romanorum* (14th century collection of tales written in Latin) — titled "The Poison of Sin."

Mayor, A. (2002). *Greek Fire, Poison Arrows, and Scorpion Bombs: Biological and Chemical Warfare in the Ancient World.* Woodstock: Overlook Duckworth.

*Variants:* The most famous literary grandchild of the "Poison Maiden" story type would be Nathaniel Hawthorne's *Rappaccini's Daughter*. Mayor lists several other variants in her book.

*Text:* Alexander the Great and his army had reached India.

The farthest limits of the known world opened up before them. On their long journey they had seen things no man had ever seen, and fought battles against people whose language and culture were unknown to the Greeks. And finally they arrived in India, the land of wonders and plenty.

But India did not give its treasures easily.

Alexander's army was powerful, but exhausted, and far from home. They did not go to battle right away. The king and queen of India took advantage of the delay, and decided to show their good intentions by sending generous gifts to the king from far away. And, if possible, also assassinate him in the process.

The queen handpicked a maiden for the task. She was not just any ordinary beauty; she was a Poison Maiden, raised from her birth on the venom of snakes and the juice of poisonous plants until they did not harm her at all. Her body was filled with poison, and even her breath carried a death sentence.

They dressed the maiden up in the finest silks and jewels, and sent her as a gift to Alexander himself. The moment he set eyes on her he felt intense desire. She was slender, proud, exotic, and moved with the menacing grace of a serpent.

Before the young soldier-king could embrace her, however, his old advisor stepped between them. Aristotle had been Alexander's teacher from an early age, and he knew a lot about the world — among other things that if a gift looks too generous to be true, especially if it comes from an enemy, it usually is deadly.

"Do not touch her," he whispered. "Bring in a man who has been condemned to death, and have him kiss her first."

Alexander did not get as far as India without listening to good advice. He ordered a sentenced criminal to be brought in, and told him to kiss the maiden.

The criminal, hardly believing his good luck, complied — and promptly collapsed to the floor, dying after a few minutes of seizures.

Alexander the Great politely returned the maiden to the Indian king.

*Comments:* Such a nice piece of ancient diplomacy.

Poison Maidens show up in many tales in India and Medieval Europe. They are the result of the discovery that the human body can develop immunity to certain toxins overtime. In some versions of the tale the maiden's kiss or embrace is deadly, in others her mere glance could kill. The high value of such a specifically trained girl is reflected in the fact that Alexander merely returns her instead of taking revenge.

Side note: Aristotle never made it to India.

◆ PART II ◆

# It's All in Your Head —
# Mind Games, Mental Prowess,
# and the Power of Knowledge

## PRECOGNITION, ALSO KNOWN
## AS FORTUNE-TELLING,
## FUTURE SIGHT, CLAIRVOYANCE
## AND OTHER FANCY WORDS

Many wise people claim that the future is best left unknown — but who would not sneak a peek if they had the chance? Knowledge of the future is as common in folklore and mythology as surplus royalty wandering the roads, yet it rarely occurs as a consciously utilized ability. Most of the time it is the privilege of witches, fairies and helpful beggars along the road, but the hero rarely ever learns the tricks to do it. But once you start scratching the surface, of course, exceptions can be found to prove the rule. With something as fluid and changeable as the future, no wonder the abilities are hard to pin down....

*Heroes that can see the future:* Blindfold (Marvel), Destiny (Marvel), Isaac Mendez (NBC's *Heroes*), Simon Bellamy (E4's *Misfits*)

## *Aicha, the Demon-Hunter*

*Ability:* Clairvoyance, exceptional fighting skills
*Source of power:* Learning (geomancy)
*Origin:* Algeria (Berber)

*Teachings:* Independence and girl power, bravery, making one's own destiny.

*Age group:* 10+

*Sources:* Cosquin, E. (1922). *Les contes Indiens et l'Occident.* Paris: Édouard Champion.

Desparmet, J. (1909). *Contes populaires sur les ogres, recueillis à Blida et traduits.* Paris: E. Leroux.

Desparmet, M.J. (1916). "Aicha, fille du marchand, la chatte et l'ogre." *Revue des traditions populaires,* 31(1–2): 12–15.

El-Shamy, H., and J. El Koudia (2003). *Moroccan Folktales.* Syracuse: Syracuse University Press.

Knappert, J. (2002). "Aicha's Tasks on Earth: Fairy Tales from Algeria, Part One. *World and I,* 17(6): 172–179.

Parker, H. (1914). *Village Folktales from Ceylon.* London: Luzac.

Pétigny, C.F. (1948). *Contes Algériens.* Paris: F. Nathan, 24–38.

Peyron, M. (2003). *Women as Brave as Men: Berber Heroines of the Moroccan Middle Atlas.* Ifrane: Al Akhawayn University.

*Variants:* I mainly focused my research on Berber tales and tales from Morocco and Algeria, but I managed to discover a few variants that are similar to the first part of Aicha's story.

Desparmet references an Indian folktale called "The Rakshasa's Claw" (Cosquin, 1922). In this version, the girl is raised by eagles, and instead of burning the demon (rakshasa) with fire, she is wounded when it leaves a claw wedged in the doorframe. The wound has a very different effect from Aicha's lust for adventure: this girl falls into a deep sleep, much like Sleeping Beauty. Another very similar version called "Black Stork's Girl" has been collected from Ceylon (Parker, 1914). In another version, titled "Seven Brothers and a Sister" (Morocco), the ogre does manage to take revenge, and succeeds in killing Aicha (El-Shamy–El-Koudia, 2003).

It looks like the wound from the ogre resulting in wanderlust and recklessness is a rare and unique variation of this story type — most versions include either sleep or death.

Peyron's version titled "Aisha and the Donkey-Eating Ogre" is also a Berber tale, but the beginning is different: in this variation, Aicha is chased away from home and becomes the adopted daughter of a female ogre that eventually rescues her from her male enemy. (Peyron, 2003).

(Yes, I have been working with this story for a long time.)

*Text:* Once upon a time in North Africa there lived a wealthy merchant who had three daughters. All three of them were pretty and clever, but the youngest one, Aicha, far surpassed her sisters in both of those fields. And that was not all; while the two older sisters busied themselves with everyday chores and gossip, Aicha learned things few people had the courage and the strength to learn.

She was an accomplished fighter who could handle the scimitar like any soldier. She could read and write and recite the holy books, and she had even learned geomancy, which is the art of reading the future from patterns in the sand. In fact, she was so famous for her skills in fighting and magic that her father could go away on business and leave the house to her, and he could be sure no one was going to bother his daughters. A man tried breaking in once, at night, just to find himself face to face with Aicha, holding her scimitar ... and word got around. No thief or robber went near that house ever again.

There was one more person in the household who the father was very fond of: Minoush, the cat. She was a large queen cat, the favorite of the family — so much so that she had her own box of sweets in the kitchen, and no one else was allowed to eat from it. Every time the father had to leave, he always reminded his daughters not to forget to give Minoush her treats.

One day while he was away, the two older sisters found the box in the kitchen, and they could not resist: they ate a piece of candy each, and it tasted so marvelous that they kept eating until it was all gone. Of course Minoush soon found out that there were no treats left, and she did what all cats would have done: she took revenge. At night when the girls were asleep, she crept into the fireplace, crouched down over the embers, and ... put out the fire.

In the morning when the girls woke up, there was no fire to cook breakfast or warm the house up. The two older sisters insisted that Aicha had to go out and borrow fire from the neighbors. They knew all too well it was going to be a long walk: their house stood alone away from the other houses, and the nearest neighbor was far away on the other side of the woods. But Aicha was not afraid. She walked along humming to herself, when she suddenly saw a light just off the path. Where there is light, there has to be fire, she reasoned to herself, and walked towards it, until she found a clearing, and in the clearing a small, miserable shack. Opening the door she peered inside, and gasped at what she saw.

In the cottage there was a fire, and a huge cauldron hung above it, filled with some gray and vile smelling goo. A man sat by the fire on a donkey's skull, and stirred the goo with a donkey's leg.

Aicha knew exactly what the man was: a ghoul, an evil monster that eats human flesh. And because she was smart, she also knew that flattery goes a long way with stupid people, so she smiled at him and said: "Good day to you, my handsome uncle!"

The ghoul smiled back at her, flashing sharp teeth, and answered: "Good day to you too, my beautiful daughter! What are you looking for?"

"I would like to borrow some of your fire," she said, "if it is not too much trouble. I wouldn't want to spoil your delicious food."

"Go ahead, take as much as you need," the ghoul waved her closer. As she leaned down to pick up some embers, he pulled a needle out of his robes and pricked her foot, just enough to draw some blood. Aicha thanked him for the fire and walked back home as fast as she could ... but when she arrived to the doorstep, she noticed the trail of blood drops she had left behind, and she knew the ghoul was going to come for her.

She went back out to the path, and dug a pit. When it was wide and deep enough, she filled it up with dry leaves and twigs, and then covered it with branches and dirt so no one could suspect it was there.

She did not have to wait long after that. As night fell, the ghoul left his house, followed the trail of blood ... and fell into the pit. As soon as she heard the crash, Aicha ran outside with a burning torch, and threw the torch down into the pit. The leaves and branches caught fire, and the ghoul started to burn. But before he died, he cried out: "If there is only a piece of bone left of me, I will take revenge on you!"

And then he burned to cinders.

People celebrated when they found out what Aicha had done. The ghoul had been terrorizing travelers for a long time, and everyone was happy to be rid of him. They called Aicha a hero, and she became so famous for her bravery that word soon reached the king's castle about her. The prince, the king's only son, told his father that he wanted to marry that brave girl everyone was talking about, and he sent messengers to Aicha's house to ask her father for her hand in marriage.

"You will have to ask Aicha herself," waved the father. "I would not dare speak for her."

When the messengers told Aicha about the prince, she shook her head. "Why did he not come to ask me himself? Is he too lazy for that?"

The messengers tried to come up with excuses but she just shook her head again.

"I don't want to marry the prince if he is not even willing to see me. Go tell him that."

But her father, who overheard the conversation, pulled her aside and begged her to accept. "You could be a queen! You are a merchant's youngest daughter, but if you married the prince, our whole family would become royalty! Think about it!"

He begged and begged until Aicha agreed to marry the prince. For her family's sake.

"I have one condition, though," she told the messengers. "Take this ring and give it to the prince. This is the token of our engagement. And also tell him that I will not marry him until he has killed all the monsters in the forest. It is a disgrace that the kingdom has a strong young prince, yet the roads are overrun by ghouls and demons. When he has gotten rid of all of them, we can get married."

The messengers took the ring and the message back to the prince. He did not like it at all. He did not like fighting, and he was scared of monsters. However, if he said no to Aicha's request his honor would be ruined and he would become the laughing stock of the entire kingdom. With that in mind, he put on his armor, took his weapons, and marched into the forest to fight monsters.

He did not have to wait long. Suddenly, out of the shadows came a small, dark figure that attacked him with fierce speed and strength. It took all the prince had to ward off the attacks of the mysterious shadow, but he still had to keep backing away, looking for a way out. Finally, his opponent knocked him to the ground, and the prince shut his eyes, waiting for the final blow ... and when he opened them, the shadow was gone. And so was his ring.

That was quite enough for the prince. He hid himself in the woods for a while, then went home and reported to his father that he had conquered the monsters and ghouls, and he was ready to marry. The king sent for Aicha, and she came to the palace dressed in her finest dress, and stood before the royal family proudly.

"My son has killed the ghouls like you have requested," announced the king. "Are you ready to marry him now?"

"Yes, your highness," Aicha answered. "As soon as he presents our engagement ring."

The prince turned red in the face. "I ... must have misplaced it, father."

"No he did not," said Aicha, loud and clear. "He lost it to me in a fight."

And with that, she presented the ring for everyone to see. The prince blushed even more and looked away.

"Your son is a liar and a coward," said Aicha, "and I do not intend to marry such a man. I apologize, your highness, but this wedding must not happen."

With that, Aicha left the court, and returned home.

As the girl passed by the pit where she had burned the ghoul, she suddenly remembered his warning. Just to make sure there was nothing left of the demon, she climbed down into the pit and started poking around in the cinders. As she turned a pile of ash over, a piece of bone was uncovered; from the sudden cold of the air it exploded, and a splinter wedged itself under the skin on Aicha's cheek.

With the piece of ghoul bone, something else also entered the girl: an unquenchable thirst for adventure. She felt uneasy, she yearned to travel, to see new lands; it felt painful to stay in one place. Confused by these strange feelings, she turned to the signs in the sand, and for the first time, she read her own future.

What she saw in the sand stunned her. She saw long roads and faraway places; she saw monsters, battles, and bloodshed. She saw cities that waited for her, and people who needed her help. And she saw that there was no mortal spouse waiting for her anywhere in the world; but at the end of the road there was the prince of the djinn, her future husband.

The next morning Aicha said goodbye to her father and her sisters, saddled a horse, and rode out into the world.

*Comments:* This is only the beginning of Aicha's story. I traced it back from a magazine to a book to the original folklore article from the early 20th century. In the earliest version, strange enough, this is where it ends. Later on, in the collection of Algerian folktales, someone added other folktale and legend fragments to it, until it became a series of exciting adventures of Aicha the demon-hunter, destined to rid the world from werewolves, ghouls and other monsters, until she could finally get rid of her curse, settle down, and become a queen. That all might not have been included in the earliest version, but it is hinted at in her vision of the future, and it makes a very compelling story. Unfortunately, it is way too long to include in this book, so I decided to stick to the original.

Aicha's story works especially well with young female audiences. Instead of being given to the prince as a prize, this heroine stands up for herself and sets out to seek her own adventures. Even though her yearning to travel is presented as a curse, she turns it into a blessing as she travels the world helping people and slaying monsters. Turning a curse into a blessing is a concept that keeps returning in modern superhero stories (just think of the Hulk), and creates an interesting, far from perfect, but still admirable hero character.

# ASTRAL PROJECTION AND OTHER OUT-OF-BODY EXPERIENCES

Astral projection is the ability to leave one's physical body and travel great distances in an ethereal spirit form. It is one of the many pseudo-scientific abilities that have been experimented with since the early 19th century, and features in countless fantasy novels and ghost stories. In popular media it is often part of a telepath's skill set, although sometimes also occurs alone.

Many traditional cultures believed that the soul (or part of the soul) leaves the body while someone is asleep and travels to faraway places. Exiting their bodies to travel into the spirit world was also the most important ability of shamans. Many tales warn about the dangers of such travels: if the body is moved or destroyed, the spirit cannot return; waking a person up before their journey is done can lead to similarly fatal consequences.

*Similar heroes:* Dr. Strange (Marvel), Emma Frost (Marvel), Professor Xavier (Marvel)

## Quiet Girl Becomes a Goddess

*Ability:* Weather manipulation, astral projection, healing powers, far sight
*Source of power:* Divine
*Origin:* China
*Teachings:* Knowledge is power, importance of bravery, girls can be heroes too (and a lot of Chinese religious history).
*Age group:* 8+
*Sources:* Irwin, L. (1990). "The Great Goddesses of China." *Asian Folklore Studies*, Vol. 49, No. 1: 53–68.

Ruitenbeek, K. (1999). "Mazu, the Patroness of Sailors, in Chinese Pictorial Art." *Artibus Asiae*, Vol. 58, No. 3/4: 281–329.

Yuan, H. (2006). *The Magic Lotus Lantern and Other Tales from the Han Chinese*. Westport, CT: Libraries Unlimited.

*Variants:* The goddess Mazu is one of the most popular deities in Taiwan, and there are numerous legends and tales about her. Only a few of them have been translated into English.

*Text:* More than a thousand years ago, on a small island near Taiwan, lived a middle-aged couple, the Lins. They had six children, five sons and a daughter, and the mother really, really wished for another girl. She prayed day and night to Kuan Yin, goddess of mercy, until the goddess appeared to her in a dream, and handed her a flower. Soon after, mother Lin was with child.

A baby girl was born. As she came into the world, the room filled with crimson light and the fragrance of blossoms, marking her as a chosen child. They named her Lin Niang, but because the first month of her life she did not cry at all, the family just called her Moliang, Silent Girl.

From her early childhood Silent Girl had always been a little strange. She was clever beyond her age, and she was soon apprenticed to a Buddhist priest. Kuan Yin gave her the blessing of far sight, which allowed her to see events that happened far away.

When Moliang was fifteen, she went to a nearby pond with her friends to admire their new dresses. As they stood by the pond, a monster erupted from the water and held out a bronze tablet. The other girls ran away screaming, but Moliang accepted the gift calmly, and soon after she started to display miraculous powers.

People in the village quickly learned about her ability to heal injuries and illnesses, and flocked to her house to ask for help. Fishermen found out that she could predict the weather and see when it was safe to venture out into the seas, and visited her daily for advice.

One day Moliang was weaving a tapestry when she suddenly fell into a trance. Through her far sight she could see her father and brother out on the sea in grave danger from a storm, their boat filling quickly with water. Using her power she left her body and transported her spirit out to the sea, grabbing her brother and swimming with him to safety. She turned back for her father and was dragging him by her teeth toward the shore, when her mother walked into her room and saw the girl's senseless body on the floor. Alarmed, the mother shook Moliang until she returned to her body and woke up ... but her father was left out in the sea, and he drowned in the storm. Silent Girl, grieving for her father, sent her spirit into the sea, and returned three days later with his body, to arrange a proper burial.

After her father's death, Moliang spent even more time studying and perfecting her skills. She was never interested in marriage or men — she only cared for making the world a better and safer place for everyone ... even if she had to fight monsters to do it.

Legend says that two giant monsters terrorized the land, one named Eyes-that-see-a-Thousand-Miles and the other Ears-that-hear-the-Wind. Some say they used to be generals under the Shang dynasty, but turned into monsters after their death. Whatever the case, no one could stop them because of their incredible size and speed. People ran and cowered, but no one stood up to fight.

No one, except for Silent Girl. She took her tablets and went to face the demons, praying and reciting and chanting calmly even in the face of danger. Her devotion and power subdued the monster-generals, and because Moliang was the chosen of Kuan Yin, the goddess of mercy, she forgave them for their sins. From that day on, they became her most devoted followers and protectors, and their statues still stand in her temples to this very day.

Temples? Yes.

When Lin Moliang was twenty-eight years old, she told her parents it was time for her to go. Climbing a mountain, she disappeared in the clouds, engulfed by golden light, and rose to the heavens to become a goddess. She became one of the most beloved Buddhist deities, Mazu, the goddess of the sea.

*Comments:* Mazu is one of the most popular deities in Taiwan, worshiped by sailors and other people who make a living from the sea. It seems unusual to Westerners for a human to become a goddess, but it occurs quite often in Chinese mythology. Silent Girl displays powers from an early age and she trains to become better at them; she uses them to help people, and it is her compassion that raises her to godhood, not the powers themselves.

Moliang has a very inspirational story that transcends religion. A quiet and strange little girl who faces water monsters without fear and discovers things through learning that make her special. Loved by the very goddess of compassion, she fulfills her destiny and makes the world a better place by doing it.

---

## The Dream House

*Ability:* Astral projection
*Source of power:* Unknown
*Origin:* Ireland
*Teachings:* Dreams do come true.
*Age group:* 8+
*Sources:* Briggs, K. (1988). *British Folktales.* New York: Pantheon.
Hare, A.J.C. (1900). *The Story of My Life.* London: George Allen.
*Variants:* Dreams come true often in folktales and legends, but this one is quite peculiar.
*Text:* Mrs. Butler lived ... somewhere in Ireland. She was clever, pretty, popular, rich, and perfectly happy. One morning she woke up with a smile on her face, and she said to her husband:

"I had the most wonderful dream! I dreamed of a lovely house, not too big, not too small, perfectly comfortable, and with such an enchanting garden! It feels like I spent all night there, oh, it was wonderful!"

Her husband smiled and said nothing. But the next morning Mrs. Butler woke up smiling again. "I have been in my house! I sat in the library; I visited the bedrooms; I walked on the terrace, and it was all so *perfect!*"

Mr. Butler said nothing.

Mrs. Butler kept dreaming about her house, night after night. It became kind of a joke in the family: people often asked her if she dreamed again, and she would throw herself into describing the perfect little house, with a bright smile on her face. Then, gradually, the dreams stopped, and so did the jokes.

A few years later the Butlers decided to move to England. The area where they lived was getting disturbed, people were moving away; since they had no children, and a bit of money, the husband and wife traveled to London to find a new home. They visited many houses in a forty-mile area around the city, looking for one to buy. Finally they heard about one in Hampshire, and they took the train to see it. The moment they arrived and walked in, Mrs. Butler stopped dead in her tracks:

"This ... this is my house!"

When the housekeeper greeted them, Mrs. Butler did not even wait for introductions. She walked around the house, knowing her way as well as if she had been living her all her life. Her husband and the housekeeper followed her around, quite puzzled, until she came to a door and stopped. "This door was not in my house," she said.

"I don't know what you mean, ma'am," said the housekeeper, "but this door has only been here for six weeks."

The Butlers decided to buy the house; it was surprisingly cheap. So cheap, in fact, that once the papers were signed they could not help but ask the agent: Why did he sell it for such a small amount?

"Well," said the agent, "for years, the house had a reputation for being haunted. But you, ma'am, do not need to worry: the ghost people claimed to see looked exactly like you!"

Mrs. Butler realized that whenever she dreamed about her house, her astral body was seen there by other people. Puzzled and delighted at the same time, she finally moved into her home, body and soul.

*Comments:* This little anecdote from late Victorian England is recorded without comments in a journal-autobiography. It does not really make or prove a point, only mentions the curious case of Mrs. Butler as an intriguing story. That is exactly what it is — a tale of astral projection that causes great delight to the person blessed with it, but is frowned upon by everyone else. Mrs. Butler's simple delight of finding "her house" makes this story kind of adorable. Because who has never dreamed of a place they would want to return to?

# TELEPATHY

Now this is a tough one. Mental powers in general have been harder to research than physical ones, simply because a couple of centuries ago everything that had to do with invisible, non-physical forces was usually chalked up to "magic." Telepathy especially, as we know it today from countless science fiction and fantasy stories, is hard to describe in "traditional" terms. Researching folktales for it has been a challenge.

I soon realized that I had to completely abandon the word itself if I wanted results. Instead I experimented with search terms such as "hearing thoughts" or "knowing thoughts" and the classic "reading minds" in order to find at least a motif or a trace that could lead me to some tales. I also had to distinguish between "hearing thoughts," "mind control," and "telepathic communication." It seems like a whole group of different abilities gets labeled as "telepathy" and with good reason.

As I continued my research in folktales and legends, I discarded tales with characters that simply stated "I know why you are here" or "I know what you wish for"— it sounded too generic for my purposes. Instead I was looking for stories where the hero (or the villain) gets to use the ability to tap into other people's thoughts. It was not an easy search, but it yielded fascinating results.

(By the way, it turns out one folktale motif for reading thoughts is V223.3, Saint Perceives Man's Thoughts. Another one is D1819.1, Magic Knowledge of Another's Thoughts.)

*Telepaths in modern media:* Emma Frost (Marvel), Jean Grey (Marvel), Kelly Bailey (E4's *Misfits*), Martian Manhunter (DC), Matt Parkman (NBC's *Heroes*), Professor X (Marvel), Psylocke (Marvel), Rachel Summers/Grey (Marvel), Sookie Stackhouse (HBO's *True Blood*), the Stepford Cuckoos (Marvel) (phew, does Marvel have a lot of telepathic heroes...)

## János Carnation-Hair (Szegfűhajú János)

*Ability:* Telepathy, knowledge, spirit travel, healing factor
*Source of power:* Magical
*Origin:* Hungary
*Teachings:* Um ... do not marry the first princess you come across? Also, bravery, kindness, second chances, friendship.
*Age group:* 8+
*Sources:* Benedek, E. (1988). *Magyar mese- és mondavilág III.* Budapest: Móra Ferenc Könyvkiadó.
*Variants:* This story is type MNK 476A in the *Catalogue of Hungarian Folktales.*

The godmother's strange way of raising the boy can be compared to the "burning for immortality" motif in Achilles's story. The copper-silver-gold kingdoms appear in many folktales internationally, most famously in Grimm's "Twelve Dancing Princesses."

*Text:* Once upon a time, there was a poor widow who only had one son. He was barely a week old when his father died, and they were left in such poverty that no one wanted to be a godmother to the child. The widow walked down to the seashore to be alone with her sadness, when suddenly a great warty toad jumped in front of her. She screamed, but in just that moment the toad turned into a beautiful woman.

"Do not be afraid of me," she smiled. "See, I am a woman, just like you. Tell me what made you sad."

"My husband died, and I am alone with a child that no one is willing to hold under the holy water."

"I will do it," volunteered the beautiful woman, who then followed the widow home. She held the baby under the holy water, and he was baptized as

János Carnation-hair, for he had beautiful hair just like carnations. The lady adored her godchild so much that they begged the widow to let her take him and raise him.

"I will love him as my own child," she promised, "and you will want for nothing."

It pained the mother to see her child go, but she wanted the best for him, so she agreed. The lady left her a bag of gold and food, and then walked back to the seashore with the baby. She touched the water with a golden wand and the waves parted, revealing her castle built of gold and diamonds.

As soon as she was home, she cut the baby into tiny pieces and left him in a bathtub for three days.

Once the three days were over, she put the pieces back together, covered them in healing ointments, and suddenly János came to life as a ten-year-old boy.

"I had such a wonderful dream, godmother! I dreamed of a kingdom made of copper, and I learned so many things!"

"You will see and learn even more than that," she answered, and cut him up again.

Three days later János was revived, older, stronger and more handsome than ever.

"Such a wonderful dream, godmother! I was in a kingdom made of silver, and I learned so many things!"

"Show me what you have learned," said the lady.

"I know my mother is on the seashore right now, crying for me. I can feel her sorrow."

"Go and bring her, then."

János went and brought his mother to the diamond palace where they feasted and had a merry time. When the visit was over and the widow went home, the lady cut János up once again and left him in the tub for three days, before she brought him back to life as a handsome young man.

"I dreamed of a kingdom made of gold, godmother," he smiled, "and now I can feel my mother walking on the seashore, waiting for me."

The widow was allowed to visit her son once again, and they were happy together. But as soon as she was gone, the godmother cut János to pieces once more. This time when he came back to life he was a dashing young man, ready to take on the world.

"I dreamed of a kingdom made of diamond, and I have seen things I have never seen before. But now I long to see my mother again."

The godmother handed him a bag of gold.

"Go and tell your mother to pay this to the king, and have a castle built for herself."

The widow went to the king, who was very surprised to see a poor woman with that much gold, and did not quite believe her. She returned to the seashore to tell her son, and János started laughing before she ever spoke.

"The king told you he wants to see me, didn't he?" he called. "I am laughing at his thoughts."

János traveled to the royal city and presented himself to the king. The princess instantly fell in love with the dashing young man, and her father secretly believed that János was some foreign prince, pretending to be a widow's son. They ordered the castle to be built immediately, with diamonds and gold, and they hoped that the handsome young visitor would grow fond of the princess and marry her.

The palace was built in no time at all, and the poor widow almost fainted with wonder when she was led across the threshold. They immediately announced a feast and invited the entire city, including the king and the princess. There was music and dancing, games and sweets and drinks and all kinds of wonders. As they were sitting at the table, János leaned over to his godmother: "I need to leave and go see the world."

"If you need to, then off you go," she smiled. "I will make sure no one follows. Remember what you learned, and go with my blessing."

As the young man walked out of the banquet hall, and the princess watched him with longing, the godmother put a spell on everyone and made them forget that János had ever existed. The feast went on.

János traveled far away. He crossed mountains, deserts, and the Red Sea, until he arrived at the Copper Kingdom he had dreamed about. He was hired by the Copper Queen who put him in charge of her horses, but warned him not to cast his eyes on her daughter, because the punishment for that was death. János guarded the copper horses on the fields, but suddenly the Copper Princess appeared out of nowhere and smiled at him, trying to convince him to become her lover. He tried to send her away but she would not go; by the time she finally left János was so tired that he lay down and fell asleep. As he did, all the horses left the fields and wandered across the border to the Silver Kingdom. János woke up and saw with alarm that all the horses were gone; but the Copper Princess appeared again and pointed him in the right direction. János walked over to the Silver Kingdom and found the copper horses in a silver castle. The Silver Princess who lived in that castle saw him from the window and instantly fell in love.

"Take the horses, János," she smiled, and let them all go; and more than that, she gave a silver horse to him that had two colts just as they were on the way home. One silver colt stood up right away and ran on its own, but the other one was weak and skinny and János had to carry it all the way home.

"Put me down, master," the colt spoke suddenly. "I will carry you now."

And as he put the colt down it turned into a wonderful, strong silver stallion.

"The Copper Queen wishes to kill you for talking to her daughter," the horse said, "but listen to my advice and you will live. I will take you to the silver castle tonight, all the queens will be there, and you can hear them talk. But if they find you, you have to run, and I will be waiting for you outside, with two stars on my saddle so you can find me in the dark."

János sneaked into the silver castle and hid himself among a crowd of guests. He could not see who was in the inner chamber, but he knew anyway, for he had the knowledge to read people's thoughts. It was the Queens of Copper, Silver and Gold, talking about him.

"We'd better look after our daughters," said the Silver Queen. "János Carnation-hair walks among us, and he makes every girl fall in love with him. And he will marry none of them, for he is destined to take the Diamond Princess as a wife!"

"Let him come to my kingdom, his pretty hair will dry on the gallows!" the Golden Queen snapped. "And he is in here right now, listening to us!"

János, hearing that, ran out of the guest room and jumped on his horse. The queens pursued him but their horses were not nearly as fast, and one by one they all fell behind. Only the Copper Princess kept riding, leaving her mother behind, calling after János desperately, and finally she managed to convince him to return home with her.

But as soon as they reached the copper castle, the queen ordered her guards to drag János to the dungeons: he was to be hanged in the morning. But even though they locked him in with seven locks, the princess still found a way to sneak in and sit by him all night. When the queen came to take a look at him and found her daughter with him, he ordered him to be dragged to the gallows right away.

János hung on the rope till sunrise. In the morning, his horse came to him and called: "Master, are you alive?"

"I am, my friend," János smiled, and the horse pulled him down, and they rode away from the Copper Kingdom. Soon they heard the sound of hooves behind them: the Copper Queen was riding after them, her sword drawn.

"You rascal, you left my daughter behind with a broken heart, and for that you will die!"

They fought for a long time, swords sparking and thundering, until finally János prevailed.

"I have never been defeated by any man," the Queen said, falling to her knees. "Take my kingdom, János, and take my daughter if you want."

"I want neither your kingdom, nor your daughter," he said, and he rode on to the silver lands.

It took János a long time to travel across the Silver Kingdom and the Gold. Both queens tried to fight him; both princesses loved him; both times he ended up on the gallows. The second time he would have truly died if the Golden Princess had not cut him down and healed him with her medicine. Still, he left her behind and rode on, seeking the Diamond Kingdom that he never seemed to reach.

"I wish my godmother was here to guide me!" he said finally, exhausted from the journey ... and in that moment, she appeared, smiling.

"Follow me, child." She led him to a land where everything was made of diamonds. "Do you remember this place, János?"

"I do. I have seen it in my dreams."

"This is the Diamond Kingdom, and its queen is my sister. She has been waiting for you ever since you were born, to marry her daughter the Diamond Princess."

János could not have been happier; neither could the princess, who fell in love with him at first sight. They held a wedding right away. The godmother transported János' mother, castle and all, to the Diamond Kingdom. There they live happily till today, if they are still alive.

*Comments:* I am going to say this up front, I have no idea what "carnation-hair" means. After a short tally of my folklorist and non-folklorist friends and acquaintances (and my audiences), I concluded that it could be silky, curly, pink, lilac, white, short, long, fragrant, or red. The latter seems the most likely, but no definite answer could be found in academic literature. Choose your preferences.

Folklorists have claimed that folktales like this are remnants of the Hungarians' old shamanistic beliefs. In many shamanistic traditions the chosen person is cut into pieces by the spirits and put back together during the initiation to come into his powers. During these visions he also travels to different levels of the World Tree, symbolized by the copper, silver and gold kingdoms (silver and gold being the moon and the sun), and fights spirits aided by his horse, the *táltos* (a symbol for the shaman's drum that carries him on these spiritual journeys). This folktale is rich in symbols and fantastic images, and surprisingly clear on János's ability to read thoughts. The story also hints at a healing factor (since he does not die from being hanged), but never explains it.

I had to shorten this tale quite a bit to fit into this book. However, I barely left anything out: the episodes that happen in the Copper Kingdom are simply repeated two more times in the Silver and the Gold, giving a steady rhythm to the story, but also stretching it to three times as long.

## Michael Scott

*Ability:* Telepathy, healing, fairy command
*Source of power:* White snake's flesh
*Origin:* Scotland
*Teachings:* Bravery, creativity, curiosity, and politeness all go a long way.
*Age group:* 8+
*Sources:* Gibbings, W.W. (1889). *Folk-Lore and Legends, Scotland.* London: Gibbings.

Mackenzie, D.A. (1917). *Wonder Tales of Scottish Myth and Legend.* New York: Frederick A. Stokes Co.

*Variants:* The "thumb of knowledge" appears in many tales, as we have already seen in the case of Sir James Ramsay. In some cases like that of Taliesin, the person cheated out of the magical powers is angered and swears revenge, while in other cases (like in Finn MacCool's), they accept their fate with resignation. The snake rolling as a wheel can be found in other folktales and fairy tales. One really good example can be found in Edmund Lenihan's book *Meeting the Other Crowd* (see Sources for "Anne Jeffries and the Fairies"). Compare this to the tale of Sir James Ramsay, who also acquired powers through eating the flesh of a white snake.

Other famous wizards with similar stories are Don Juan de Salamanca, Doctor Faustus and Pietro Baillardo (later in this book).

*Text:* When Michael Scott was a young man, just like any other ordinary young man (or maybe a little bit braver), one day he set out on a journey to Edinburgh. Because walking alone was boring and the road was long, he decided to travel with two of his friends as companions.

One day after climbing a steep hill they sat down to rest for a while, and as they looked around they saw a very strange sight. Something that looked like a big white wheel was rolling towards them — up the hill! The two companions scampered away in fear and ran for their lives, but Michael stood his ground, armed with nothing but his walking stick, and waited. As the wheel got closer it turned out to be a great white snake with its tail in its mouth. Moving toward Michael it uncoiled itself, ready to spring; the young man swung his staff, and hit the beast with enough force to snap its body into three pieces.

Michael soon caught up to his companions, telling them what happened, and they continued their journey. As night fell, they came across a little hut where an old woman lived, and they asked for lodgings for the night. Telling stories by the fire, one of the companions recounted how Michael had killed a great white serpent. The old woman gave him a strange look.

"Are you sure the serpent is dead?" she asked Michael.

"Quite sure. I cut it into three pieces."

"That means nothing. The white serpent has great powers. If its head can crawl to a stream of healing water nearby, it can reattach itself to the body, and it will not stop till it hunts you down and takes revenge. Even if you run to the end of the world, it will still find you. Only if a man reaches the stream before the head does would the serpent die."

Now Michael was worried. "What should I do?"

"You need to go back to the mountain and bring me the middle part of the serpent. But hurry, run fast, lest you run out of time."

Michael ran back to the mountain, and found the still wiggling middle part of the snake. The head was nowhere to be seen. He hurried back to the old woman's house. He was sure the serpent's head would follow him for vengeance, but as he reached the door he noticed that there were charms around it to keep evil spirits from entering.

The old woman looked delighted to see the piece of white snake flesh — so delighted, in fact, that Michael grew suspicious, and wanted to see what she was going to do with it. He pretended to fall asleep just like his companions, but he kept an eye on her. He saw her put the snake flesh into a pot and start boiling it over the fire, checking every once in a while to see if it was cooked. Michael walked over to the fire and told her he could not sleep from some pain, and asked her if he could sit by the warmth of the flames.

"If you are going to be awake," she said, "then I am going to sleep. Make sure to keep an eye on the pot, and wake me up first thing when the meat is cooked."

Michael sat by the fire all night. He did not know when the meat was going to be ready, or what was going to happen when he woke the old woman up. But toward dawn he looked inside the pot, and dipped a finger in it to see how it was going. The tip of his finger was burnt and he took it into his mouth to cool the sting down ... and as he did, something changed. The rooster on the roof crowed once, and the old woman woke up with a scream.

Michael sat by the fire, stunned by the new powers the snake's magical flesh had given him. He now had the power to foretell events, to cure illnesses, and to read people's thoughts. When the old woman said to him, "You did not call me," he knew instantly that she wanted to taste the flesh first, and have the powers for herself.

"I killed the serpent," he answered. "It was my right to taste it first."

"I cannot scold you now for what you have done," she sighed. "You are wiser than me now, and you possess great power. You can see my thoughts, and read the future, and you can command the fairies of the invisible world. All I can ask of you now is your friendship."

"My friendship shall be yours," Michael smiled. They sat together by the fire as the sun came up, and she asked him many questions. Michael found that he could answer them, even though he did not remember learning the answers. When the two companions woke up the old woman made breakfast, and after the meal she said goodbye to the travelers.

"Do not forget me. You owe me much," she said to Michael.

"I shall never forget you," he promised, and he walked out into the world.

*Comments:* Michael Scott is regarded as one of the greatest Scottish wizards of the Middle Ages. He was born in the 13th century, worked for the Pope and the Holy Roman Emperor in Italy, and his influential life soon seeped into legend and folklore.

I know I made a point of not including wizards and magicians in this book. But I also made a point of including at least one story for all the powers listed, and two are even better. Supernatural knowledge and the reading of thoughts more often than not fall into the realm of magic in traditional stories, and they are not always as specifically stated as in this tale.

In terms of story, I admire the bonding moment between Michael and the wise woman he cheated out of the magical powers. She handles defeat with grace and dignity, and only asks for answers she has been seeking.

This is only the beginning of Michael Scott's story; legend goes on to tell of his exploits and magical tricks. Some deal with his "second sight" and command over fairies (or devils). I found no tale specifically dealing with his ability to read people's thoughts, though, so I leave the story here, at the point of acquiring powers, the doorstep to a life of adventures.

# TELEKINESIS

To tell the truth, this is one of the powers that almost beat me in my research — once again simply because objects moving on their own are usually labeled "magic." Moving them with the power of one's mind and sheer will seems to be a fairly modern thought that developed as science took over from religion. With that said, telekinesis is a major power on the list of superpowers, and as such I could not leave it unmentioned.

Telekinesis, also known as psychokinesis, has been researched extensively but has never been proven to exist. The basic idea is the ability to move or influence physical objects without the use of any kind of a physical force, rather the "power of the mind." In comic books and films powerful telekinesis often also gives a person the ability to fly (or, literally, lift him/herself into the air), which would add many tales with flying objects (e.g., broomsticks) to the list.

In the end, in order to illustrate telekinesis, I decided to choose a folktale where objects seemingly move on their own accord, but they are clearly obeying the will of a person present in the room. This is as close as I could get.

*Telekinetic heroes:* Andrew, Matt and Steve (*Chronicle*), Finn (E4's *Misfits*), Hellion (Marvel), Jean Grey (Marvel), the Jedi (*Star Wars*), Richard Tyler (CBS's *The 4400*)

## The Man Who Had No Story

*Ability:* Telekinesis (or at least moving objects somehow without touching them)

*Source of power:* Unknown

*Origin:* Ireland

*Teachings:* Everyone has a story.

*Age group:* 6+

Sources: Foss, M. (1977). Folktales of the British Isles. London: Macmillan.

Lindahl, C. (2001). *Perspectives on the Jack tales: And Other North American Märchen.* Bloomington: Folklore Institute / Indiana University Bloomington.

Niles, J.D. (2006). "Bede's Caedmon 'The Man Who Had No Story' (Irish tale-type 2412B)." *Folklore*, Vol. 117, No. 2.

O'Sullivan, S. (1968). *Folktales of Ireland.* Chicago: University of Chicago Press.

*Variants:* This story type (AaTh 2412B) is extremely popular in the Scottish-Irish storytelling tradition (as well as with modern storytellers all around the world). There are several different versions and their combinations circulating around (see the sources).

*Text:* There was a man called Rory O'Connor. He was a good man, he was a decent man, he was a hard-working man ... but he was not really an *interesting* man. Now, that seems like a disadvantage that would be easy to live with. But you need to know that back in the olden days in Ireland it was common courtesy to entertain people one visited ... and Rory was a peddler. He traveled from house to house, with short stops at pubs in-between. And whenever he sat down for a spell to talk to people, someone always, *always* asked him to do something. Often they wanted him to sing a song. Or tell a joke. Many people were interested in news from the next town over, and some insisted that Rory should play some music on a penny whistle. And every once in a while — way more often than poor Rory was comfortable with — someone would ask him to tell a *story*.

Rory had no story.

It was so rare for an Irishman to not know even a single anecdote that everyone who met Rory thought he was more than a little bit strange. The whole thing got to the point where he would rather leave the pub or the house when people started gathering for entertainment. And all the time he felt miserable.

One day Rory was walking home from the market, and he got caught in a storm. As the rain started pouring down he spotted a little house just off the road among some trees, and thought he might get some shelter there for the night. He had barely knocked once on the door when it opened, seemingly on its own, and revealed a cozy little room.

"Welcome, Rory," a voice rang out cheerfully. An old man was sitting by the fireplace, all shaggy beard and bright smile. "Would you fancy some dinner?"

Rory nodded mutely, then remembered his manners and nodded again, thanking the old man for his hospitality.

"Take a seat," his host pointed. A chair suddenly skidded across the room and positioned itself behind Rory, who, once again, was rendered speechless.

"Your coat is soaked," the old man continued, and the coat slid off Rory, hanging itself neatly on a peg. Rory collapsed onto the chair, his eyes wide.

"Let's have something to eat, then," the old man continued without missing a beat. Knives and forks and plates jumped off the shelves in the kitchen, drawers opened and closed, and soon a pot hobbled over to the fireplace, full of fragrant thick soup. Before Rory could gather his wits (or what was left of them) dinner was ready. The old man stood and walked over to the dining table, followed by Rory, and the two skittering chairs in tow.

The food was good, but Rory barely tasted it; he kept an eye out for any more utensils flying his way. When they were finished with dinner, the tablecloth lifted itself and cleaned the table while the chairs walked back to the fireplace.

"Now, Rory," the old man smiled a sweet smile, and said the words Rory had always dreaded the most: "Tell me a story."

"I ... I don't know any stories."

"Sing me a song, then."

"I ... am not good at singing."

"Is there any kind of entertainment you can offer for my hospitality? Music? Dancing? News? Anything at all?"

"I am afraid there isn't."

"Then out you go."

The door opened, and the coat flew off the peg. Rory shuffled to the door and muttered an apology and a goodbye to the old man, before he stepped outside. The door banged shut and hit him on the back.

Rory walked down a path through the woods, wrapped in his coat and feeling miserable. Suddenly he saw light through the trees, and as he got closer, he realized it was a campfire, surrounded by rough-looking men. What was even worse they had a bagful of stolen goods, and they were arguing over how to divide them. Rory backed away as quietly as he could ... which, as it turned out, was not very quiet at all. Twigs snapped under his feet and the bandits jumped up.

Rory ran for his life, though mud and bough and scraping branches, with the bandits and their weapons hot on his heels. His foot slipped, he skidded down a hillside ... and fell head first into an icy-cold river.

The next moment he was sitting up in bed, gasping for air. The old man was sitting by the bedside with an all-knowing smile, and patted Rory on the shoulder.

"*Now*, son, you have a story to tell."

*Comments:* I stitched this story together for a few variants I have read and heard. The middle part with the house and the mysteriously moving objects belongs to the Irish version published by both Foss and O'Sullivan, and the rest is a mix-and-match of other Scottish and Irish tales.

Technically the story never states that the old man is making the objects move, but it is clear that they obey his will. It is never stated what he *is* either, and knowing Irish folklore there is a good chance he is not (quite) human at all. But this is as close as one will get to telekinesis in folklore, and the story is great fun to tell. The fact that the old man uses his power over inanimate objects for mischief (but, in the end, he still helps Rory) is another example of creative use of a supernatural ability.

# INFINITE KNOWLEDGE

Infinite knowledge (also known as omniscience), given its nature, is kind of hard to define. In some cases (and stories) it encompasses everything in the past, present and future, and thus includes future sight. In other cases it means the knowledge of everything that is happening at any given moment in the world, which makes it an omnipotent version of far sight (and a lot of multi-tasking). Sometimes it is the knowledge of the answer to any question — as long as a question is asked. Finn MacCool, the leader of the Fians, had infinite knowledge from burning his thumb while cooking the Salmon of Knowledge (that, in turn, had been feeding on the magic hazelnuts of knowledge) — but he had to put his thumb in his mouth to access it. Sometimes knowledge includes practical magical powers, other times it is purely theoretical. The folktale motif for magical knowledge is D1810.

With infinite knowledge comes infinite possibilities — and a lot of power. Infinite knowledge also makes for challenging storylines (what could possibly surprise a person that knows everything?). For that reason most tales, young and old, place limits on a (mortal) person's omniscience. They work the same way Achilles's heel works with invulnerability.

*Heroes with (almost) infinite knowledge:* Dr. Manhattan (*The Watchmen*), Mimir (Marvel, originally from Norse mythology), Prodigy (Marvel)

## The Serpent Wife

*Ability:* Infinite knowledge, omnilinguality (the ability to speak all languages)

*Source of power:* Natural (serpent)

*Origin:* Cossack

*Teachings:* Respect for women, division of work in the household, adult relationships rely on communication.

*Age group:* 16+

*Sources:* Bain, R.N. (1894). *Cossack Fairy Tales.* London: Lawrence & Bullen.

*Variants:* This story belongs to the story type sometimes called a "Melusine tale" after one of the most famous versions, the French legend of Melusine. These stories usually tell of a supernatural wife that stays with her human husband as long as he does not intrude on her privacy and see her true (monstrous, often serpent-like) form. This motif appears at the end of "The Tide Jewels" tale later in this book.

*Text:* There was once a man, and there are only two things you need to know about him: he worked as a farmhand, and he liked to be alone. Whenever the other workers went to the tavern after a long day of hard work on the fields, he liked to take a walk in the woods, or sit on the hillside watching the sunset. People knew that about him, and they only invited him along out of courtesy every once in a while.

One day he was strolling in the woods as usual when he came across a huge serpent, coils upon coils. At the sound of his footsteps the creature reared up and opened its mouth. The man looked at it without fear, accepting his fate as dinner ... but the snake did not bite.

"You are not afraid of me."

"If I have to die, I have to die," the man shrugged.

"You will not die today," answered the serpent. "Go back to your master and help him bring in the corn from the fields. Leave one small sheaf standing, and when he asks about your payment, just ask for that one sheaf of corn. When it is yours, burn it, and you will earn yourself a wife."

The man, surprised at the strange instructions, turned around and returned to the fields where the corn was still standing. He worked hard for the rest of the day, and by the time night fell he piled all the corn on the cart and brought it to his master's house. The rich man was very pleased with his work — and very surprised when all he asked for was the one sheaf left standing.

"Take it if you like," he waved. The farmhand went back to the fields and set fire to the sheaf of corn. As the flames grew he saw a glimmer of scales, and the next moment a beautiful green-eyed woman stood before him.

The new wife was everything the man could wish for. She was sweet and kind, and a hard worker; everything around the house seemed to go smoothly, as if by magic. In fact, the house itself went up like magic — the husband barely touched it with the tools before it was finished, neat and tidy and bigger than most of the other houses in the village.

The young couple lived content for a while; everything they needed seemed to be provided in some mysterious way. But one day as the husband (who did not work as a farmhand anymore) was on his way home, walking across his fields, he noticed that the corn was still standing, even though it had been harvested everywhere else.

"What is the meaning of this?!" he huffed to himself. "She should have taken care of the harvest! This is what I get for marrying her. Once a serpent, always a serpent."

He called his wife's name when he walked into the house, but she did not answer. He searched high and low until he found her — a great, shining emerald serpent coiled up on the pillow in their bed.

"You called me a serpent," she hissed in a sad voice. "I hoped you would never do that. Now I am truly a serpent again, and I will never return to you."

She slithered off the bed and out the door. Her husband cried out in despair and ran after her, chasing her all the way to the woods. She wrapped herself around a hazelnut bush and looked up.

"I must say goodbye to you," she said, "but you can kiss me one last time." The man leaned forward and kissed the snake very gently.

"How do you feel?" she asked.

"I feel like I suddenly know everything that is happening in the world."

"Kiss me again. What do you feel now?"

"I understand all the languages spoken in the world."

"Kiss me one more time. What do you feel now?"

"I know everything that is under the earth."

"Go now. Visit the tsar. Prove to him what you know. He will give his daughter to you for a wife. Remember me, and pray for me. Go." The snake disappeared in the shadows with a glint of emerald scales.

*Comments:* Once again, supernatural knowledge comes from a serpent — this time, in a very unique way. The abrupt ending is not due to editing — the original text ends the same way, after stating that the man did, in fact, end up marrying the tsar's daughter. It is slightly disappointing that we do not see him use his newly acquired abilities. Still, the emotional weight of the story makes up for the lack of action. This tale resonates very well with adult female audiences, and sparks (often emotionally charged) discussions about relationships and gender roles. The Melusine tale type is a feminist classic, and this story is no exception.

# ILLUSION

Powers related to illusions come in two forms: the ability to create one, and the ability to see through the ones created. There is a folktale type that includes both of those, known as ATU 987 (False Magician Exposed by Clever Girl).

Because illusions are very useful for misleading people and making things seem something other than what they really are, they are often associated with villains and tricksters. They are also often used by the fairy folk and other supernatural creatures to veil their true nature and make their lairs appear more splendid than what they really are.

Maya (Sanskrit word for "illusion") was embodied as a goddess in India. She represented the illusions of the senses the mind had to overcome to reach enlightenment. "The veil of Maya" became a phrase used for the illusions separating the mind from experiencing the ultimate truth.

One of nature's most well-known illusions is the mirage, an optical illusion that makes faraway objects appear displaced on the horizon. One of the many names of the mirage is Fata Morgana, named after Morgan Le Fay, King Arthur's sorcerer sister. In Hungarian folklore (and the folklore of Slavic countries) it was believed to be a kind of witch or fairy, toying with people's minds in the midday heat.

*Characters with illusion powers:* Candice Willmer (NBC's *Heroes*), Dani Moonstar (Marvel), Mastermind (Marvel), Mesmero (Marvel)

# The Rooster Beam

*Ability:* Illusion / Clear sight

*Source of power:* Natural

*Origin:* Germany

*Teachings:* Do not believe everything you see.

*Age group:* 8+

*Sources:* Grimm (KHM 149).

Kennedy, P. (1866). *Legendary Fictions of the Irish Celts.* London: Macmillan and Co.

O'Conner, B. (1890). *Turf-Fire Stories and Fairy Tales of Ireland.* New York: P.J. Kennedy.

*Variants:* ATU type 987, Sham Magician Exposed by Clever Girl, and type AaTh 1290, Fool Mistakes Flax Field for Lake. See some Irish versions in the sources listed above. Herbs and plants having magical powers over vision or visibility appear often in folklore (see the fern seed under Invisibility).

*Text:* A magician was in town. People gathered around him, gaping at the wonders he had shown them, and the images he had conjured. He brought in a rooster that walked up and down on the stage, carrying a large wooden beam in its beak as if it had been light as a feather. People stared and clapped in amazement.

There was a girl in the crowd. She had just found a four-leaf clover, which is known for being able to break enchantments. It made her vision clear, and she could see things for what they really were.

"All of you people, can't you see it is all just a trick? That is a straw the rooster is carrying, and not a beam!"

The moment she called out the magic vanished, and magician stared at the girl furiously. She had ruined his show and his livelihood! He watched her walk away and swore to himself that he would take revenge.

Time passed, the girl got older, and she was about to get married. As the wedding procession walked towards the church, suddenly a swollen brook appeared across the road and there was no bridge over it. The girl, determined to not let anything stand between her and marriage, picked up her skirts, lifted them around her waist, and started wading through the water. She was in the middle of the brook when a mocking voice called out: "What eyes do you have that see water where there is none?!"

In that moment, the enchantment vanished. Looking around, she realized she was standing in the middle of a field full of blue flax flowers, with her skirts hitched up around her waist, and all the people in the village laughing at her.

The magician had taken his revenge.

*Comments:* This story makes a lot more sense if one knows that in medieval Europe a lot of women only wore petticoats for underwear.

I personally like the character of the girl in this story. She calls the magician out on his tricks, and she is unstoppable on her way to the church. She sees things for what they are (most of the time) and calls them by their name; but she is still vulnerable to the same powers she had made fun of.

Magic in this case is pure illusion: the magician makes people see things the way he wants. His illusions are countered by the clear vision granted by the four-leaf clover, a symbol of luck. However, seeing things is one thing — confronting the magician is another, and that does not come from the clover, it comes from the heroine's own personality.

# TECHNOMANCY

Technomancy is described as the ability to interact with technology on a telepathic or supernatural level. It includes manipulating electronic and mechanical objects, inventing and creating advanced technology, and even communicating with machines (known as technopathy). Sometimes it is also described as magic that deals with technology. It is clearly the invention of the modern age, but some seeds of the idea, in the form of marvelous inventions, can be found in legend and folklore.

One of the most famous inventors in mythology is Daedalus. He did not only design the Labyrinth of Knossos and then mechanical wings to escape from it, but he also built Talos, the bronze giant that guarded the island of Crete from its enemies. In the Middle Ages there were many legends circulating in Italy about Virgil as a wizard who designed many a useful and miraculous creation for the emperors of Rome (including an alarm system that warned of approaching armies from any province). Inventions that were ahead of their time have always fascinated people — and many of them became reality later on.

*Heroes with technological abilities (in a broader sense):* Box (Marvel), Forge (Marvel), Iron Man (Marvel), Kelly Bailey (E4's *Misfits*), Micah Sanders (NBC's *Heroes*)

## *The Ebony Horse*

*Ability:* Technomancy (magical inventions)
*Source of power:* Natural
*Origin:* Arabian Nights

*Teachings:* Honesty and bravery, respect, never give up on the person you love.

*Age group:* 8+

*Sources: Arabian Nights,* nights 358–371.

*Variants:* Chaucer's "The Squire's Tale" (in *The Canterbury Tales*) includes a horse made of bronze with similar abilities. Another tale from the *Arabian Nights,* "The City of Brass" (nights 567–578), mentions a brass statue of a horseman that turns on its foundation and points travelers in the right direction.

*Text:* The Shah of Persia was a wise and generous king. He was just, open-minded, and good to his people; he cared for the poor and helped the weak, and was beloved by all his subjects. Twice every year, for Nowruz, the New Year, and for Mehrgan, the autumn equinox, he opened the doors of his palace and held great festivals where people could come and salute him. The shah was famous for his love for science and curiosities, so many craftsmen brought him presents on these occasions, hoping to win his favor.

On one of these splendid days three craftsmen arrived at court, all three of them master inventors, skilled in creating rare and curious things. They came from three different corners of the world: one from India, one from Byzantium, and one from Persia. The Indian stepped forward first and presented his invention to the shah. It was a statue of a man made of gold and set with gemstones, with a trumpet in its hand.

"Put this statue at the gates of your city," he said, "and if the enemy approaches it will blow the trumpet and warn you of the danger. Even more than that, from the sound of the trumpet the enemy will drop down dead in a seizure."

"If you are telling the truth," said the shah, "you shall have whatever you wish for."

Next the Greek stepped forward and bowed to the shah. He brought a silver bowl with a golden peacock in it, surrounded by twenty-four chicks.

"Every hour of the day and night this peacock will cry out and peck one of the chicks, and remind you of the time," he explained, "and at the start of every month it will open its mouth and show the crescent moon."

"If it indeed works, I will grant you whatever you desire," nodded the shah.

The Persian stepped forward last, leading a horse made of shining black ebony, inlaid with gemstones and gold, saddled and bridled fit for a king.

"This horse will carry you on land or through the air wherever you wish to go," he said, "and it will cover a year's journey in a day."

The shah was satisfied with the gifts. He tried all three of them and saw how they worked; he entertained the craftsmen for three days, and when the feasting was over he asked what they wished in exchange for their gifts. They said that they had heard about the shah's three beautiful daughters, and they wished to marry them.

The shah consented, and he ordered the wedding arrangements to begin. But the three princesses had been looking through the curtains, and the youngest, as fair and lovely as a flower, was horrified when she saw her husband-to-be, old and wrinkled and ugly. She ran to her room and threw herself on the bed, wailing and tearing her clothes, until her brother, Prince Kamar al-Akmar, Moon of Moons, came to see what made her so upset. She told him, crying, that she was to marry a frightening old magician, and that she would rather die than be his wife. Prince Kamar marched up to his father and asked him why he would give his loveliest daughter away to an ugly old man like that.

"If you saw his gift, you would understand," the shah said, and he ordered the Persian (who was not at all happy to be called an ugly old man) to show the prince the horse and how it worked. The Persian pointed at the pin that made the horse ascend into the air, and then watched as the prince flew away on the magical creation.

"He is never coming back, sire," he said to the shah, "I forgot to show him how to make the horse descend."

The shah glared at the craftsman in anger, and ordered him to be thrown into prison; then he and his entire family dressed in mourning for the prince who was lost in the skies.

In the meantime Kamar flew higher and higher, and realized what the Persian had done. He started feeling around on the horse, sure that someone who made a pin for flying must have also made a pin for landing. Finally he found the other pin on the horse's shoulder, and as he turned it, the horse started to descend. He soon figured out how to steer the creature, and he had great fun flying around on it, seeing cities and places he had never seen before.

As night fell he started looking for a good landing place, and when he saw a splendid palace he decided to spend the night on the roof. Once he was safely on solid ground he examined the horse, marveling at the details of construction; then he realized he was hungry and thirsty, and decided to take a look around in the palace, hoping to find something to eat.

What he did not know was that he landed on the roof of the king of Yemen.

First he came across a guard sleeping in a chamber, and he found some food on a table that he quickly ate. Then, taking the guard's sword, he moved on to the next room, and the room after, and he ended up in a bedchamber where he found a princess sleeping, surrounded by her maids. She looked so beautiful and lovely in her sleep that he leaned over and woke her up with a kiss on her cheek.

"Who are you?" she said, alarmed as she opened her eyes.

"I am your servant and your slave," the prince answered, and she blushed in delight. She had been asked to marry by the prince of India the day before; she thought this young man was him, and she was happy that her future husband was so handsome. But as the maids woke up and in turn, they told her this was not the prince, but a stranger, and confusion broke out; the guard ran for the king, and the king soon marched into the room with a scimitar in hand, demanding to know who the strange man was in his daughter's bedroom. Even though he could tell Kamar was from royal blood, he could not let him get away with sneaking into the palace and leaving his daughter's virtue in doubt.

"It seems to me you have two choices, your highness," said Kamar very politely, but keeping his eyes on the scimitar. "You can fight me here in single combat, but people will always doubt what happened in this room, and if I manage to kill you, your kingdom will be mine. Or you can allow me to put up a fight in public, at dawn, against your entire army."

The king thought the prince was surely mad, but he consented anyway. "You will fight my entire army at dawn," he declared, and he sent for his vizier to start the preparations and rally the troops. Dawn came all too fast, and forty thousand soldiers were lined up on the field, waiting for the young madman who proposed to fight them single-handed.

"The only thing I ask," said Kamar to the king, "is permission to fight from horseback. I came here on my own horse, and I would like to ride it into battle today."

"I will grant you that," agreed the king, and then he watched in amazement as the prince sent the servants to fetch his horse — from the roof. Everyone stared at the magnificent creature, and Kamar smiled as he mounted it. As soon as he was in the saddle he turned the ascent pin, and the horse flew up into the air. No matter how much the king yelled after him, Prince Kamar was gone.

The princess fell into deep sorrow when she heard the news. She refused to eat or drink or talk until her love returned to her.

As for Prince Kamar, he flew straight home and gracefully landed the horse on the roof of his own palace. He found his family in mourning, but their tears soon dried up when they saw that Kamar was alive and well. Mourning turned into celebration and the Shah ordered a general pardon for all prisoners, including the Persian who had made the horse. He was given generous gifts for his creation (but was not allowed to marry the princess) and the ebony horse was officially in the possession of the royal family.

Once the festivities were over, however, Kamar started thinking of the Yemeni princess, and his heart ached for her so much that he woke up in the night, left his room, took the ebony horse from its stables and flew away. When the shah woke up in the morning and saw his son was gone, and so was the ebony horse, he swore he was going to destroy the creature if his son ever returned. Then, as most parents do, he went on worrying.

Kamar flew all the way back to Yemen, and landed on the roof of the palace. He found the maids asleep and the princess awake on her bed, weeping bitterly. He soon dried her tears up and made her smile, and they spent the night together. When morning came Kamar said goodbye and promised the princess he would visit her once every week. However, the princess was not at all content with that, and she insisted on going with him. Taking some of her most precious jewels and treasures, she followed him to the roof, and they flew away on the ebony horse, back to Persia.

They landed at dawn in the royal gardens. Kamar told the princess to wait for him there, while he went and announced their engagement and got a procession ready to escort her to the palace. He hurried home, told his father all the great news about the princess of Yemen whom he intended to marry, and organized a procession of maids and servants and gifts to the gardens.

But when he returned to where he had left the princess and the ebony horse, they were both gone.

People who had been working in the gardens told the prince that they had seen the old Persian walk around earlier, gathering spices — and that was enough for Kamar to know exactly what had happened. Saying goodbye to his father once again, he set out on a journey to find his bride.

He traveled for a very long time before he arrived to Byzantium. As he stopped at an inn to eat, he heard the merchants talking about miraculous things that had happened in the kingdom.

"The emperor was out hunting," one said, "and he came across a shining maiden on an ebony horse. She was arguing with an old, ugly Persian who claimed to be her husband, but she said he was a liar and a villain. The Emperor ordered him to be beaten, and took the maiden into his palace. No one knows what happened to the strange horse."

Kamar, happy to hear the news that his bride was near, moved on and befriended the palace guards. Sharing food and drinks with them, he asked them about the emperor's new maid.

"She is beautiful," they all agreed, "but she is quite mad. The emperor cannot go near her without her trying to claw his eyes out! He promised wealth to whoever can cure her, so he can marry her. The horse? The horse is in the treasure rooms."

That was all Kamar needed to hear. He went and presented himself to the emperor, and claimed that he was a man skilled in medicine who could cure all illnesses of the mind. The emperor greeted him with eagerness, hoping he could finally cure the princess. Kamar said he needed to see the horse first, to make sure it was not cursed somehow, and when he made sure the horse was unharmed and functional, he went to the princess's room, and made plans with her.

When he emerged, he smiled at the emperor.

"I have discovered her illness, and I have cured her for you. Be kind to her and she will be grateful."

They brought the princess out for the court to see, and she was as lovely and polite as any maiden. The emperor thanked Kamar, but he shook his head.

"Don't thank me yet, your highness," he said. "The illness was caused by a demon, and if I do not exorcise it, it will return. We need to go to the woods where you found her, and put her back on the horse, so I can say the proper prayers and spells."

The emperor did not doubt a word. They all went back to the woods, put the princess on the horse, and stood back to watch the rituals. As soon as they were clear Kamar jumped up in the saddle behind the princess, turned the pin, and flew away.

The emperor eventually consoled himself by saying the princess must have been an enchantress or a demon, and he was better off without her anyway. Kamar returned home on the ebony horse, married the Yemeni princess, and eventually found a way of making amends with his father-in-law. The shah destroyed the ebony horse — they all agreed they were safer without it. When the old shah died, Kamar became the new ruler over the kingdom, and he lived a long and prosperous life with his queen.

*Comments:* Characters in this story show a lot of ... character. Kamar is a responsible brother to his sister, but easily distracted by the flying horse; he cares for the princess, but would settle for visiting her once a week (we all know from Rapunzel how that would end) until she steps up and demands to go with him. But when push comes to shove and the princess is kidnapped, he grows up to the task of rescuing her, showing perseverance and cunning, and earns a happy ending for his family. Quite the coming-of-age story for a young prince.

"The Ebony Horse" is one of the most well-known tales from the *Arabian Nights* (fun fact: it is also a *Magic: The Gathering* card). It does not only present the idea of a king who loves science, but it also gives us a glimpse of the vast world that these tales inhabit, from Yemen all the way to Byzantium.

The exact workings of the magical inventions are never explained. People repeatedly refer to them as magic, and call the craftsmen magicians, but most of them proved to be scientifically possible by our time. Still, in the given time and place, the ability to create (and operate) these objects was regarded as a form of supernatural knowledge, and thus they have a place in this book. The miracle of flight pairs up with the skill of steering a vehicle, and the horse is destroyed in the end because it held too much power for evil or good. That is one way of dealing with great responsibility.

# ANIMAL SPEECH

Speaking the language of animals could run for "most common supernatural ability in folklore" with a good chance of being in the top three. The motif number is D1301 and it comes in many sub-motifs depending on how the power is acquired. It can come from eating a dragon's heart (as Sigurd does in the *Völsunga* saga), various magic items, or simply learning (as we saw in "The Gold-Spitting Prince"). It is interesting to note that this power is not always a requirement for heroes to be able to communicate with animals. Sometimes animals simply speak.

The animals most often communicated with are birds. In many cultures they have been seen as messengers between heaven and earth, and thus the holders of secret knowledge. They make many kinds of sounds to communicate, and many of them copy sounds they hear, including human speech. No wonder that talking to birds became a popular motif in folklore.

*Heroes with zoolingualism (animal speech):* Aquaman (DC), Beastmaster (*Beastmaster*), and of course Dr. Dolittle (*The Story of Doctor Dolittle*)

## The Gold-Spinners

*Ability:* Understanding the speech of birds, shape-shifting
*Source of power:* Learned / Magical
*Origin:* Estonia
*Teachings:* Creativity, bravery, freedom, standing up for yourself and the ones you love, friendship, sisterhood, harmony with nature.
*Age group:* 6+
*Sources:* Kirby, W.F. (1895). *The Hero of Esthonia.* London: John C. Nimmo.
Lang, A. (1889). *The Blue Fairy Book.* London: Longmans, Green & Co.
*Variants:* Spinning gold features into Grimm's famous story, "Rumpelstiltskin." One also can't help but think of Rapunzel, kidnapped by a witch and kept in a tower, putting her golden hair to good use. I have not found another version of this tale apart from the two listed above.
*Text:* Three girls lived in the forest with their mother. They were all lovely and beautiful as flowers, but there was no one to admire their beauty: their old mother barely allowed them out of their little house. They had to work day and night, summer and winter, spinning fine golden flax into shining thread. Once all the flax was spun the mother locked it away, and by the time the girls woke up, a new bundle of golden flax would be ready for them to spin. The work

never ended, and they never knew where the flax came from, or where the thread went.

Every summer the mother would go on journeys for days, sometimes for weeks at a time. She always returned by night so they never saw when she arrived or what she brought back. Every time she left the girls with a heavy workload and a warning: "Don't let your eyes wander, and hold your fingers carefully, because if the thread is broken or loses its shine, that will be the end of your good fortune!"

The girls did not understand this — how would gold suddenly lose its shine? — but they never argued. Then, one day, they found out exactly what it meant.

It happened on that day that a prince from the blood of Kalev was out hunting in the woods, and he was separated from his companions. Lost and confused, he kept wandering without a path. He spent the night under a tree, and the next morning as the sun shone through the trees he finally stumbled upon the little cottage in a clearing.

The three girls were scared of the stranger, but soon their fear turned into curiosity. Since their mother was not home to watch them, they put the spinning aside and treated the prince as a guest, delighted to hear his stories about the world beyond the woods. And even after the two older sisters went to bed, the youngest one sat on the threshold with the prince, and they talked and laughed all through the night.

In the meantime, the prince's hunting companions had been searching desperately for their lost leader. They yelled his name and combed through the woods, but to no avail. Finally they sent the sad news home to the king, who ordered his entire army to spread out and keep searching until they found the prince. Three entire days passed before one of them finally came across the footpath than led to the cottage in the woods.

The prince enjoyed his time away from the world, but now it was his duty to return home. Before he left he promised the youngest girl that he would come back for her and make her his bride.

The two older sisters did not know about this — but the mother found out anyway. When she came home in the night she found the spool of the youngest daughter broken, and the golden thread dull and rough. Waking her daughters one by one she questioned them and threatened them until she found out about the royal visitor. She became furious; she cursed till the sky grew dark and the earth trembled, and the girls were so terrified of her that they could not even speak. She threatened to kill the prince, to break his bones and give his flesh to the wild beasts if he ever showed his face again.

The youngest girl was desperate. She stole out of the house at dawn, but she had nowhere to go. Everyone was asleep around her, except for a raven that had been ruffling its feathers on a nearby pine tree.

"Oh wisest of the wise birds, please help me!" the girl said. And the raven listened. When she was very young, the girl had learned the language of birds from her mother, and now it proved to be very useful.

"What help do you need?" asked the raven, cocking his head.

"Fly to the royal city and tell the prince that I am in trouble," she begged, and she told the bird the entire story. The raven promised to help, provided he could find someone to translate for him, and took wings towards the royal city.

Fortunately enough, the prince had a friend who was the son of a wizard. Working in the gardens, he heard the raven's voice and delivered the message to the prince. In return, they gave a piece of meat to the bird and told him to tell the girl to stay awake on the ninth night, and her prince would rescue her from her mother's wrath.

Nine days felt like an eternity for the girl. She was not allowed to spin anymore, but she was kept busy with other chores, and her mother scolded her day and night, making her life miserable. When the long-awaited night finally came, she sneaked out of the house and waited till the hour before dawn. For a long time it was quiet all around ... then she heard the muffled sound of hooves, and the prince appeared with his guards. He had been following the secret marks he put on the trees to find his way back to the girl he fell in love with. Lifting her up into the saddle, he rode away from the house and never looked back.

The sun came up, and birds started to twitter and sing. If the girl paid any attention to them she would have known she was in danger ... but she was so happy with her love, she did not hear the warning.

Her mother woke with the sun, and soon discovered one of her daughters had escaped. Her fury was terrible, but she knew the lovers were too far ahead to pursue. Instead of chasing them, she decided to turn to dark magic. Picking up a handful of nine herbs, she mixed them with magical salt and tied them in a bundle, then she evoked the wind. The wind carried the bundle after the fleeing lovers, and the mother's curse with it.

In the meantime, the prince and the girl were about to cross a river. There was a single, narrow bridge over the water, and horses could only cross it one at a time. Just as they slowly rode to the middle, the bundle came flying from the air and attacked the horse like a gadfly. The horse reared up, and before anything could be done, the girl slid off the saddle, and the river swallowed her up.

The prince was devastated. He would have jumped after her, but his guards held him back. He fell so ill from sadness that the king, his father, feared for his life. All the doctors and wise men failed at curing the prince. Finally, the son of the wind-sorcerer who was his friend suggested that they should send for the old wizard of Finland, for he was wiser than any other man.

The message was sent, and the wizard arrived a week later on the wings of the wind.

"Your highness," he said to the king, "the prince's illness came from the wind. An evil witch robbed him of half his heart by a curse. Send him outside so the wind may carry his sorrow away."

The king listened, and the prince was sent outside for a walk. The more he walked, the more it seemed like he was slowly forgetting his sorrow; but even after a year of mourning, he refused to even hear about choosing another bride.

One day, he finally found the strength to return to the bridge where he lost his love. He sat there, crying, when he suddenly heard a whisper of a song, carried by the wind over the water.

"By the mother's curse she's taken,
Sank in flood the helpless maiden,
In the watery grave the fair one,
And in Ahti's waves your darling."

The prince looked around, but there was no one who could have been singing. Yet he heard the song again, and again, and as he walked along the river he noticed a water-lily on the waves. He stared at it for a while, listening to the song ... but he knew that flowers cannot sing. Yet, sometimes the wind brings good ideas to men, and so it happened this time, because the prince remembered the cottage, and decided to visit the two older sisters, and ask for their advice.

It was hard to find the cottage again; the woods had grown a lot in the past year. Finally he came across the path that led him to the clearing. He waited until one of the girls came outside to wash her face in the spring, and then talked to her quietly, fearing the mother would notice.

Fortune was with the prince: the mother was away. The girls invited him in and asked about their sister. The moment he told them what happened they knew their mother must have cursed the poor girl, and they started devising a plan to set her free.

The oldest sister gathered strong magical herbs and baked them into a pork pie. The prince, who was famished from his wanderings in the woods, ate the entire pie and soon fell into a deep sleep. In the morning he woke up with a smile: "I had a wonderful dream! I dreamed that I was in the forest, and I could speak the language of the birds."

"Your dream is true," said the older sister. "The pie I made you gave you the gift of hearing. Listen carefully to what the birds say, because they are very wise creatures. And if you manage to break the spell, please do not forget about us!"

The prince gave them his word, and rode away. At first it was confusing for him to hear all the birds around him speaking, because they talked about people he did not know, but slowly he managed to hear them more clearly, and finally he caught a magpie and a thrush gossiping about none other than the prince himself.

"Men are truly deaf sometimes," said the thrush. "For a year that poor girl, the foster-child of an old hag, has been singing her sorrows by the bridge, but did anyone listen? No, they did not! Her lover rode by yesterday, and he did not listen either."

"The maiden was cursed by her foster-mother," the magpie added. "She has to stay a flower unless the curse is broken."

"And it would break easily, too," the thrush agreed. "The old wizard of Finland knows how."

"Talking about Finland," said a swallow to her friends on a nearby tree, "I want to move there. Let's go right now!"

"Wait!" yelled the prince. "Please, give my regards to the old wizard of Finland, and thank him for his help! Please ask him to tell me how to break the spell on my bride!"

The swallows, surprised that the prince understood them, promised to carry his message and flew away. The prince returned to his home, and waited anxiously for an entire week. He was just about to give up, thinking the swallows forgot their promise, when he suddenly saw the shadow of wings, and an eagle descended to give him the old wizard's message.

The prince made sure every word was etched into his mind before he set out for the bridge once again. On the riverbank he took off his clothes and he smeared himself with mud all over, uttering the magic words: "Let the man become a crayfish."

He could feel his body transform into something small, something different ... and in a few moments he was not a man anymore. The crayfish scampered to the river, dove into the water, and swam down to the roots of the water-lily. Digging in the soft mud very carefully he freed the roots one by one until the flower pulled free. Holding on to his flower, the crayfish floated down the river and around the bend until he saw a rowan tree and a large stone beside it. As soon as he saw that he said the magic words: "Let the flower become a maiden, and let the crayfish become a man!"

They both turned back into their human form once again, and swam to the shore. But the girl was so ashamed to be naked that she refused to come out of the water.

"I will close my eyes," said the prince, "and you can go hide by that rock while I go and find my clothes and horse.

The prince walked back to the bridge ... but his horse and his clothes were gone! He walked up and down searching desperately until a splendid chariot happened to pass by, with a maid inside. They offered the prince a horse and clothes, and he sent them on to the girl hiding by the rowan tree, to dress her up too.

When they finally made their way back to the castle, they found the kingdom in mourning. The prince's horse and clothes had been found by the bridge, and people believed he had drowned himself. Magic works in strange ways: what he thought were only a few hours in the water had been several days on the surface. The king and the queen were overjoyed to see their son alive and happy, with a beautiful bride at his side.

A wedding was celebrated, and the couple lived happily for a while. Summer turned to fall, fall turned to winter, winter turned to spring. In the spring, one day the prince heard a magpie chattering outside the window: "What an ungrateful man! He rescued his bride, but he forgot his promise to the sisters! They are still prisoners, working night and day, for a woman they think is their mother! She kidnapped them when they were just children, and makes them work for her! She deserves death and nothing better, for she would curse the girls again if they escaped!"

The prince remembered his promise and he was ashamed. He ordered his guards right away to get ready, and set out for the cottage in the woods. He waited until the mother left, and then told the girls he was going to set them free. Getting rid of every piece of food in the house he replaced the herbs with boiled hemlock. When the mother returned, famished from her journey, she ate all the hemlock before she fell into bed ... and never woke up.

The girls were free, and overjoyed to see their little sister again after two years. The guards found fifty loads of golden thread in a secret chamber, which the prince divided between the sisters. As they were going through the rooms of the house, the prince heard the rooster crow on the roof: "Catch the cat! Catch the cat and it will all come to light!"

The found a great black cat trying to sneak away. As soon as he was caught, the cat spoke up in a human voice: "Don't hurt me! I used to be a man just like you! I served a great king in a castle where the old hag was a maid. We plotted to take the king's wealth for ourselves, we kidnapped his daughters when the oldest was three years old, and took all the gold from the treasury. The hag was afraid I would betray her so she changed me into a cat, and the gold into flax. The girls are all princesses, and the gold belongs to their father!"

The cat was killed by the guards for his wickedness, and buried together with the hag, in a place no one knows anymore. The three girls never found their father, but they married as princesses, with a rich dowry of gold, and they all lived happily ever after.

*Comments:* Ahti is the god of the waters, in case you were wondering.

I chose this story for animal speech because it shows a very active use of the ability. Instead of simply overhearing birds like many other heroes, both the prince and the princess use them as messengers and regard them as advisers. In addition, we encounter two different ways of acquiring the same power: by learning, and by the use of magical herbs. Interesting to note that apparently only the youngest sister learned how to speak to birds, while the two older girls have no "magical voice" to call for help — they have to wait until they are rescued. Shape-shifting also figures into the story for a single occasion, but the transformation is commanded by the prince himself, so it definitely counts.

The story is surprisingly practical in a lot of ways in terms of handling problems. The prince needs signs to find the cottage again, time passes, scenery changes. A translator is needed for passing on the message of the birds. A minor yet intriguing character is the "son of a wind sorcerer" who acts as an intermediary between the prince and the supernatural. The "wizard of Finland" plays a similarly small but important role, and reminds the reader of Veinemöinen, the old wizard of the Finnish epic *Kalevala*.

# ◆ PART III ◆

# At the Mercy of the Elements — Powers of Water, Fire, Earth and Weather (and Ice)

## FIRE MANIPULATION

Ever since mankind first discovered how to tame and cultivate the red flower, fire tales have been abound in folklore, legend and mythology. Fire is still the most mysterious element, representing life, danger, change, rebirth, warmth, light, and cooked food.

The ability to create and manipulate fire is known as pyrokinesis. Sometimes it includes the creation or summoning of fire, while in other cases a pyrokinetic can only manipulate flames that are already there. One of the most spectacular and dangerous supernatural abilities, pyrokinesis is often featured in visual media, used both by heroes and villains.

The history of mastering the flames, however, goes back much farther in time. Many cultures around the world tell stories about gods, heroes and animal spirits that first brought the fire to the people. For some American Indian tribes like the Navajo, the fire thief is Coyote the Trickster (this story is very popular with storytellers as well as young audiences), while for others like the Choctaw, it is Grandmother Spider. For the Greeks it was Prometheus, and in the considerably less well known Nart sagas (Northern Caucasus), it was Pkharmat the Blacksmith.

Once the fire is stolen or otherwise introduced, a whole range of stories blossom from it, ranging from Anansi the Spider's short-lived romance with Miss Flame all the way to epic battles like that of the Chinese Monkey King and Princess Iron Fan. Many times fire clashes against ice or water, as we will see in some of the tales later in this chapter. In one colorful and grand Inca epic, water and fire redesign the Andean landscape as they battle for dominance over people's life, while on the Hawaiian Islands Pele, powerful goddess of volcanoes, embodies the entire range of personalities and emotions associated with heat and flame. Fire is one of the core motifs that feature into every mythology one way or another, and plays an essential role in such well-known folktales as "Vasilisa the Beautiful" or the haunting image of the Russian firebird. It is interesting to note that in most of the tales fire embodies the entire circle of life, both destruction and rebirth.

In 2009 I was invited to a high school physics day to tell stories — the theme was fire. I spent the better part of three months collecting and crafting folktales, myths and legends about fire, and it was a fascinating journey into the world of symbols. When the day of the physics fair finally arrived, I had enough stories collected to last me the entire eight hours (with short breaks in-between). Classes came and went, some stories were repeated, some were not; teenagers came in with suspicion and eye-rolling, and stayed to ask questions in the end. I went home at about four o'clock in the afternoon, collapsed, and slept for fifteen hours. I drew a conclusion: telling stories about nothing but fire, no pun intended, burns a storyteller out more than any other genre I have ever tried. And I would do it again in a heartbeat.

Without further ado, let's see some of those stories.

*Similar heroes:* Firebenders (*Avatar: The Last Airbender*), Human Torch (Marvel), Magma (Marvel), Meredith Gordon (NBC's *Heroes*), Portgas D. Ace (*One Piece*), Pyro (Marvel)

## The Daughter of the Sun

*Ability:* Fire manipulation, phasing, healing factor, flight, and girl power
*Source of power:* Natural
*Origin:* Italy/Algeria
*Teachings:* Independence, respect for women, stand up for yourself and the ones you love, also, jealousy does not pay off.
*Age group:* 8+
*Sources:* Calvino, I. (1980). *Italian Folktales.* Orlando, FL: Harcourt.
De Nino, A. (1997). *Le piu belle fiabe abruzzesi.* I Tascabili d'Abruzzo, Vol. 32. Cerchio: Polla.
Knappert, J. (2002). "The Lion's Daughter. Fairy Tales from Algeria: Part Two." *The World and I,* 17(7): 172–179.
*Variants:* Different variants of this tale contain different tricks the heroine presents. In the Algerian variant, she takes her eye out and puts it on the win-

dowsill while bathing to make sure men don't sneak up on her. The version presented here is my own creation, patched together from the three sources quoted above. Be advised. Be very advised.

*Text:* Once upon a time there was a king. He had a beautiful young queen, but their happiness was not complete: for the longest time, they were not blessed with a child. They hoped and they prayed and they wished, until finally their dream came true: the queen gave birth to a beautiful, healthy baby girl. The day the little princess was born, the king sent for all the fortune-tellers and wise men of his kingdom to tell him the future of his daughter. The fortune-tellers and wise men looked at the stars, consulted their charts, stared deep into their crystal balls, and then returned to the king and bowed low with sorrow.

"We are deeply sorry to tell you this, your highness," they said, "but all the signs say the same: your daughter will bear a child to the Sun before she turns sixteen years old."

The king was shocked and worried. His daughter, having a baby without being married? The Sun was royalty, but he lived way up in the sky, he was never going to marry a mortal princess! Fearing that his daughter was going to live in shame, he came up with a plan. He ordered a tower to be built, with only one window at the very top, high enough that the sunlight would never reach the bottom inside. He sent his newborn daughter with a nurse and the nurse's child to be locked in that tower, and the princess was not allowed to leave until she turned sixteen and the prophecy was broken. He thought that if he kept her hidden away from the Sun, she could avoid her fate.

All parents wish fate could be avoided so easily.

The princess grew up in the tower and she never saw the outside world. The only companions she had were the nurse and the nurse's daughter. One day, just past her fifteenth birthday, the princess was left alone with her best friend while the nurse went out to bring them some food from the castle. The girls got bored of playing their usual games, and gazed up at the window at the top of the tower, wondering that the outside world looked like. Curiosity took over: they started putting all the furniture on top of each other, first the drawers then the chests, tables and chairs, until they had built themselves a ladder that reached the window, and then they both climbed up, and looked outside.

It was a beautiful spring day. The trees were in bloom, there was a sweet scent in the air, birds were singing, rivers were glittering, and the sun shone bright and warm. The Sun looked down from the sky, saw the princess in the window of the tower, and instantly fell in love with her. It only took a slight touch from his warm rays to bring a blush to her pale cheeks ... and nine months later, much to the nurse's surprise and alarm, the princess gave birth to a shining, smiling baby girl.

The nurse was scared: what if the king found out that she had not kept the prophecy from coming true? She was responsible for the princess! The king would surely punish her and her daughter. Maybe even have them beheaded! In her fear, the nurse picked up the baby, carried her outside at night, and left her in the woods, hoping no one would ever finds out that she existed.

A few days later, the princess turned sixteen. The tower's gates were opened with great fanfare and celebration ... and nobody knew about the Sun's daughter, except for the nurse, the nurse's daughter, and the princess herself.

The daughter of the Sun was all alone in the woods, crying, cold and hungry. The king of the neighboring kingdom happened to pass by while hunting for deer, and he heard the baby's cries. Seeing that she was a beautiful little girl, he picked her up, and carried her home to raise her together with his son, the prince, who was almost the same age. The children grew up together, played together, learned together, and when they were grown, they fell in love.

Playing and learning was all nice and fine, but the king did not want his son to marry a nameless orphan girl. He was the heir to the throne! Worried for the future of his kingdom, the royal father made a decision: the girl had to leave the court. He had a cottage built for her far away from the castle, and for the second time in her life, the daughter of the Sun was all alone in the woods.

Soon after the king found a suitable bride for his son: a princess that was beautiful, noble, rich, and from a good family. A wedding was planned, and messengers were sent out to deliver invitations to all the neighboring kings and nobles. An invitation was sent to the daughter of the Sun as well — she was a close friend of the prince's, after all, and he insisted she should be included on the guest list.

The messengers went to the cottage in the woods, and knocked on the door. They could hear light footsteps inside, and a moment later, the daughter of the Sun opened the door ... and her head was missing!

The messengers opened their mouths to scream, when suddenly they heard a cheerful voice from inside the house:

"Oh, I am so sorry! Silly me, I was brushing my hair, and I forgot my head on the table! Just a second, please, I will be right back!"

The girl's body walked back inside and a moment later appeared again, her head back in its place, and smiled at the messengers. They handed over the invitation, told her she was invited to the prince's wedding ... and ran away.

The daughter of the Sun put on her best dress, and went to the wedding. When she arrived, she looked around, and saw a long line of people waiting to hand their wedding presents over to the prince and his new bride. The daughter of the Sun slapped herself on the forehead: "How could I forget about bringing a present?! Silly me! What should I do, what should I do? ... I know!"

Walking over to the fireplace, she called out: "Fire, burn!" In a moment, bright flames burst out of the fireplace with such heat that people had to step back and cover their faces. But not the daughter of the Sun. She stuck her hands into the fire, and when she pulled them out, her fingers were on fire, like ten thin white candles! People gasped, but she kept smiling, and looked like the flames did not hurt at all.

She bowed before the prince and his bride: "Your highness, I will present you a dance to celebrate your wedding!"

And so she danced, with the flames on her fingers, sparks falling all around her, and she was such an amazing dancer that people just stared at her in silent amazement. The one who stared the most was, of course, the prince, who was smiling a happy smile and looked so much in love that his new bride grew jealous.

"If she can do that, I can do that!" she complained, and, marching over to the fireplace, she stuck her hands into the flames. Next, there was a lot of screaming and a lot of confusion, and by the time they put the fire out, the bride's hands were badly burned, and the wedding was cancelled.

This, however, did not convince the king to allow the young lovers to marry. Quite the opposite. He soon found another princess that was young, pretty, and rich, and another wedding was arranged. Messengers went out to carry invitations to friends and family, and, once again, the prince made sure that the daughter of the Sun was invited. The messengers went to the house in the woods, knocked on the door ... and then they watched in horror as the girl walked out of the house through the wall, like a ghost.

"I am sorry," she smiled cheerfully. "The door is stuck, I can't open it from the inside. What can I help you with?"

The messengers handed over the invitation ... and ran away.

The girl once again put on her best dress, and went to the wedding. When she arrived, she looked around ... and buried her face in her hands. "Oh no! I forgot to bring a gift again! How can I be so absent-minded? ... What should I do now? ... Oh, I have an idea!"

Once again, she walked over to the fireplace. "Fire, burn!" When the flames sprang up, she walked into the fireplace ... and disappeared. People watched in horror, thinking she must have burned to cinders ... when she walked out of the fireplace again, not even a hair singed on her head, wearing the most beautiful cape anyone had ever seen. It was all the colors of a sunset, red and gold and violet, and it was fastened at her neck with a golden pin. The girl took the cape off, folded it over her arm, and presented it to the prince as a wedding gift.

The prince looked at her with deep love in his eyes, and the new bride grew green with envy.

"That is nothing!" she pouted. "That is how I make *all* my clothes!"

"Is it?" asked the prince. "Well, I would like to see that!"

The bride marched over to the fireplace, but as soon as she stuck one foot into the flames, her slipper caught fire, and she started screaming and crying ... and the wedding was cancelled.

But the king was still persistent to find a princess for his son to marry. And he did. Don't ask me why, after all the stories that were going around about the daughter of the Sun, but he did, and yet another marriage was arranged. Messengers went out, invitations were carried, and, once again, the daughter of the Sun was on the guest list. When the messengers arrived to the cottage in the woods (they drew straws to determine who had to go), they knocked on the door ... and nothing happened.

They knocked again. Still no sign of the girl.

At the third knock, there was a voice right above them in the sky: "I am so sorry! Have you been waiting there for long? I just went for a quick flight around, I didn't mean to make you wait!"

And with that, the daughter of the Sun descended from the sky, floating as easily as a cloud, or a butterfly. The messengers handed over the invitation, and ran away.

Once again, the daughter of the Sun went to the wedding, and once again, she forgot to bring a gift with her. She panicked for a few moments, trying to figure out what to do, and then she picked up a knife from a table, cut off her own ear, and started pulling a wedding veil out of her head. It was made of the most delicate golden lace, light as a spider's web and shining like the sun. When it was long enough, she folded it up, and handed it to the bride as a gift ... then, she picked up her ear and put it back to its place, where it promptly grew back.

The prince, of course, stared at her with love in his eyes, and the bride, of course, grew jealous.

"That is nothing! I can do that!" She stomped her pretty feet, and picked up a knife from the table. But she barely sliced into her own ear when she started crying and blood dripped onto her dress, and there was a lot of confusion ... and the wedding was cancelled.

By this time, the prince was so deeply in love with the daughter of the Sun that he fell ill from sheer longing. No physician, no doctor, no wizard could heal him, and his father was worried for his life. Finally, he had to swallow his pride, because he knew that there was only one person powerful enough to cure the prince: the girl who lived in the cottage in the woods. Once again, messengers were sent, and they brought her back to the palace, where the king begged her to cure his son. The daughter of the Sun did not say anything; she just went to the kitchen and started cooking a soup full of herbs and secret ingredients. When it was ready, she went to the prince's bedroom, followed by the entire court, and sat down on the edge of his bed, feeding him the soup.

Now, here is the thing: the daughter of the Sun was good at magic, but not so much at cooking. The soup was so sour, so bitter, that the prince barely tasted it before he spat the entire spoonful back into her face.

"How dare you!" the girl yelled, wiping soup from her eyes. "How dare you spit into the face of the daughter of the Sun!"

Well, after that, there was some more yelling, and more confusion, but this time, nobody was hurt. Quite the opposite: the king finally realized that the girl was not just an orphan. She was the child of the Sun, and as such, she was royalty! Now he had no more worries about the future of his kingdom, and he gladly allowed the prince to marry the love of his life. A fourth wedding was arranged, people were invited ... and they all lived happily ever after.

*Comments:* Or, you know. They didn't. It really depends in which version you go with. In the version from the Abruzzi, the daughter of the Sun gets fed up with the fact that the prince never stands up for her, and when the last bride is defeated, she returns to the sky to her father. In the Algerian version she marries the prince first, but since she refuses to talk to him, he takes other wives that are all, in turn, tricked into hurting themselves, until the spell that keeps her silent is finally broken.

This story speaks of relationships on many levels. There is the overprotective father who just makes the forbidden fruit all the more alluring, and the nurse who would rather sacrifice a child then take the punishment for her own mistakes. And then there is the prince and the daughter of the Sun, with their many facets of love and spite. The more I work with this story the more I feel like it is a multi-sided Rubik's cube that one can twist to show different colors, from star-crossed lovers all the way to mismatched couples that were doomed for the start.

As for the superpowers: this gal has quite a few of them. Her healing factor would put Wolverine to shame, she flies, she phases, and she is impervious to fire. Still, since she has sunlight in her veins, fire is at the core of her personality and her power. I personally could never picture her in any other way but with flaming red hair and clothes in all the colors of the sunset. Fire is much more than just an element she controls. It is her personality, volatile, playful, warm and explosive at the same time.

Daughters of the Sun tend to make a career for themselves in folklore and mythology. One of the most famous ones is the Greek Circe, the enchantress of the *Odyssey* who commands powerful magic and spites most men (excluding Odysseus, who gives her a son). Her niece, the infamous Medea, is also an exotic mix of power, love and cruelty. In many Hungarian folktales the Sun is represented as "a woman dressed in sun." Light and fire have long been associated with strong, independent women who make their own way in the world.

## Pietro Baillardo

*Ability:* Fire magic
*Source of power:* Magic book (Book of Commands)
*Origin:* Rome, Italy (Middle Ages)
*Teachings:* Redemption, bravery.
*Age group:* 8+
*Sources:* Busk, R.H. (1874). *The Folk-Lore of Rome.* London: Longmans, Green & Co.

Gatto Trocchi, C. (2002). *Leggende e racconti popolari di Roma.* Roma: Newton Compton.

*Variants:* Very similar stories have been told in the Middle Ages about Virgil as a sorcerer, even though the affinity for fire seems to be Pietro's own.

*Text:* When they hear the word "wizard" people usually think of two things: old men with long white beards, robes and funny tall hats with stars and moons on them ... or Harry Potter. But before Harry Potter, it was just wise old man studying the secrets of magic in tall towers and peering over ancient books filled with secret signs. Everyone has seen that picture before, I am sure you have too.

Forget it.

Pietro Baillardo was young and handsome with flaming red hair and a really bad reputation. All over the city of Rome he was known as Trouble, with a capital T. Even when he was a child, he was the kind of child who opened all the forbidden doors, got into fights with boys who were bigger and slower, and never wore clothes that were clean for more than ten minutes after he put them on. When he was old enough to go to school, his parents were glad to see him go. He was curious and sharp-minded, eager to learn new things ... even when he was not supposed to learn them. One day when the teacher went home early, Pietro snuck into his study room and explored the bookshelves, pulling down one book after the other ... until he found something very interesting. In a hidden, cobwebbed corner of the study, behind a pile of papers and trinkets, he found an old, old book, bound in leather, decorated with flames of copper and gold, the pages filled with curious signs ... and his life was changed forever.

It was a book of magic. The moment the little red-haired boy took it into his hands he became the master of that book, and the powers in it. He grew up practicing his newfound tricks and spells, and soon he discovered that he had an exceptional knack for commanding fire. By the time he was a grown man, he had figured it all out, and he had gained a reputation, both as a sorcerer and as a troublemaker. There was a saying about him in Rome: "Wherever he goes, the Devil follows him."

The first time he fell in love with a girl, she rejected him ... and disappeared the next morning. Woodcutters found her two days later up on Mont Cavallo, three days' walking from Rome, surrounded by a ring of fire that no amount of water could put out. Pietro did not return to the city for a few weeks after that one.

At the beginning of our story, Pietro was sitting in prison for starting a fight in a tavern. He was sitting in one corner of the cell, and all the robbers and thieves were huddled in another, too afraid to look at him. Pietro was bored. He did not like being in prison at all. After a few hours he stood, and looked at the other prisoners.

"I have had enough," he announced. "We are going."

The prisoners laughed nervously and looked at each other. "Going? Going where? No one has ever escaped from this prison!"

They were right. The guards who arrested Pietro knew all too well who he was, so they took him to the most secure place in the city of Rome: the Castel D'Angelo, the old fortress that was supposed to keep the Pope safe from all dangers in case the city ever fell to a hostile army. In times of peace, they used the strong walls and secure cells to keep some of Rome's most notorious criminals from escaping.

"Well I am not staying here a minute longer," shrugged Pietro, and walked to the wall of the cell. He picked up a piece of charcoal (later on no one was sure where he got it, or if he had it in his hand all along) and drew a boat on the wall, with sails, ropes and all. When the drawing was done, he leaned down, drew a circle around himself, and then murmured a few words ... a deafening explosion and a blinding flash later, there was a gaping hole where the wall used to be, and outside, suspended in mid-air, there was a flying boat, ready to sail away. Pietro and all the prisoners got in the boat, except for an old man who was sitting in the corner. Pietro gave him a gold coin and told him to wait for the guards, and tell them what he had seen. After all, what use is magic and trickery, if the people who have been tricked do not know who did it?

They say that after the escape Pietro returned to the mountains, allowing some time before he showed his face in Rome again. As he was walking along he came across the sparkling blue waters of Lake Scanno, and stopped to admire the view. When he started on his journey again, his foot slipped in the mud, and he slid down the slope into the water. Now, someone as used to fire as Pietro getting soaking wet was similar to how a cat feels about bathing, and his reaction was exactly the same. He clambered out of the lake, sputtering and cursing, taking off his clothes to dry them. As he was standing there, the lake started to ripple, and then to bubble, and then to boil, and right before his eyes a beautiful young woman rose up from the water and glided toward the shore. She was wearing a sky blue dress and her hair was long, wavy and dark mossy green. Pietro forgot about his cold, half-naked state and stared at the lady as she smiled at him.

"Greetings, Pietro," she said. "I can see you are shivering. Do you need a place to warm yourself up?"

Pietro smiled back, and at a snap of his fingers, a nearby pile of twigs burst into blazing fire. "Thank you my lady, I will be fine on my own."

"I can see that," she smiled. "Still, I wish you would visit my palace under the lake. I have heard a lot about you, Pietro, and I would like to get to know you better."

Pietro, of course, could not say no to such a graceful lady, and he gladly followed her into the lake, to her underwater palace. In his haste, however, he forgot his book on the shore, by the fire.

Pietro had a great time with the lady, who turned out to be Madama Angiolina, the sorceress of the lake. Even though they were as different as water and fire, they understood each other, as one sorcerer to another, and the more time they spent together, the more Pietro forgot about the world outside the lake.

Then, one morning he woke up and he was alone. Angiolina the sorceress was gone. She had gotten bored of Pietro and decided to go and seek the company of other men ... and Pietro was trapped. He tried getting out of the underwater castle, but without his book, he did not have the right spell ... so he sat down and waited, hoping against all hope that someone would come along and rescue him.

He did not hope in vain. Up on the surface his friend and apprentice had been searching for him, and as he passed by the lake, he found the campfire that was still burning, and the pile of discarded clothes. Sorting through them he found the book and opened it, even though Pietro had warned him many times not to do that. As soon as the book was open, a group of demons appeared and bowed before him: "Master, what is your wish?"

"Do you know where Pietro Bailliardo is?" the apprentice asked, and the demons nodded.

"He is trapped in the castle of Angiolina, under the lake."

"Build him a way out of there," the apprentice ordered, and as soon as he said the words, the water started boiling with demons that flew back and forth, carrying stones to build a bridge out of the lake. When the bridge was ready, the gates of the castle opened, and Pietro walked free. It only took him one good look to guess what had happened; the demons were already swarming around him. "Master, what is your wish? Master, what is your wish? Master, what is your wish?"

Everyone who has ever used magic can tell you that if you summon demons, you need to keep them constantly occupied, or they will get bored and take your soul. Pietro took the book, snapped it shut, and looked at the demons: "Build me a road across the sky, and build it from stones from the deepest bottom of the sea." The demons hurried away to busy themselves with the impossible task. Some say this is how the Milky Way came to be.

Pietro returned to Rome, furious at Angiolina's betrayal. It was already night by the time he arrived. Walking down the empty streets he extended his arm. A candle flame in a nearby window quivered then sprang up into the air and flew into his hand. He walked on, and another flame joined in from behind a door, then another; flames from fireplaces and sparks from under cooking pots, hearth fires that were keeping people warm, and all the flames of the city of Rome flew to Pietro's command, until he had gathered every single one of them ... and then he closed his hand, and all the fire was gone.

In the morning, the people of Rome were all out in the streets, grumbling and shouting about their fires. Houses were cold, food was uncooked, and they had to spend the night in complete darkness. Who took the fire? It was not long before they found Pietro sitting on one of the squares, waiting patiently for a crowd to gather. When he decided there were enough people around him yelling and accusing him of fire theft, he stood and said:

"People of Rome! Why would I steal fire from you? You know how much I like the flames, why would I want them all gone? Think about what you are accusing me of! Is it not more likely that someone else took the fire, hoping you would blame me first? There is a sorceress in a nearby lake, she commands water the way I command fire. It is the nature of water to put out fires! It is not me you are looking for, it is Angiolina, the sorceress of the lake!"

The crowd agreed; they needed someone to blame, and they believed Pietro's words. Pouring out through the gates of the city they marched down to the lake. Angiolina, who was on her way back home, caught sight of them just in time, and she barely escaped into her underwater palace without being attacked by the mob.

She knew instantly who set the people of Rome after her, and her fury rose like the tide on the sea. She swore she was going to take revenge on Pietro — and the people of Rome for believing him. Summoning all her powers she moved the waters of the lake out of the valley and she marched on the city of Rome, followed by the tide, to flood and drown everyone she was angry at.

Pietro caught sight of the tide, and he knew the rivalry had gone too far. He might have been a troublemaker, but he did not want the people of Rome to suffer for his mistake. It was *his* city and *his* people, and he was not going to let Angiolina cause as much as a puddle on the streets. Gathering all the fire he had stolen from the people he met her outside the walls.

They say it rained fire that day. They say that flames fought waves on the outskirts of Rome, that trees were scorched and ponds overflowed. As water boiled into steam thick clouds covered up the hills, but no matter how many flames the water put out, new ones sprang up everywhere. Some people who were brave enough to look watched the fight from the walls of Rome, and for the first time they saw Pietro Baillardo in a different light. The battle between water and fire raged on for what seemed like hours ... but then, slowly, the water started to seep away, and the tide retreated into the lake.

No one ever saw the sorceress Angiolina again. Pietro, on the other hand, returned to Rome, and continued his life of troublemaking ... but now people were looking at him in a different way, and for the most part, they put up with his pranks. All his life, the power of the magic book followed him everywhere, and he knew that one day he would have to pay the price ... but that is another story, for another time.

*Comments:* I put this story together from bits and pieces. Some I found in a book of Roman legends; others I found in Medieval poems, or Italian collections of notable places in Rome. Since the first time I read about Pietro I have been fascinated by his story, so I kept looking, and searching, and it all slowly came together.

This is by far not the most popular tale about Pietro. Most legends concern his deal with the devil and his eventual redemption before his death. According to the most common version, one day Pietro summoned a demon and took a trip to Hell to see if it really existed. Seeing it for himself scared him enough to realize he did not want to end up there after his death, and he turned to the Roman Inquisition for advice (because where else?). They told him he needed to take a pilgrimage and attend mass in three great churches of Europe, to redeem himself from his sins. Pietro, of course, was too used to his own ways, so he summoned the demons again and made them take him to all three masses in one single night — one in Rome, one in Paris, and one in Constantinople. Upon his return he told the Inquisition he had completed the task, which of course horrified the good fathers, and they told Pietro what he had done was worse than not going to church at all. Eventually, just before his death at the age of 90 years, 6 months and 6 days, Pietro really repented and prayed in a church, and died with a clean soul. As the story says: "He lived with the Devil, but he died as a saint."

I have noted in the Rules that magic does not qualify as a superpower, unless it is very specific. I wrote that with Pietro in mind. Although the command of fire is by far not the only trick in his book, he still has an unquestionable specialty in it. Angiolina, who also owns a "book of commands" makes a perfect nemesis for him in that matter. The rivalry of the wizard and his lover is an age-old motif in legend — remember Merlin and Nimue (or Vivian, or Morgan, take your pick), but there are also stories about Virgil the Wizard who was suspended from a tower in a basket by his lady love. Pietro and Angiolina's fight is by far the most intense: it is not only sorcerer against sorceress, but it is also fire against water, resulting in quite the apocalyptic scene.

While I was piecing the story together I wanted to make sure to keep it as close to the original tidbits as I can. Minor details, like Pietro's flaming red hair, are mine (but with the side note that some sources claim his family was English, so he might as well have been a ginger). I could not include all the interesting details I found, but I did add the names of real places from the original legend to ground the story in the Italian landscape. I have visited Avezzano and L'Aquila many times, and I have seen the mountains that surround Lake Scanno. Talking about the lake: Angiolina also has her own backstory, connected to the legends of Charlemagne. A poem from the 15th century tells about a king called Corburante who kidnapped the wife of the famous knight Orlando, and as a punishment after his death his entire castle was sunk by a spell under Lake Scanno. Angiolina, our sorceress, happened to be the sister of that king.

# WATER POWERS

If mastering fire has been a milestone in the history of man, water has been with us right from the start. The source of all life on Earth, it has to be present in one form or another for us to survive and thrive. Some scientists have gone as far as suggesting that at some point in our evolution we spent a significant amount of time swimming, which accounts for many of our physical attributes such as hairlessness and extra fat (this became known as the much-argued Aquatic Ape Theory). The last unexplored boundaries of our planet, the depths of seas and oceans have always been populated with countless creatures of our imagination, from mermaids to krakens. We value things that come from under the sea such as pearls, coral and seashells, not to mention hundreds of types of seafood, and thus water became the ultimate legendary source of abundance and wealth. The most splendid tales of the *Arabian Nights* (such as "Julnar of the Sea") tell us about the land of the people who live underwater, and immortal heroes like Sindbad roam the surface of the Seven Seas, seeking adventure. The Water of Life brings many a folktale hero back to life, and water divides the world of mortals from the Islands of Eternal Youth.

With all that said, our control over water is very different from fire.

We have tamed fire: we know how to create it, we know how to put it out. Water, on the other hand, is an entity on its own. Control over water in tales is limited to crossing it and walking on it, or manipulating the source it comes from. Most of the time great bodies of water are far too powerful for a mortal to command — it requires the power of a deity to make the seas roar or calm down. In Greek mythology rivers, lakes and seas are inhabited by many different species of nymphs such as Naiads (fresh water), Nereids (the nymphs of the Mediterranean), and Oceanids (salt water). They are much more than just protectors of nature; they are the embodiment of the water they inhabit.

In modern media, water manipulation is known as aquakinesis. It includes breathing water, manipulating and moving bodies of water, and sometimes even manipulating water that is inside living bodies (known in *Avatar: The Last Airbender* as "bloodbending"). Modern heroes seem to have a better grasp on commanding this element than their traditional ancestors. We learn.

*Heroes with control over water:* Aqualad (DC), Aquaman (DC), Namor (Marvel), Tracy Strauss (NBC's *Heroes*), Waterbenders (*Avatar: The Last Airbender*)


## Fergus Mac Léti

*Ability:* Breathing underwater
*Source of power:* Fairy
*Origin:* Ireland
*Teachings:* You have to face your fears.
*Age group:* 8+
*Sources:* "The Saga of Fergus Mac Léti," ed. D.A. Binchy, *Ériu* 16 (1952): 33–48.

Watkins, C. (1995). *How to Kill a Dragon: Aspects of Indo-European Poetics.* New York: Oxford University Press.

*Variants:* Walking under water appears in other tales (see "Tide Jewels" for another example) but usually with a guide, and not as a supernatural power given and practiced. Dragon-killing is also fairly common, and dragons are often associated with water (see "The Gold-Spitting Prince").

*Text:* Fergus Mac Léti, the King of Ulster, had a bit of a ... cosmetic issue. His face was on backwards.

It's not like he was born with it, though. Back in those days in Ireland one could not become king unless he was physically fit and perfect for the task. No, when Fergus Mac Léti started his rule over Ulster, his face was by no means better or worse than any other face.

That is, until he saw the dragon.

But let's tell the story from the start.

One day Fergus and his charioteer, a man named Muena, rode by the seashore and they stopped to rest for a while. The king soon fell asleep. As he was lying in the sand unprotected, three spirits happened to pass by and they decided it would be great fun to drag the king out to sea and make him take a dive. They gathered him up and carried him over the waves, but the moment they prepared to drop him, as soon as his feet touched the cold water, the king woke up, and grabbed the spirits, one in each hand, one pressed to his chest. He was a strong man, a warrior, and no matter how the spirits struggled, they could not break free.

"A life for a life!" cried their leader.

"Fulfill one wish each, and you are free to go," answered the king.

"Name them!"

Legend does not remember what the first two wishes were. We only know one for sure: Fergus Mac Léti wished for the power to be able to walk under water. The spirits fulfilled his wish and gave him a cloak that he had to wrap around his head. As long as he was wearing the cloak, he would be able to breathe under water, and explore the mysterious world below. Before they were set free, the spirits also gave the king a warning: he could walk under every sea, river or pond, except for Loch Rudraige, which was on his own lands.

Taboos are dangerous things. For a long time, King Fergus was happy exploring rivers, lakes and oceans, walking anywhere he pleased ... but the more he had seen, the more he wished to see the one place he was not allowed to go. Finally one day he decided to ignore the warning, and set out straight for Loch Rudraige.

Leaving his charioteer on the shore, he walked into the water and disappeared. But he did not wander in the green gloom of the waters for long before he saw something that froze the blood in his veins: a *muirdris*, a dragon, more terrifying than any creature he had ever encountered. It was huge and scaly, and as its sides expanded with every breath, it made waves all across the lake.

When King Fergus clambered out of the lake a few minutes later, his face was so distorted with fear it was practically backwards. His charioteer was frightened at the sight, and the king knew something was wrong.

"How do I look?"

"You look upset, your highness," Muena said tactfully, "but it's nothing a good night's sleep cannot cure."

While the king slept, Muena went to consult the men of Emain Macha, the advisers of the king. A blemished king cannot rule Ulster, that was the law — but everyone loved dear curious Fergus too much to let him go. Finally the people decided to bring him home to his castle, and make sure he never found out his face was disfigured.

The entire court was in on the plan. They allowed no fools in the king's presence lest one of them would mention it; they washed the king's hair and face with him lying on his back so he could not see his reflection in the water. For seven years Fergus Mac Léti lived with his face distorted, and he did not even know about it.

One day a maid was washing the king's hair, and, maybe because she was scared of his face, or maybe just because she was clumsy, she accidentally pulled on the king's hair. Fergus, angered by the discomfort, struck her. The maid was so angry at being abused that she started yelling at the king, and she threw his ugliness in his face. By the time people ran in, it was too late; the king was so furious and so confused that he struck the maid again, and this time, he killed her.

The secret was out. Fergus was desperate to get his real face back, and set things straight. He returned to Loch Rudraige with a sword in his hand, and walked under the water once again to face the *muirdris*. King and dragon fought a fierce battle that raged on for an entire day and a night, and waves crashed against the shore as people watched in fear. Finally on the next morning Fergus emerged from the lake, dragging the dragon's head behind him.

"I am the survivor," he announced ... and then he fell down dead.

They say the water of the lake remained red from the dragon's blood forever.

*Comments:* Loch Rudraige is actually a harbor known as Dundrum Bay in County Down, Northern Ireland. In other translations the "spirits" are mentioned as dwarfs or leprechauns. In some versions of the tale the king has herbs he has to put in his ears to be able to walk underwater. Water-walking shoes are also mentioned.

There are different ways of describing what happened to Fergus under the waters of Loch Rudraige. Some say his face was distorted with fear, others that his face turned all the way around (although if the king does not notice that for seven years, there is something clearly wrong), and the text of "The Saga of Fergus Mac Léti" claims that his mouth extended all the way to the back of his skull.

There is something endearing about how the entire kingdom plays along to keep Fergus on the throne despite his disfigurement. Apparently he is loved as a king, and even after he kills the maid that reveals the truth, people still watch by the lake and wait for him to return victorious. Finally, the king has to face his demon in order to redeem himself.

I told this story for a MythOff USA event when I drew Secrets as a category. It has a lot of comedic potential, but in the end, it is more touching than funny. The audience, just like the court, grows fond of King Fergus.

---

## The Tide Jewels

*Ability:* Control tides
*Source of power:* Magic jewel
*Origin:* Japan

*Teachings:* Politeness, forgiveness, honor, and respect for one's given word.

*Age group:* 6+

*Sources:* Aston, W.G. (1896). *Nihongi: Chronicles of Japan from the Earliest Times to A.D. 697.* London: Kegan Paul, Trench, Trubner &Co. Ltd.

Griffis, W.E. (1911). *Fairy Tales of Old Japan.* London: George G. Harrap & Co.

James, G. (1923). *Green Willow and Other Japanese Fairy Tales.* London: Macmillan & Co.

Ozaki, J.T. (1903). *The Japanese Fairy Book.* Westminster: Archibald Constable & Co.

Pfoundes, C. (1878). "The Lost Fish-Hook," *The Folk-Lore Record* 1:126–129.

Roberts, J. (2004). *Japanese Mythology A to Z.* New York: Facts on File.

*Variants:* There is a similarly well-known Japanese tale about the Empress Jingu conquering a Korean kingdom by using the same tide jewels (see Griffis, Aston). "The Lost Fishhook" exists in many variations, Aston alone lists several of them.

*Text:* Hikohohodemi, Fire Fade, the fourth Mikoto of Japan, was a strong and fearless man, known for his favorite pastime as "The Happy Hunter of the Mountains." His elder brother, Fire Flash, preferred to fish rather than hunt, and people named him "The Skillful Fisher of the Sea." The brothers were happy and content for a long time.

That is, until one day Happy Hunter turned to his brother with a new idea.

"We have both been pursuing our own pastimes for a long time now," he said. "What would you think about switching them for a day? I could try my hand at fishing, and you could see how you like being a hunter."

Skillful Fisher agreed, and the two brothers switched places. Happy Hunter marched down to the sea with his brother's prized fishing rod and favorite hook, and waited impatiently for the little buoy to disappear. But, you see, Happy Hunter knew nothing about fishing, so naturally he did not catch a single fish all day. As evening fell, the frustrating day took a turn for the worse: the emperor discovered that he had lost the fishing hook. Thinking he must have dropped it somewhere on the shore, he started looking all around in the fading light. In that moment Skillful Fisher arrived at the scene, already in a bad mood because he had killed nothing that day either, and he had to admit he was a really bad hunter.

"What are you looking for, brother?"

"I have done something very bad!" wailed the emperor. "I have lost your fishing hook...."

"My fishing hook!" the brother yelled. "I knew this was a bad idea! We should have stuck with what we do best, and not meddled into each other's affairs! Now look what you have done! I will not return your bow and arrows until you return my hook!"

Happy Hunter, now a lot less happy, searched all over for the hook, but he could not find it. In desperation he went home, broke his favorite sword apart, and made five hundred hooks out of it — then added another five hundred. But no matter how many hooks he made, his brother refused to forgive him.

"I want my own hook, and nothing else!"

The truth was, Skillful Fisher was not all that fond of that hook. He just saw an opportunity: since his younger brother owed him obedience, even as an emperor, he wanted to find a way to get rid of him, and usurp his throne. Happy Hunter suspected this as well, and he was desperate to find the hook somehow. Returning to the beach he started looking all over, to no avail, until he bumped into a little old man.

"What are you searching for, your highness?"

"I lost my brother's prized fishing hook," the emperor explained, "and I really, *really* need to find it."

"It is probably in the sea, or in some fish's body," the old man suggested. "You should go ask Ryujin, the Dragon King, he is the only one that can help you."

"That is a splendid idea," said the emperor. "The only problem is that Ryugu-jo, the palace of the Dragon King, is on the bottom of the sea. How am I going to get there?"

"I can make something for you," the old man shrugged, and set to work. He made a small basket, just big enough for the emperor to sit in, and promised it would take him all the way to Ryugu-jo. Happy Hunter thanked him a thousand times and promised he would reward him greatly upon his return — then he sat in the basket and floated out to sea.

The basket-boat seemed to know its way. In no time at all the emperor caught a glimpse of the Dragon King's palace, and realized that no story he had ever heard had done the place justice. The palace was grand, built of coral, pearl and precious stones, surrounded by blooming trees.

Climbing out of the basket Happy Hunter tried the great coral gates, but they were locked. Looking around he discovered a well, and decided to wait there until someone came outside. He did not have to wait long before the gates opened, but instead of the dragons and sea monsters he expected to see, two beautiful young maidens appeared carrying golden buckets. He hid himself in a tree and waited for them to come closer. They did not see him among the branches, but they did notice his reflection in the well and they leaned over to draw water from it. At first they were scared to see a stranger, but the young emperor's politeness soon convinced them that there was nothing to fear. Happy Hunter begged them for a cup of water, and they handed him a golden cup; he handed it back, dropping a jewel from his necklace into it as a payment and a sign of gratitude.

"Who are you?" they asked, because they could tell from the rare gem that he was no ordinary fisherman.

"I am Hikohohodemi, the fourth Mikoto, grandson of the goddess Amaterasu, also known in Japan as the Happy Hunter."

"We have heard about you!" smiled the older girl. "I am Princess Toyotama, the eldest daughter of the Dragon King."

"And I am Princess Tamayori, his younger daughter," bowed the other girl.

The emperor was delighted to hear that. He told the girls his story, starting with the lost fishing hook and ending with the basket, and begged them to take him to their father, so he could have a word with him.

"He will be delighted to see you," the princesses said. "We do not get such esteemed guests very often."

Bowing low they led him into the palace, and announced his arrival to the Dragon King. Ryujin was excited to greet the grandson of Amaterasu — mortals only visited his palace once every few hundred years. He ordered all his subjects, every fish in his court, to line up at the door and greet Happy Hunter as he walked in. The Dragon King himself and his queen bowed to the ground to honor their esteemed guest.

"I am sorry for the trouble I caused you with my unexpected visit," said Happy Hunter.

"We are grateful to have you as our guest," the Dragon King answered. He ordered a feast and a celebration, and soon the banquet hall was filled with fishes carrying trays of delicacies. The two princesses danced and played music, and the evening passed in such good spirits that the emperor almost forgot why he was there. But his guilt still haunted him about his brother's fishing hook, so after a while he turned to Ryujin.

"Your daughters might have told you the reason why I am here. I lost my brother's favorite fishing hook, and I was hoping you would be able to help me find it."

The Dragon King clapped, and summoned all the fishes of the sea at once.

"My esteemed guest has lost a fishing hook," he told them, "and I want to know if you have seen it. If any one of you knows anything about this, come forward."

There was some murmur and some whispering, and finally someone in the crowd spoke up.

"I think it was the *tai* fish! He has not been eating since yesterday, and complaining of a sore throat!"

The Dragon King realized that the *tai* was the only fish who had not obeyed his summons. He sent for him at once, and the *tai* was brought to the court, looking pale and sick.

"Why did you not come when I summoned everyone?" the King demanded.

"Forgive me, your highness! I have been sick!" croaked the poor fish "There is a hook stuck in my throat and I cannot get rid of it!"

"You are the thief, then!"

"No, no, your highness, I did not mean to steal it! I just snapped at the bait, and the hook stuck in my throat. Believe me I want nothing more than to return the hook to its owner!"

"Let's return it, then," the king said, and ordered the cuttlefish to pry the hook out of the *tai*'s mouth. The Dragon King still wanted to punish the little fish for theft, but Happy Hunter begged him not to do it, saying that no one was at fault in the accident. The fish celebrated and praised their honorable guest, asking him to spend some time in their magical underwater realm.

Before the emperor noticed, three years went by. There was something new and amazing to see every day, but finally he grew homesick, and he longed to return the hook to his brother, and put the whole affair behind them. He said goodbye to the Dragon King and his court with a heavy heart.

"We are sad to see you go," said Ryujin, "but we understand that you have your own kingdom to govern. We hope that the friendship between Land and Sea will grow stronger with us."

The two princesses handed two presents to the emperor: two shining, brilliant pearls.

"Nanjiu and Kanjiu, the Tide Jewels," Ryujin explained. "We inherited them from our ancestors. They are powerful treasures that control the movement of the sea. Nanjiu, the Gem of the Flood Tide, draws the waves in; the Kanjiu, the Jewel of the Ebbing Tide, pushes them away."

Ryujin showed the emperor how to use the jewels — but that was not the only gift he gave. Over the three years, Happy Hunter had grown fond of Princess Toyotama, the luminous jewel of the dragon court, and now that he was about to depart, the Dragon King gave his blessing to their engagement. The couple said their final goodbyes to the family of dragons together, and the emperor left richer with three new precious jewels.

When Happy Hunter walked out of the palace through the coral gates, however, he found a giant shark waiting for him instead of the basket he had arrived in. The Dragon King ordered the sea monster to take the emperor and his bride home to Japan.

As soon as he was on dry land once again, Happy Hunter hurried home, bowed down before his brother, and begged for his forgiveness. When Skillful Fisher saw his own hook returned, he feigned a smile, but he was secretly furious.

For the past three years he had been ruling over Japan, rich and content, and he had no intention to return the reign to his brother. He started making plans for getting rid of the true emperor once and for all.

A few days later Happy Hunter was walking along the rice fields. He was aware that his brother was following him, and he had no doubt about his intentions. Feeling more disappointed than afraid, he decided it was time to put the Tide Jewels to use. Taking Nanjiu out of his pocked he touched it to his forehead.

The waves of the ocean came roaring into the fields. One minute Skillful Fisher was staring in disbelief, and the next he was swept off his feet by the swirling tide, begging his brother to spare his life. Fortunately for him, Happy Hunter had a kind heart, and once he thought his brother had learned his lesson he pulled out the Kanjiu and made the tide ebb away, leaving Skillful Fisher soaked and shaken, but alive.

The wicked brother realized his mistake; he could not possibly try to overthrow an emperor who could command the tides of the sea. He bowed down and begged for forgiveness, promising to mend his ways.

This time he was telling the truth. Happy Hunter returned to the throne, and his reign was long and plentiful. His brother stood by him and helped him in everything, and together, with the help of the Tide Jewels, they made Japan a flourishing kingdom.

*Comments:* First of all, about the bounty of names in this story. "Fire Fade" is a literal translation of Hikohohodemi, while "Fire Flash" stands for Honosuseni. They have also been translated as Fireshine and Fireshade. For clarity's sake I decided to go with the less well-known names describing the two brother's favorite pastimes, solely because they are harder to confuse with each other. The emperor is also known as Hoori while his brother is known as Hoderi.

The *tai* fish is also known as the red sea bream (*Pagrus major*), and is a delicacy in Japan. The word used in the story for shark is also translated into "crocodile" in some versions, but given the deep sea setting of the story, I decided to go with shark.

In the continuation of the legend, Toyotama the sea princess gives birth to a son. She swears her husband to secrecy, but he sneaks a peek anyway, and sees her in her true dragon form, which embarrasses the princess so much that she goes home and never returns. Walking in on wives' secrets is a common theme in folklore and mythology (see the stories of Achilles or "The Serpent Wife" in this book, or the French legend of Melusine).

Once again, water control in this case is not a power the emperor is born with — it requires magical items, and the use of magical items requires learning. And who better to teach him than the Dragon King, the ruler of the Sea? Ryujin plays an important role in Japanese mythology, and, unlike Western dragons, is not only able to take on human form, but is also quite the polite and respectful host to his visitors. The fact that more than one person uses the pearls in Japanese mythology is also intriguing — the powers that come with them are so great that they can defeat armies (see the legend of Empress Jingu). One has to deserve the gift of the pearls though, by being worthy not only in behavior, but also in heart.

# Earth Manipulation

Of the four basic elements earth is the one that seems to be the hardest to manipulate by mortal heroes — I needed to look really hard to find a folktale that fits the description. While fire, air and water are naturally mobile and volatile, earth feels very solid under our feet, and when it does move, it does it with such incredible force that it must be the work of some higher divine power. Gods and goddesses have long been responsible for the ground shaking, be it Poseidon in the form of a bull, Loki chained in a cave, or Hawaiian goddess Pele throwing a jealous fit from a volcano. Regions with less stable geological conditions naturally have more stories to explain what happens beneath our feet.

There are some folktales where characters display the power to mold earth and metal, usually through extraordinary physical strength. An example that every child in Hungary knows is the (fairly shamanistic) tale of "Son of the White Horse" who is accompanied by three men, one that tears up trees from the ground, one that molds metal in his hands, and one that crumbles stones into dust. Some folklorists suggested that they could be the embodiment of wind, fire and water respectively. In any case, breaking stone into sand is more a feat of strength than an earth-bound superpower.

In modern media earth manipulation is also known as geokinesis or terrakinesis. Just like water manipulation, it shows a lot more variety, ranging from creating earthquakes and manipulating magma all the way to creating sandstorms or burrowing underground.

*Heroes with earth powers:* Avalanche (Marvel), Earthbenders (*Avatar: The Last Airbender*), Geo-Force (DC), Magma (Marvel), Rictor (Marvel), Samuel Sullivan (NBC's *Heroes*), Terra (DC)

## The Son of the Hunter

*Ability:* Geokinesis, sharp hearing, extraordinary capacity for drink and food, far-jumping, resistance to heat, turning people into animals, kiss of youth

*Source of power:* Unknown

*Origin:* Greece

*Teachings:* Teamwork and cooperation, honesty, hard work, respecting one's given word.

*Age group:* 6+

Sources: Courlander, H. (1955). Ride with the Sun: An Anthology of Folk Tales and Stories from the United Nations. New York: Whittlesey House.

Dawkins, R.M. (1950). *Forty-Five Stories from the Dodekanese.* Cambridge: Cambridge University Press.

Dawkins, R.M. (1953). *Modern Greek Folktales.* Oxford: Clarendon Press.

Dawkins, R.M. (1955). *More Greek Folktales.* Oxford: Clarendon Press.

Geldart, E.M. (1884). *Folk-Lore of Modern Greece.* London: S. Swan Schonnenschein & Co.

*Variants:* Once again, this is the (in)famous folktale type AaTh 513, this time combined with the motif of the villain trying to destroy the hero through seemingly impossible tasks. Dawkins lists several Greek versions from different parts of Greece in *Modern Greek Folktales*, and some in *More Greek Folktales.*

In many ways this story resembles the ancient Greek myth of the Argonauts. Even the power of the princess to turn people young again dates back to Medea who uses her magic to destroy King Pelias.

*Text:* Once upon a time there was a hunter who worked for the king. One day, as he was carrying game to the palace, he ran into the vizier who wanted the rich meat for himself. He tried to pay the hunter off to give him the game, but the hunter refused: he had orders to bring everything to the king. The vizier let the issue go, but secretly he swore he was going to destroy the hunter.

Time went by, and no opportunity presented itself. The hunter was an honest man, and the vizier could not find a reason to have him banished from court. But as he grew old, the hunter grew sick, and he felt his death was near. On his deathbed he made his wife swear that she would not allow their son, Yannakis, to become a hunter, for the vizier was still looking for a way to take revenge on the family.

Once the hunter died, his allowance from the king stopped, and the widow and her son sank into poverty. Yannakis, who was used to being dressed nicely and going to school, could not bear being mocked by his friends, and one day he turned to his mother. "Mother, tell me, what was my father's trade?"

"He was a hunter, my son, in the court of the king. But you must not become one. That was his dying wish."

Yannakis did not say anything, but the next day he sneaked out of the house, took his father's bow and arrows, and went to the forest to hunt. He shot some large, fat birds, and took them to the king's court. The king was so satisfied with his meal that he wanted to meet the person who brought in the meat. "Are you the son of the huntsman I used to have?"

"I am, your highness."

"Then you shall take your father's place. Whatever game you kill, bring it straight to me."

After that, Yannakis and his mother lived comfortably once again. The king paid him well for the game, and was satisfied with his new huntsman.

One day as Yannakis was carrying the game to the palace, he ran into the vizier, who did the same thing he had done to the hunter's father: he offered money for the first pick of the kill. Yannakis refused, just like his father, and the old wound flared up in the vizier's dark heart. Now he was out to destroy the young huntsman, once and for all.

A few days later the king sent Yannakis out with very specific orders: he was to bring enough game for a Saturday feast. The young hunter walked the woods all day, but he could not even glimpse a single bird or deer, let alone kill one. He was starting to get desperate, when he caught a glimpse of something else: bright gold. Waking closer he discovered a beast, stranger and more magnificent than anything he had ever seen. Its skin was gold, covered in diamonds and precious gems. Yannakis drew his bow and fired arrow after arrow till he brought the beast down, and since he caught no game he decided to ease the king's anger with the gift of the gold-and-diamond hide. On the way to the palace, he met the vizier once again, who tried to pay him for the rare treasure, but Yannakis refused. He was right to do so, for the king gave him ten thousand piasters, while the vizier had only offered a hundred.

As the court gathered to admire the treasure, the vizier leaned over to the king's ear. "That is all fair, your highness," he whispered, "but wouldn't it look a lot better in a palace built from ivory? Send the young hunter out for elephant tusks, and make him build a palace that no king has had before!"

The idea appealed to the king's vanity, so he ordered Yannakis to set out right away, and bring him the ivory — or perish trying. The young hunter returned home to his mother and told her about the order. He was sure he could not do it alone.

"I will tell you something your father told me a long time ago," said the widow. "Up in the mountains there is a lake. Elephants go there to drink every day at noon. If you fill that lake with wine they will fall asleep, and you can cut off their tusks."

Yannakis returned to the king and told him that he could bring him the ivory if he gave him twenty barrels of *raki* and twenty barrels of wine, and twenty young men to work with him. The king granted this wish and Yannakis set out for the lake in the mountains.

The little group of young men carried out the plan perfectly. They drained the lake and filled it up with a mix of wine and *raki*, then waited in the bushes while the elephants drank their fill and collapsed into a drunken sleep. It was not long before Yannakis returned to the king with a huge load of tusks, and a new palace was built from the ivory.

"This is all fair and well, your highness," whispered the vizier to the king, "but there is something even more desirable than a palace of ivory. There is a princess called Dartane, fair and beautiful, with a very special gift: her kiss turns a man young and strong, no matter how old he may be. You should send the young huntsman to bring back the princess for you."

What the vizier did not tell the king was this: Dartane was the little sister of forty dragon brothers who guarded her from every danger. The Russian czar alone had lost five thousand soldiers when he tried to take her as his bride. Yannakis did not know this, but his mother did.

"Tell the king you need a good horse to travel to Dartane's kingdom," she suggested, "and when he grants you the horse, leave and never come back. Take all the money we have left, and settle in a far away country."

Yannakis kissed his mother on the cheek, and said nothing. He did ask the king for a good horse, and when he received one, he set out on his journey.

He did not travel far before he came across a man with skin dark as ebony, who was busy drinking up a river. "I am always thirsty!" the man complained, while Yannakis waded across on the river that was reduced to a stream. "And I am always traveling alone!"

"Travel with me, then," the hunter offered, and they went on together. Soon they came across another man who huddled by a blazing fire, complaining of the cold, then another one who was always hungry. Both of them were welcomed into the slowly growing party of travelers. So was the man they met a short way down the road. At first they thought he was dead for he was lying on the ground, but he soon turned out to be listening — to the affairs of the World Below. Yannakis hired him too for his sharp hearing. The next to join the group was a jumper: he held two stones in his hands and he threw them behind his back when he jumped, pushing himself sailing through the air faster than any man could run. The last companion was a man who could make the earth shake and rumble, and he made the seventh member of the group.

The seven companions finally crossed the border of the kingdom of the forty dragon brothers, and the snow-white royal castle opened up before their eyes. When the dragons discovered them and wanted to know why they came, Yannakis stepped forward and extended the king's request to marry Princess Dartane. The dragon brothers laughed, and told the companions that they would agree to the betrothal if they completed four tasks.

For the first task, someone had to eat forty oxen boiled in huge cauldrons. The companions sent the man who was always hungry, and even after licking the bottom of the last cauldron, he was still asking for seconds. Next, the dragons gave them seven jars of water, and the ebony skinned man drank them all, and claimed he was still thirsty. Desperate to win the challenge, the dragons declared that the next contestant had to endure the fiery heat of a steam bath. The man who was always cold volunteered happily, and for a long time there was no word from inside the room. But when the dragons peeked in to see if he was dead, they were met with an angry yell: "Close the door, the cold air is getting in!"

There was only one task left.

"On the next mountain over there is a spring," the brothers explained. "Whoever brings water from it first will win the challenge. You will be competing with our sister."

Princess Dartane set out, and so did the man who could jump far. He swayed his arms, tossing the rocks behind him, and jumped all the way over to the next mountain, filled his pitcher, and walked back towards the castle, taking his sweet time. Halfway back he met the princess, still on her way towards the mountain. They sat down to talk and rest, and as they did, the jumper felt terrible sleepiness come over him, and he lay down on the ground. The moment his eyes closed, the princess picked up his pitcher and started on the way home.

"We have a problem," Listener told Yannakis, pressing his ear to the ground. "I can hear our friend snoring, and the princess on her way."

"I will wake him up," the seventh companion volunteered, and he made the earth shake and rumble. The jumper sat up, rubbing his eyes, and realized the water was gone. He picked up two stones, threw them behind his back, and jumped after Dartane; grabbing the pitcher from her hands he jumped again, and made it back to the castle before her.

All the challenges had been won; the dragon brothers had to let their sister go. Yannakis took Princess Dartane back home to the king's court. But when the princess saw the old king, she turned, and looked at the young hunter again, then back at the king. "Who brought you the ivory of this palace?"

"The huntsman," answered the king.

"And who built you the palace?"

"The huntsman."

"And who won me from my brothers and brought me here?"

"The huntsman."

"And if he did all that, why should I marry you and not him?" Dartane asked, and she clapped her hands. "May the vizier be a mouse, and may the king be a cat," she declared. In that moment the king turned into a large cat, and the vizier into a tiny mouse, and the cat chased the mouse of the palace, and that was the last anyone had seen of them.

Yannakis married Dartane and became king. They lived happily in the ivory palace ever after.

*Comments:* I pieced this story together from several of the variants mentioned above. The beginning was taken from Geldart's version, while the companions and tasks are mostly from Courlander, and Dawkin's *Modern Greek Folktales*. I took the princess's name from Dawkin's *More Greek Folktales*, which is a very similar tale, but does not include the companions. According to Dawkins, the name means "a woman of slow movements and plump." I personally like the idea of a plump princess (or a princess with a name in general).

I was tempted to take pieces from *More Greek Folktales*, but decided against it. In that version the huntsman has to bring the mother-of-pearl bones and golden feathers of a magical bird instead of ivory. I was not entirely comfortable with the mass elephant mutilation either, so take that with a note of caution. Sometimes when I tell this story to children (or easily upset adults) that can't yet grasp the concept of a different historical era with different values, I just substitute an elephant graveyard for the lake, so no live animals are hurt in the creation of the story. But for this volume I felt like leaving the original episode, mostly because it falls in line with the rest of the old hunter's legacy.

The person who is the main reason for this story being included in the book only shows up in two of the variants, Courlander's and *Modern Greek Folktales*, and despite the great number of variants around the world, I only found his earth-trembling powers in the Greek versions. We do not find out much about him, other than what he can do. It feels very appropriate that a country with many earthquakes would be the one to include a character like that in a folktale. Another Greek addition is the long jumper (instead of the usual swift runner) who throws stones behind him as he jumps. This is a way of jumping featured at the ancient Olympic games where athletes used weights to stretch the length of their jump.

The archer that often shows up in AaTh 513 type folktales in this case is the hero himself, who is a very capable hunter of his own (unlike many other heroes of the same tale type who tend to be foolish or lazy). Yannakis is the Greek version of the name often translated as Little John.

# WEATHER MANIPULATION

I realize that "weather" is not one of the four elements, but it is the most spectacular way of influencing the forces associated with air. Controlling the weather (that, in turn, controls most of our lives) has been an age-old dream of humanity, and one we still haven't mastered (not intentionally, anyway). From rain dances to human sacrifice, humanity has tried a wide spectrum of rituals, prayers and spells to bring rain, stop rain, or otherwise make the forces of nature bend to our will.

If we took the narrowest definition of "air manipulation" as wind, we could still find plenty of examples in folklore and mythology. We have already seen examples in the tale of Princess Szélike and the story of the gold-spinners. Another famous one would be Odysseus who held the four winds in a bag (courtesy of Aeolus, God of the Winds), but let them escape and earned years of exile for his clumsiness. A similar folktale exists in Hungary in which a monster called Kalamona binds the winds and causes great environmental distress until the hero sets them free. Another folktale from Transcarpathia tells about an old woman whose godmother was the Wind herself, and helped her whenever she needed her clothes dried.

There is a whole series of modern fantasy terms for air and weather manipulation: atmokinesis, aerokinesis, aeromancy, anemokinesis etc. They usually involve flight, bringing or calming storms, creating tornadoes and hurricanes, calling down lightning, and controlling precipitation. The most famous character associated with weather powers is probably Marvel's Storm, incidentally also the first black female superhero to play a major role in comic book history.

*Heroes that control air and weather:* Airbenders (*Avatar: The Last Airbender*), Red Tornado (DC), Storm (Marvel), Thor (Marvel), Wind Dancer (Marvel)

## Garabonciások

*Ability:* Weather control, luck, teleportation, flight, dragon command
*Source of power:* Learning (and magic book)
*Origin:* Hungary
*Teachings:* Never refuse a gift to someone who asks nicely. Respect people less fortunate than you. Wealth does not equal happiness.
*Age group:* 6+
*Sources:* Ipolyi, A. (1854). *Magyar mythologia.* Pest: Heckenast Gusztav.
Tőke, P.M. (1987). *A szerencsés aranyász.* Budapest: Móra.
*Variants:* This is the only version I know of this particular folktale, but there are many other tales and legends that feature the garabonciás. The sky-high tree (or World Tree) is an old mythical motif that appears in the stories of many nations, and is especially important in Hungarian folklore.
*Text:* In the northwestern part of Hungary there is a village called Ásvány. Once upon a time it used to be famous for a tree—a tree that was so high its top branches were permanently hidden in the clouds. Even though there are many tales and legends about this sky-high tree, sadly it does not exist anymore: A storm uprooted it some time ago. It wasn't an ordinary storm, either.

The story goes like this:

One day a poor fisherman was walking home from the river. As he passed by the sky-high tree, he suddenly heard ... laughter? ... Music?! Looking around he saw no signs of a feast, until he finally realized that the merry noises were coming from *above*. His curiosity taking the better of his instincts to run away, he tried to climb up the tree. And failed. He tried again, and failed again, many times, since the tree was so huge even the lowest branches were out of reach.

Suddenly, there was a voice.

"You should wait for the giant."

"Wh..." the fisherman blinked and turned around, nervous like a thief caught in the act. Behind him there was a stranger wrapped in a black cloak and wearing a black hat. "What giant?"

"*That* giant," the stranger pointed, and sure enough, there was a giant strolling peacefully down the road towards them. "If you hold on to the back of his shirt, he will take you up the tree."

It was easier said than done. The giant was, well, a giant after all, and the poor man could not even reach his ankles, let alone the back of his shirt. Finally the stranger rolled his eyes and pulled a great leather-bound book from the folds of his black cloak.

"*Térdelj le!*" he read aloud, and the giant knelt down. The fisherman clambered up its back and grabbed two fistfuls of his shirt.

"*Állj fel!*" read the stranger in a commanding voice, and the giant stood. And started to climb.

They rose higher and higher until the clouds rolled in around them, and the fisherman could not see the ground anymore. He screwed his eyes shut, and held on for dear life ... until the giant finally came to a halt.

The poor man opened his eyes, took a quick glance around, then dropped down from the giant's back and rolled under a table.

Yes, a table. There were tables on top of the sky-high tree, and around them, feasting, drinking, and being merry, there were hundreds of witches. (And the occasional giant.)

The poor man huddled under the table and hoped no one would discover him and curse him into something ugly. But the more time he spent there, the more glances he stole at the feast happening over his head. And one of the things he noticed was the plates and cups made of solid gold.

He was afraid, but his greed was stronger. If he could just steal a single plate and a cup, he could be rich! Very carefully he reached out from his hiding place and felt around the corner of the table until he managed to sneak a plate and a cup away, and hide them inside his shirt.

Once the feast was over, the giant said his goodbyes to the witches, and started his descent from the tree. The fisherman jumped onto his back as he passed by, and traveled down the way he came.

Except, when they arrived to the bottom of the tree, there was no sign of the helpful stranger.

Before the giant could carry him off to only God knows where, the fisherman made a desperate decision: he screwed his eyes shut, and let go of the shirt. He landed in the bushes, scratched and bruised but alive, and ran home to his wife.

The plate and the cup were made of solid gold. They yielded enough money for a new house, new clothes, and good food, and the couple lived happily in their newfound wealth ... for a while.

"You should go back to that tree," the wife suggested one day. "You could steal another plate and a cup, and make us even richer."

It might have sounded like a suggestion, but in the fisherman's house, it was an order. He returned to the tree, waited for the giant, somehow managed to grab hold of the hem of the giant's pant leg (the black-cloaked stranger did not show), and traveled once again up the tree to the witches' feast. He stole a plate and a cup, survived the journey back down, and returned to his wife.

The second plate and cup, once again, yielded a great deal of money. Now they had servants, and horses, and acres of land ... but still not quite enough for the wife's taste. She kept sighing and hinting at how they could be as rich as the king, if only he would go back to the tree and steal another plate and the cup. Finally, the husband gave in.

"But this is the last time!" he promised. "After that, if you want more gold, you can go and get it yourself!"

He returned to the sky-high tree. He waited for the giant. He traveled up the tree on the giant's pants, hid under a table, stole a plate and a cup, and traveled back down. He scratched and bruised himself as he fell into the bushes, then ran back home, and sold the plate and the cup.

Now they had more money than the king himself. They lived in a mansion, ate food fit for royalty, and wore the finest clothes.

And then, one evening someone knocked on the door.

The lady answered the door, but she did not recognize the strange man standing outside. He was wearing a black cloak and a black hat, and holding a heavy, leather-bound book under his arm.

"Good evening, my lady," he tipped his hat politely. "I am tired and hungry. Could I bother you for a cup of milk and a slice of bread?"

"We don't have enough for ourselves! Go away," she snapped, and shut the door in his face.

That ... was a mistake.

Back in the old days everyone in Hungary knew that a stranger in a black cloak carrying an old book was a garabonciás — a weather wizard. They went to study the art of magic in faraway places like Italy, and completed thirteen schools of learning. When their time was up, thirteen students had to sit on a wheel of fortune, balanced above a deep, deep pit. The wheel would spin, and one of them would fall off, and the rest were endowed with great power.

Their power was held in their magic book. If they wanted to travel fast, they could turn a page and appear wherever they wanted to go. If they wanted to travel high, they could put a stick in the ground, and it would grow until it reached the moon. And if they wanted to travel far, they could summon a dragon from the lakes and the rivers, and saddle it like a horse.

They used to travel from village to village, from house to house. They would ask for milk and bread, to test people. If they were generous and kind, the garabonciás would put a sign on their door, and good luck would come to the house, crops would grow, cows would give milk in abundance, and children would be healthy. But if the people of the house refused, another sign would appear on the door, and bad luck would soon follow.

As soon as the lady shut the door in the stranger's face, there was a sound outside: the whistling of wind. By the time she and her husband ran to the window, the whistling grew into a hiss, and then a roar, and before their eyes stood the stranger, his book open in his hands ... with a whirlwind forming around him.

A terrible storm broke out that night over the village of Ásvány. It leveled the fisherman's mansion, tore up his fields, and before it was over, it uprooted the sky-high tree. When the storm was over, the fisherman and his wife were just as poor as they had been before — and there was no tree to climb, no more plates to steal.

They remained poor for the rest of their life.

*Comments:* And that, kids, is why you should not refuse a bite of food or a cup of drink to those in need.

Ásvány or Ásványráró is the name of a village that still exists today. "Térdelj le" means "kneel!" in Hungarian; "Állj fel!" means "stand up!"

The figure of the garabonciás is a well-known one in Hungarian folklore. Some researchers suggested that it has its origins in medieval times when young men traveled abroad (mostly to Italy) to study medicine and other sciences, and returned home with their traveling cloaks covered in dust, their heads filled with strange knowledge, carrying books written in mysterious languages. Even at the beginning of the 20th century a new doctor in town or a well-educated visitor was suspect for being a garabonciás.

Sacrificing one of the students to gain power also has its roots in medieval legends, and appears in many stories about wizards and magicians. It is usually suggested or flat-out said that the one that dies is claimed by the Devil in exchange for teaching the rest the Dark Arts. But unlike many other humans who were said to possess magical powers, garabonciás were not thought to be evil. They appear more as mysterious characters distributing justice, assigning bad luck to bad people, and good luck to the good. They are often seen fighting witches, countering evil spells, or showing people hidden treasure, much like in this folktale. They are especially often mentioned in stories from Northwest Hungary, and they also appear in the folklore of neighboring countries. One of the most well-known recent examples of similar tales is the Czech story of Krabat, which was turned into a German feature film in 2009.

(I am well aware that I am breaking the "no magic" rule again, however, garabonciás are first and foremost seen as weather wizards, their image merged with the idea of storm and hail and water dragons. Many other examples featuring a similar level of weather control usually deal with deities.)

# ICE AND SNOW

Control over ice and cold is also known as cryokinesis. Even though technically ice is still water, the ability to control temperature as well as the element deserves a separate category. Many times when elements clash fire is opposed by ice, as cold opposes heat, instead of water.

In many cultures that have to deal with cold, harsh winters, Cold itself is regarded as a person. We could mention Jack Frost (who gained modern media fame recently through *Rise of the Guardians*), Santa's Russian ancestor, Grandfather Frost, the Norse frost giants, or Pakkanen, the frost-spirit of the Finnish epic *Kalevala*. Humans are not built for cold weather, and when it comes to fighting it, ice is an opponent that's hard to defeat.

Just like fire, ice manipulation makes some spectacular displays of power.

*Heroes with ice powers:* Ice (DC), Icemaiden (DC), Iceman (Marvel), Jack Frost (*Rise of the Guardians*), Polar Boy (DC), Waterbenders (*Avatar: The Last Airbender*)

## Snow Daughter and Fire Son

*Ability:* Fire body, ice body, heat and cold manipulation
*Source of power:* Natural
*Origin:* Bukovina (Armenian)

*Teachings:* The importance of family, or the lack thereof.

*Age group:* 8+

*Sources:* Lang, A. (1906). *The Yellow Fairy Book.* London: Longmans, Green and Co.

Wislocki, H.v. (1891). *Märchen und Sagen der Bukowinaer und Siebenbürger Armenier.* Hamburg: Actien-Gesellschaft.

*Variants:* I have not found another version of this tale; the one in the *Yellow Fairy Book* is a direct translation from the German original. Snow Daughter's story is very similar to the Russian folktale of the Snow Maiden.

*Text:* Once upon a time, there was a poor man and a woman who did not have children. They waited and waited to be blessed with a child, but their prayers remained unanswered. One bright winter morning they were standing outside their home, watching the icicles on the roof glitter in the sunlight.

"I wish we had as many children as icicles on this roof!" the wife sighed, and her husband chuckled at that. As they watched, an icicle detached itself from the roof. The wife caught it and popped it into her mouth.

"Maybe I will have an ice daughter now," she said, and they laughed at the idea together.

But soon after to their great surprise and joy, the wife discovered she was with child. In due time a baby girl was born, white as snow and cold as ice. At first they were alarmed that she was ill, but she ate and grew just like normal children. There was only one curious thing about her: she seemed to suffer in the heat. Whenever they brought her near the fire she screamed till they put her into a cooler spot. When she learned to walk she went outside at night to sleep in the snow, and in the summer she hid in the cellar and complained about the heat. Her parents called her "our Snow Daughter," and it fit so well they never gave her any other name.

One evening husband and wife were sitting by the fire, talking about their daughter who was dancing in the snowstorm raging outside. "I wish I would have given birth a fire child instead!" the wife sighed. In that moment a spark flew out of the fireplace and landed on her lap.

"Maybe now my wish will come true," the wife smiled, and they laughed together.

Soon after she found she was with child again, and in due time a baby boy was born. He was hot to the touch like an ember, and yelled himself into a fit if he was not close enough to the fire — or if his sister came anywhere near him. He was red as flames and grew like them too, and his parents named him "our Fire Son," and that was the only name he needed. Soon he was running around the house, going wherever he pleased — except near his sister.

In fact, the two siblings could not stand each other: when Snow Daughter was in the room, Fire Son almost crept into the fireplace, and she complained about the heat. In the summer he was outside basking in the sun and she hid in the cellar; in the winter she slept in the snow and he spent his time plastered against the hot surface of the fireplace. Brother and sister barely ever met.

Just when Snow Daughter turned into a young woman and her brother into a young man, their old parents passed away. When they had been laid to rest Fire Son turned to his sister, "I am going to seek my fortune in the world. There is no reason for me to stay here."

"I will go with you," Snow Daughter answered. "You are the only one left for me in the world."

"I love you with all my heart," said her brother, "but how can we ever travel together? I am freezing whenever I go near you, and you can barely stand my heat...."

"I have an idea," she said. "I will make a fur coat for both of us, and that will shield me from the heat, and protect you from the cold."

Once they put on their fur coats, brother and sister were happy in each other's company for the first time in their lives. They traveled all summer and fall, and when winter approached they decided to stay in the forest and build a home. Fire Son spent the winter days and nights inside the cottage by a roaring fire, while his sister walked outside enjoying the cold, not wearing more than a slip of a dress.

One bright winter day the king of the land was out hunting in the woods, and saw Snow Daughter dancing with the falling snowflakes. Amazed by her beauty and her strange state of undress he stopped to talk to her, and she told him her story. They did not talk long before the king was completely in love with her, and asked her to become her queen. Snow Daughter consented, and together they traveled to the royal city for the wedding.

The king built a palace of ice under his own castle for the new queen, so she could live in the cold even during the summer. He also built a palace for his brother-in-law, a palace heated day and night by large ovens. Fire Son lived there and his body filled up with so much heat that it was dangerous to go near him.

One day the king held a feast and invited everyone in his court, including Fire Son. The brother-in-law was the last to arrive, and when he walked into the hall he carried so much heat in his body that people fled outside in panic. Seeing his banquet destroyed, the king grew angry.

"I should have never brought you here!" he yelled. "If I knew you were so much trouble I would have left you in the woods!"

"Don't be angry, dear brother," Fire Son smiled. "Just let me embrace you, and I will go home."

Despite the king's efforts to flee, Fire Son caught him and embraced him. The king cried out in agony, and Snow Daughter, who fled to the other room from the heat, hurried to his rescue ... but she was too late. When she saw her husband burnt into ashes, she flew at her brother in a furious rage. A fight began, unlike any other fight ever before, and it raged on until the castle was destroyed, burnt and frozen to a ruin. After, when everything was quiet, people found a puddle that used to be Snow Daughter, and a pile of cinders that used to be Fire Son. This was the end of the two unfortunate siblings.

*Comments:* Strange, strange story. Sometimes when I tell it I call the siblings Spark and Flake, simply because it rolls off the tongue easier than Snow Daughter and Fire Son. Much like in the Snow Maiden tale, there is no happy ending for either of them because of their supernatural nature. Their birth is miraculous, but their life follows the rules of heat and cold, and of human relationships.

In this case we cannot really talk about supernatural powers — heat and cold are in the sibling's nature. They are hot or cold to the touch, and they do not handle the other extreme well. Fire Son apparently also absorbs heat until his body is burning too hot for humans to handle. They both release all their heat and cold in a final epic fight, and they prove to be equal, causing serious destruction.

# ◆ PART IV ◆

# Transitional Powers — From One State to Another

## WHEN DRAWINGS COME TO LIFE

Had I been only looking to fill in a list of superpowers that are popular in modern media, this one would not have made the cut. Even though there is a significant amount of folktales and legends of pictures coming to life (mostly from East Asia and India), this ability has not made the jump to the big screen just yet.

Storytellers, on the other hand, are quite familiar with it. A famous and beloved story of many audiences is "The Golden Paintbrush" (China), closely followed by "The Boy Who Drew Cats" (Japan). Both have been re-told and re-imagined by many storytellers around the globe in the past decades of the modern storytelling revival.

I decided to include this ability in the book as an example of powers that feature often in folklore, but seem to have been neglected by popular media. Of course when one looks hard enough, exceptions can be found. As usual.

*Characters with similar powers:* Erazer (E4's *Misfits*), Sai (*Naruto*)

## *The Legend of King Vikramaditya*

*Ability:* Bringing pictures to life
*Source of power:* Magic item (chalk)
*Origin:* India
*Teachings:* Knowing what is truly important (also, watching too much television is bad for you and your kingdom).
*Age group:* 8+

173

*Sources:* Edgerton, F. (1926). *Vikrama's Adventures; or, The Thirty-Two Tales of the Throne, a Collection of Stories About King Vikrama, as Told by the Thirty-Two Statuettes That Supported His Throne, Edited in Four Different Recensions of the Sanskrit Original (Vikrama-charita or Sinhasana-dvatrincaka).* Cambridge, MA: Harvard University Press.

Haksar, A.N.D. (1999). *Simhāsana Dvātriṃśikā : Thirty-Two Tales of the Throne of Vikramd"itya.* New Delhi: Penguin Books India.

Nivedita, S., and A.K. Coomaraswamy (1914). *Myths and Legends of the Hindus and Buddhists.* Boston: D.D. Nickerson.

Sagar, R. (1995). *The Folk Tale Reader: Selections from Indian Folklore.* Delhi: Ratna Sagar P. Ltd.

*Variants:* This story comes from a 13th century Sanskrit collection of tales called the *Vikramacarita* (also known as "The Thirty-Two Tales of the Throne"). It includes — surprise — thirty-two stories told by the statues that surround the great throne of King Vikramaditya. For different retellings of the story, see sources above.

*Text:* King Vikramaditya believed that the best way he could govern and protect his kingdom was to stay in his palace for half of the year, and travel the neighboring lands the other half. He wandered near and far, visiting holy places, meeting wise people, seeing other kingdoms, other cities, forests, mountains and rivers with his own eyes. The things he learned during his travels were often useful when he had to make decisions and dispense justice from his throne.

One day he traveled to a city called Padmalaya. Sitting by a clear, calm lake in the company of other travelers, he overheard them talking about holy men, saints and yogis who live in such harsh, faraway places that one cannot visit them without risking their life. The travelers all seemed to agree that a man's first responsibility is to take care of himself in order to avoid paying more than his goals are worth.

At this point King Vikramaditya could not listen quietly any longer. He spoke up and reminded the men that everything seems impossible to achieve until someone has the courage to try. "Great men do not just sit around waiting for things to fall into their lap. A ditch can fill up with rain falling from the sky, but it can also fill up from below. Fate is powerful in this world beyond measure, but is human effort not powerful too?"

The travelers all turned to listen to him, and nodded quietly at his speech.

"Twelve leagues from here there is a mountain surrounded by a dark forest," the king continued. "I heard that on top of the mountain lives the great master yogi Trikala Natha. He grants the wishes of anyone who visits him in his seclusion. I will go and see him today."

"And we will go with you!" cried the other travelers, excited about the prospect of meeting the famous saint. But once they set out on the road, through the forest and up the mountainside, the followers quickly started to lose their initial momentum.

"How much farther is it?" they demanded to know.

"Eight leagues more," the king answered, walking forward at a steady pace.

"We should go home," one traveler suggested, and many others agreed.

"Are you giving up already?" Vikramaditya shook his head. "Nothing is too difficult for the capable, no place is unreachable for the educated, and nothing is too far for those who have a purpose."

They traveled another six leagues up the mountainside when a giant serpent appeared in their path, spitting poison and flames. The rest of the travelers ran away but King Vikramaditya kept walking forward, even when the snake coiled itself around him and sunk its venomous fangs into his skin. Dizzy from the poison and staggering from the constriction of the serpent, the king walked the last two miles, and reached the yogi's cave. At the sight of the master the serpent dropped to the ground and slithered away, and the venom left the king's veins.

"What brings you here on such a dangerous path?" Trikala Natha inquired from his royal guest.

"I wanted to see you with my own eyes, and hear your wisdom with my own ears."

"Did you have trouble on the road?"

"Nothing that would be worth mentioning. A man should improve his knowledge and acquire wisdom while he is still young and capable in body and mind. It is too late to dig a well when the house is already on fire."

The sage liked King Vikramaditya's answer, and granted him gifts. One was a quilt that provided food, money, clothing, and other things a king could wish for.

The other gift was a piece of chalk.

"Whatever you draw during the day will come to life at night."

The king could hardly wait to get home to his palace and try the magic of his gifts. Even though the quilt could conjure up food, treasures and clothes in great numbers, he was more fascinated with the properties of the piece of chalk. He locked himself up in his chambers and spent the day drawing men and women, gods and goddesses on the walls. As night fell, the images all came to life before his eyes. He spent the night conversing with them, and in the morning, he moved on to another portion of the wall. He drew an army, with horses, elephants, warriors and heroes, and in the night it all came alive with the thunderous sound of an army passing by. The next day he drew dancers and musicians, and spent the night enjoying their performance.

Days passed after night, night passed after day. Vikramaditya forgot about his duties as a king, and as a husband. His wives wept and complained, and missed him terribly. Finally they all gathered up and visited the king in his chambers.

"My dear ladies, why are you so pale?" he asked, alarmed when he saw their eyes fill up with tears.

"Maharaja, you promised to never leave us!" they cried. "Why have you abandoned us all these days and nights? What is more important to you than your kingdom and your family?"

King Vikramaditya knew that he had done something wrong ... but the spell of the moving images was still on him, and his attention wandered. The queens left, and returned in the morning when the pictures were still.

"We want to ask you for a boon," they told him. A king could not refuse a boon, even if he wanted to — and because he knew he had wronged his queens somehow, he agreed eagerly to make things right.

"Give us the piece of chalk that is in your hand."

The queens hid the magic piece of chalk in a place where Vikramaditya could not find it again, and everything in the kingdom returned to the way it should have been. Never did any pictures in the court come to life again.

*Comments:* Moving pictures distracting husbands from their duties around the home? Who would have thought that could ever happen....

I pieced this story together from two different versions. The beginning is from the Haksar version, while the chalk and the story of the moving images are from Sagar and Nivedita. In the second half of Haksar's story, the king gives the chalk to an exiled prince he meets on his way home, so that the prince can take back his kingdom with the army he drew. In the other two versions, Vikramaditya receives the chalk from two wise men who had been arguing about Intelligence and Wisdom, and asked the king to be a judge in their argument.

Once again the supernatural power is possessed by an object rather than a person. However, it needs someone with imagination and talent to bring the power to life. If the king can imagine it, and draw it, he can create it. The first version with the exiled prince also suggests that the pictures do not only move, but they come to life altogether, since he is ready to use a hand-drawn army to take back what was rightfully his.

## Painted Dragons

*Ability:* Bringing paintings to life
*Source of power:* Unknown
*Origin:* China
*Teachings:* With great artistic talent comes great responsibility.
*Age group:* 6+
*Sources:* "Dragons." (1917). *Ch'en Jung's Picture of Nine Dragons.* Museum of Fine Arts Bulletin Vol. XV, No. 92: pp. 67–73.

Giles, H.A. (1918). *An Introduction to the History of Chinese Pictorial Art.* London: B. Quaritch.

Karetzky, P.E. (1996). *Court Art of the Tang.* Lanham, MD: University Press of America.

*Variants:* If one is looking for tales about painted dragons, China is the perfect place. In another story master painter Chang Seng-yu (6th century) paints dragons without eyes to keep them from coming alive. When he is forced to finish his paintings, the dragons fly off the walls of a temple, leaving only ruins behind. For more stories on painters and dragons, see the sources above.

*Text:* More than a dozen centuries ago there lived a painter called Feng Shao-cheng who was famous for his art. He painted birds and dragons that were so life-like people often thought they could catch a glimpse of them stirring from the corner of their eye. People admired his work, and he lived to amaze them with every picture.

It happened in those years that Emperor Xuanzong of the Tang dynasty decided to build a magnificent palace by the Huaqing Hot Springs for himself and his concubine, the legendary beauty Yang Guifei. He wanted the walls of the palace decorated with the paintings of the best artists, and so he summoned Feng Shao-cheng to his court.

As the painter traveled to the emperor's court he saw desiccated fields all along the way. The kingdom had been suffering from a terrible drought; not a single drop of rain had fallen for months. As Feng Shao-cheng thought about the emperor's new palace by the hot springs, an idea started to dawn on him.

He set to work as soon as he arrived, choosing his paints and brushes very carefully. First he drew the outline of a dragon, its long serpent-like body twisting and undulating as it flew through lightly sketched clouds. Then he painted the scales, shining and iridescent, and before the eyes of the emperor and his court, drops of water started to gather on the dragon's body. By the time the colors and details were filled in, the body of the magnificent creature seemed to be straining against the lines on the wall, trying to break free. At the same time, storm clouds started to gather as if called by some mysterious voice, and the wind picked up. When the last line was finished on the painting, the great white dragon broke free from the wall, rose into the storm clouds, then plunged into the nearby lake, bringing a torrential downpour of rain.

The earth drank, the drought ended, and people still tell tales about master painter Feng Shao-cheng to this very day.

*Comments:* Chinese dragons are associated with water and rain. It is a very conscious choice on the painter's part to paint a dragon that would come to life and bring an end to the drought. It is never quite explained how he does it, though, it is only said that he is aware of his ability to bring the picture to life, and that it somehow draws on his artistic talent for making images extremely life-like.

This story is as much fun to tell as it is short. I often use it in art classes and then encourage children to paint their own dragons.

# TELEPORTATION

Following the obscure ability of bringing art to life is one of the all-time most popular superpowers of fantasy and science fiction: teleportation. The ability to appear in an instant wherever one wishes to be, has intrigued mankind for centuries. The folktale motif D1521, Magic Object Offers Miraculous Transportation, has more than two dozen sub-categories with every possible object in mind, from capes through boots to stones, and, as we shall see later, pocket knives (for the boots example see the story "The Gold-Spitting Prince" from earlier in this book).

Teleportation has definitely made the jump (no comment on the pun) into popular media. Not only that, but it is still considered a scientific possibility that might be realized, at least to some extent, in the near-distant future. In the meantime it continues to be a favorite of comic book writers and science fiction fans.

When one looks at folktales, it is not always clear if what we see (and don't see, and see again) is indeed teleportation in the modern sense of the word, or just really, really fast flight. Sometimes it is stated that the hero, with the help of magic boots/cape/charm, travels "as fast as thought." If you are wondering exactly how fast that would be, I recommend reading Gresh's *The Science of Superheroes* (see further readings at the end of this book). Story-wise it rarely ever makes a difference, so for all intents and purposes, the idea of teleportation has been nesting in the human mind for a very long time.

*Heroes with teleportation abilities:* Blink (Marvel), Cloak (Marvel), Dr. Manhattan (*The Watchmen*), Magik (Marvel), Nightcrawler (Marvel), Nikki (E4's *Misfits*), Pixie (Marvel), Rachel Mills (NBC's *Heroes*)

## The Three Soldiers

*Ability:* Teleportation, infinite monetary resources, military summoning
*Source of power:* Magic objects (knife, purse, horn)

*Origin:* Scotland

*Teachings:* Keeping your word, stealing is wrong, just because someone is a princess it does not mean she is always right.

*Age group:* 6+

*Sources:* Barbeau, M. (1958). *The Golden Phoenix and Other French-Canadian Fairy Tales.* New York: H.Z. Walck.

Campbell, J.F. (1890). *Popular Tales of the West Highlands I.* London: Alexander Gardner.

*Variants:* The French-Canadian version of this tale is known as "The Princess of Tomboso," and features fruit that makes the princess's nose grow. Campbell lists several different variations from the West Highlands.

*Text:* Two soldiers deserted from the British army; one of them was Irish, the other Scottish. The army sent a sergeant after them. When he finally caught up to the deserters, they convinced him that there was a better life waiting for poor devils like them in America, and the English sergeant decided to join them instead of returning to the army. Together they sailed over the ocean and started out looking for a new home.

One night, wandering in the endless forests of the New World, they saw light in the distance. It turned out to be the light of the fire inside a small house by a lake, and the three soldiers were grateful to have found shelter for the night. As they walked in they noticed food on the table and three beds, but there was no one inside or around the house.

"We should eat and sleep," the Irish soldier (his name was John) suggested. "If they come home in the morning, we can pay them back."

They all agreed, ate their fill, and went to bed. But when they woke up in the morning, there was not only fresh food on the table, but also clean clothes for all three of them by the beds — and still no one in the house. The soldiers had breakfast, and while the other two suggested they should leave, John convinced them to stay another night. Everything happened the same way. Without ever catching a glimpse of anyone, or hearing a single footstep, there was fresh food in the morning, and clean clothes.

This time, John was too curious to leave things alone. He walked out of the house and around the lake, trying to find the mysterious host. Instead of a host, however, he found three swans swimming on the lake. He pulled out his gun and aimed at one of them ... but the swans suddenly spoke.

"Don't hurt us! We are human beings just like you, under an enchantment. We have been waiting for a very long time for someone to break it. If you had stayed in the house one more night without questions, we would have been free...."

John was ashamed to find out he missed his chance to help the swan-maidens.

"Is there any other way we could help you?" he asked. "Anything at all?"

"There is an old tree by the house," the swans answered. "If you return here exactly a year from today and uproot it, we will be free."

The three soldiers promised they would return, and the swans gave a parting gift to each of them. John received a purse that was always filled with coins and jewels. The Scotsman got a knife that, when opened, transported its owner to wherever he wished to go. Finally, the sergeant received a horn that could summon an army when blown through one end, and make it disappear when turned the other way. Happy with their magical gifts, the three soldiers moved to the nearest town and set up a household to wait out the year.

They were content for a while, until one day John woke up with a shiny new idea: he was going to visit the king's daughter! He had heard tales about her beauty, and now that he had a purse full of coins and jewels, he thought he might have a chance at an audience. Putting on his best clothes he walked up to the palace gates and knocked.

At first the servants did not want to let him in, but the moment he showed them gold and diamonds they rushed him straight to the princess's audience room without any questions asked.

The princess, on the other hand, had a lot of questions.

"How can a soldier like you have such treasures?" was the first one when she saw John's gifts.

"Oh, they come from this purse," he said with an innocent smile. "It never runs out of coins and jewels no matter how much I spend."

"That is amazing! Can I take a look?" the princess asked, and John placed the purse in her hands without a second thought. The moment she had it she summoned her guards and had John thrown out of the palace, poor as he had been before. And she didn't even feel bad about it.

It was hard enough for John to confess to his friends that he had lost the magical gift; it was even harder to convince them to help him get it back. He begged and reasoned and coaxed until the sergeant agreed to lend him the magic horn.

John marched back to the palace and blew into the horn. The next moment he was surrounded by an entire army of soldiers. The princess (and the rest of the court) ran to the windows to see who was out there. Their initial shock at the sudden siege was followed by annoyance on the princess's part when she realized who was leading the hosts.

"What do *you* want here?"

"I came to get my purse back," John declared. "If you don't return it, I will order my army to take your castle."

"How do I know this army takes orders from you? You are just a simple soldier!"

"They listen to me because I have the magic horn!" John countered.

"I'll believe it when I see it!" the princess stomped.

In response to the stomping, John turned the horn around and blew into the wide end — and the army disappeared in a puff of smoke. With a triumphant grin on his face, John blew into the right end again, and the army returned, ready to march.

The princess was fascinated. She came out of the castle with a charming smile on her face.

"That is truly a rare treasure you have," she said, inching closer to John, "and you use it so well too! It is hard to believe that all of this great army came out of that horn!"

"Oh, it did!" John promised, and to prove his point, he turned the horn around again, and made the army disappear. As soon as they were gone, the princess snatched the horn from his hand, and blew into it herself.

John returned home late that night, beaten and exhausted, and without a horn. The sergeant was furious at him for losing his magical gift, and claimed that John got what he deserved. The Scotsman, suspecting his gift was next, hid the knife and refused to lend it to John, even though he asked and begged and reasoned, swearing on everything he could think of that he would get the other two gifts back.

In the end, John just stole the knife at night and went back to the princess's castle.

The princess was greatly amused when she saw the poor soldier return to her castle for the third time.

"What have you brought me this time?"

"Come closer and take a look," John offered. When the princess was at arm's length, he grabbed her by the hand, snapped open the knife, and thought of the farthest island out on the sea ... and in the blink of an eye, they were on that island, surrounded by nothing but trees, and endless water.

John told the princess they were going to stay on the island until she agreed to return the magical gifts. But if John was determined, the princess was downright stubborn, the way only royalty can be. They were at a stalemate, and stranded on the island.

The princess never quite figured out how John transported her so far away in a blink, so no matter how she tried, she could not sneak away. Then, one day while John was asleep she looked at her hands, and to her dismay she had to discover that her nails had grown terribly long. Looking around for something to cut them with she saw the handle of a knife poking out of John's pocket. Switching the knife open she started poking at her nails, wishing to be home in her own comfortable room once again.

The next moment, she was.

When John woke up and found both knife and princess gone he knew instantly what had happened. He spent the next day wallowing in despair, and planning all kinds of revenge ... until he grew hungry, and kind of bored. Wandering around the island he found trees he had never seen before: one was heavy with shining red apples, and the other with green ones. John picked a red apple and bit into it, not even noticing as he wolfed it down that his head was growing heavier ... and heavier with every bite. Only when he was down to the core did he finally realize that his head was tilting sideways, pulled down by some unexplainable weight.

He had antlers. Heavy, magnificent antlers that would have made a stag jealous.

At this point John was sure his day could not possibly get any worse. Staying away from the red apples he moved on to the green ones, and because he was still hungry, he threw caution to the wind. To his utter surprise, this choice turned out to be more fortunate: after the first few bites his head grew lighter, and finally both antlers fell off.

That gave John an idea. Gathering some of the green apples and some of the red ones he walked back to the beach, and waited patiently till he saw a ship passing by. He yelled and waved until the sailors noticed him and brought him on board, and then conveniently placed the bundle of red apples where they would find it.

After that, it did not take long for the plan to start working. The sailors found the fresh apples and started eating them. By the time the captain noticed they all had great ten-point antlers and they were running around in panic, getting tangled in the ropes and sails.

"What have you done to my crew?!" he cried, but John just shrugged in response.

"They should not have eaten my prized possessions," he pointed out. "Those magic apples are worth a fortune."

"I will give you this ship and the cargo if you stop them from ruining it all!" the captain promised, and John took him by his word. He gave some of the green apples to the sailors, who promptly shed their antlers, and they sailed safely back home, with John as their new captain.

Once they were anchored, John went back to the palace and sent a basket full of the most beautiful red apples to the princess as a gift from a secret admirer. The princess (who clearly had not heard enough tales about princesses and apples as a child) was delighted, and ate three of them before she noticed the antlers growing out of her head.

The entire court was in panic. Physicians were summoned, wise men were consulted, and the princess locked herself in the bedchamber. After all possible treatments had failed it all came down to the old solution: the king declared that whoever could cure his daughter would have his blessing to marry her.

The next morning John knocked on the castle door, carrying a basketful of green apples.

"I have something that will cure you for sure," he told the princess before she could open her mouth to complain. "But you have to return my purse first."

Royal pride or not, the fair patient was in no position to argue. She told her servants to return the purse to John, and once he made sure it was his own purse, he gave a green apple to the princess.

"I will return tomorrow with the rest of the cure," he promised, and walked away with a happy smile.

Sure enough, the next morning there he was again, and the princess, with one lopsided horn left on her head, waited for him eagerly. "Give me another one of those apples!"

"Give me back the magic horn and I will."

"Take your stupid horn and go!" she said, and John obeyed, but not before he handed another green apple to the princess.

The apple however, did not have the effect the royal patient had hoped for. It reduced the remaining antler to a mere two-point, but it was still there, firmly planted on her head. She had to give up the last of her pride, and send for John one more time.

"This one will cure you for sure," John promised, with the last green apple in his hand. "But you need to return my knife first."

"Take it," the princess sighed, and bit into the apple.

The antler fell off, and the court rejoiced. John smiled a small smile.

"Are you going to marry me now?" the princess asked with a smile of her own.

"Not now, and not ever." John shook his head, opened the knife, and he was gone.

The year was almost up. Once John arrived home to his friends with all their magical possessions, the three soldiers set out to the swan maidens' house in the woods.

The tree was easy to find, and almost just as easy to uproot. The moment it fell to the ground three red-haired maidens appeared, inviting the soldiers into the house, and greeting them as their saviors.

The three soldiers found love with the swan maidens, and a new home in the woods. The magical gifts provided everything they needed. No one knows what happened to the princess, but as for John and his friends: they lived happily ever after.

*Comments:* I am going to say up front that I absolutely adore this tale. I first encountered it in the French-Canadian version, and then stumbled upon it again among the West Highland tales. It is one of those inter-generational stories that entertain every age group from elementary school to senior center.

It feels fresh among all the other fairy tales with the mean princess and the very human hero. It is equal parts humor and magic with a dash of badassery on the side (teleporting by flicking open a switchblade has to look cool, no questions asked).

I stitched and pieced this story together from the versions listed above. The princess snatching the horn is from "The Princess of Tomboso," but the rest is from the Scottish variants. Tellers and audiences are probably very aware of the fact that there are no princesses or castles in America ... but it does not take much to make them willing to suspend their disbelief.

---

## The Magic Book

*Ability:* Teleportation, flight

*Source of power:* Magic book

*Origin:* Hungary

*Teachings:* Do not poke your nose where it does not belong. Also, knowledge is power.

*Age group:* 6+

*Sources:* Holló, D. (1934). "A garabonciás diák alakja a magyar néphagyományban." *Ethnographia* Vol. 45: 19–34, 110–126.

Ipolyi, A. (1854). *Magyar mythologia.* Pest: Heckenast Gusztav.

*Variants:* This is another one of the many garabonciás tales circulating in Hungarian folklore. There are many different versions where the civilian who finds the magic book takes a peek inside, and gets into all kinds of trouble: summons a dragon, makes a cart fly, transports himself into a faraway land, or even summons little devils who demand tasks to do. The latter can be familiar by now from the legend of Pietro Baillardo.

*Text:* A poor man was driving an oxcart home from the fields when he noticed a stranger on the side of the road. He was one of those ragged, dust-covered travelers that wandered the roads all the time, without letting anyone know where they came from, or where they were headed. No one really trusted them. There were strange tales whispered around the countryside about sudden storms, untimely hail, and whirlwinds that twisted and turned just like the body of a giant serpent.

Still, the traveler looked weary and limped heavily, leaning on a staff. The poor man stopped the oxen and leaned over.

"I can take you to the inn in the village," he offered. "You can travel in the back."

The stranger did not say a word, but nodded with a tired smile and climbed into the back of the cart. He lay down, wrapped his ragged cloak around himself, and instantly fell asleep.

The only possessions of the stranger were the staff, and a big leather bag that opened up when he hung it on the back of the driver's bench. The corner of a large, leather-bound book was poking out of it. The poor man kept stealing glances over his shoulder, wondering what was in the book. He had heard about strange travelers who kept great wisdom in their books, and he decided that he wanted a taste of that wisdom.

He reached over and quietly pulled the book from the bag. It opened with a creaking sound and a rustle of thick pages. The poor man could not read the strange words and signs that filled them, so he licked his fingers, and turned a page.

There was a whistle of wind, and when he looked up, he was in the middle of a marketplace.

People hurried around the cart as if nothing strange had happened. The stranger was still asleep in the back. The poor man stared at the crowd and at the buildings around the square until he realized that he knew the place: it was the market in Miskolc. Three days' journey from his own village.

Panicked, and worried that the stranger might wake up and question what he had done, the poor man turned the page back. There was another whistle of wind, and the next moment he was back on the road just outside his home.

Although he was still scared of the book's power, his curiosity was stronger. He poor man looked at the writing on the page and recognized a single word, written in neat bold letters: "Rise." As soon as he read it, moving his lips quietly, the cart, together with the oxen, started to rise into the air. It soared higher and higher, and the poor man held onto the book and the bench for dear life, his eyes searching frantically to find another word that would put the cart down. As he prayed and searched, the stranger stirred in the back. He sat up, rubbed his eyes, and it only took him one glance around to know exactly what had happened. Reaching over he lifted the book from the poor man's shaking hands, and read another word aloud: "Descend."

The cart descended until it gracefully touched down on the road.

"You are lucky you did not close the book up in the air," the traveler grumbled as he climbed off the cart. "We would have fallen to our death. Good day, sir."

He walked away, and was never seen again.

*Comments:* I put this story together from two variants of the same tale: one with teleportation, and one with flying. Once again, the powers come from the book rather than from the person, although there are some garabonciás folktales where the wizard merely spins around on his heel and appears wherever he wants to go. The book is a symbol of learned knowledge, a tangible proof that the garabonciás has completed his training and the 13 schools of magic, and possesses powers that opened up to him with achieving the book at "graduation."

On that note, here is an interesting bit: according to some legends, only twelve of the garabonciás students receive a magic book; the thirteenth in the class receives another that specifically deals with summoning and controlling dragons. How cool is that?

# PHASING

Phasing (also known as intangibility) is the ability to walk through solid objects. In folklore it is mostly the privilege of ghosts and other beings that lack a physical body. In popular culture it allows heroes and villains alike to walk into locked rooms and other secure places. One example of this ability can be found in the tale "The Daughter of the Sun." Even though it is not a very popular superpower, it is a well-known one, probably due to popular comic book characters such as Kitty Pryde and the Flash. It deserved a mention, and a good story.

*Heroes that phase:* Cipher (Marvel), D.L. Hawkins (NBC's *Heroes*), Flash (DC), Martian Manhunter (DC), Shadowcat (Marvel), Silver Surfer (Marvel)

## The Taoist Priest of Lao-shan

*Ability:* Phasing and illusions
*Source of power:* Divine (or at least religious magic)
*Origin:* China
*Teachings:* Learning and wisdom do not come overnight. Hard work earns lasting results.
*Age group:* 6+
*Sources:* Sung-ling, P. (1916). *Strange Stories from a Chinese Studio.* 3d ed. Shanghai: Kelly & Walsh, Limited, pp. 10–13.
*Variants:* This is the only version of this story (published in English) that I managed to trace back, although it is quoted in many different books and publications.
*Text:* Mr. Wang was interested in becoming immortal.

Back in the old days Taoist priests were said to possess the secrets of immortality, as well as other miraculous powers. Anyone who was determined enough could become a disciple of one such priest, and learn the secrets through hard work and devotion. Wang was not particularly fond of hard work, and the only thing he was really devoted to was his own life, but he decided to give learning a try anyway. He had heard tales that on Mount Lao-shan immortals were so thick you could not throw a stone without hitting one, so he packed his bag and set out on a journey for enlightenment.

Climbing the peak of the mountain he came to a monastery that belonged to an old, well-respected priest. Wang bowed before the master and asked him to take him on as a disciple.

"I am afraid it will be too much work for you," said the priest (who was not a sage for nothing).

"Try me!" Wang insisted. He was taken as one of the disciples, and the next morning he started his studies in immortality — by chopping firewood. By the end of the day, his hands were blistered and his legs were shaking, and the day after was not any better either. Chopping firewood must have been an essential part of training, because Wang did nothing but chop and chop and chop for almost three months in a row. He was becoming tired, disappointed, and suspicious that the priest had no real secrets to disclose whatsoever.

But he was wrong.

One evening as he returned from work he found the old priest in the company of two guests.

"It is getting dark, but we should not end our feast just yet," the sage smiled, and, picking up paper and scissors, he cut out a circle and put it on the wall. It did not only stick there, but immediately became a brilliant silver moon, flooding the dining hall with smooth moonlight. Disciples crowded in through the door in amazement, and the guests smiled.

"Indeed. And we should all have some more wine."

One guest handed a kettle of wine to the nearest disciple, who hurried to fill his cup, thinking there could not possibly be enough in the kettle for everyone. But as they passed the kettle around, it did not only fill all the cups, but it was also still full when they returned it to the table. Amazed by all this, the disciples sat around in quiet awe, waiting for the next miracle.

"We should have some entertainment," the old sage observed, and picking up a chopstick, he hurled it at the moon on the wall. Brilliant rays burst out of the circle, and then a girl appeared, gracefully stepping down onto the floor. It was Chang'e, the woman in the moon who had stolen the elixir of immortality from her husband oh so many years before. She smiled as she grew to the height of a normal woman, and started dancing an enchanting dance that left the disciples speechless. When the dance was finished she twirled around in the air, her toes gently tapping on the table ... and she turned back into a chopstick.

Wang had no more doubts about the old priest's magical powers. However, despite the night's entertainment, his studies still solely consisted of chopping wood from dawn till dusk. After a few more days, he decided he had had enough.

"Master, I have never worked so hard in my entire life," he told the priest one evening. "Surely there has to be some small and easy trick I am worthy of learning!"

"I told you it would be too much hard work for you," the priest shook his head slowly. "You can return home in the morning."

Wang knew then that he should let it go ... but he didn't.

"I have worked for you for more than three months now!" he reasoned, not unlike a stubborn child. "Teach me one thing, *one* thing only, and I will return home content that I have not wasted my time."

"Very well. What art would you like to learn?"

Wang was taken aback by the question. It took him a few moments to make up his mind.

"I noticed that whenever you come and go, there are no obstacles for you, master. I have seen you walk through walls. I want to learn that, it seems useful."

"Done," the priest nodded, and he taught Wang a short chant he had to repeat while he walked through things. Once he had learned it, his master told him to give it a try.

"Right now?" Wang hesitated. He looked at the wall. The wall looked solid.

"Go ahead," the priest encouraged him. "Run a few steps, it will be easier."

Wang did not really believe that, but did not want to make a fool of himself either. Repeating the chant furiously in his mind he took a few steps back ... then ran straight at the wall.

It worked. The next moment Want was outside the building, grinning happily. He walked back in through the wall, and bowed to the old priest.

"Use it wisely," the master warned him. "No power is too small to be taken seriously."

The next morning, Wang returned home, and the first thing he did was brag about his newfound powers to whoever was around to hear it. Mostly it was his wife, who had soon had enough of the tales of miracles and powers, and refused to believe a single word until she had seen it with her very own eyes. Wang, who was not going to have his one and only power questioned by his spouse, recited the chant, and ran into the living room wall with great confidence.

This time, however, the chant did not work. Instead of his wife's respect, all Wang earned was a bump on the head, and a bruise on his pride.

*Comments:* And thus "Don't try this at home" was invented.

There are many, many Chinese tales about miracles and illusions Taoist priests can work. Even in tales that celebrate Buddhism like "Journey to the

West," Taoists miracle-workers appear around every corner, and their repertoire of powers ranges from shape-shifting through healing to, apparently, walking through walls. The power is clearly an acquired one, since Wang, who is not even in the ballpark for achieving enlightenment or immortality, can master the chant that makes him able to phase. However, when he uses it irresponsibly and for his own pride, the power fails him. The story has a moral, without a truly tragic ending: a power alone is not enough to make someone exceptional. But at least Wang got a good story out of the deal....

# SHIFTERS, CHANGERS AND INDIVIDUALS OF MULTIPLE SHAPES

If I had to name a single supernatural ability as the most common one in legend and folklore, my money would be on shape-shifting. It does not even have a motif— it has an entire range, D500–D599, in the Thompson index, listing various means and ways of changing one's shape. Within this range the most common would be animal shifting, but people changing into other people, plants or even inanimate objects also occurs quite often.

Here is the catch: as I have stated in the rules, at least for the purposes of this book, I have been using a narrow definition for shape shifting, based on two principles: 1) It has to be voluntary and controlled (or managed) by the person; 2) It has to go both ways. This ruled out a great number of tales such as transformations from curses ("The Frog Prince"), origin stories of plants and animals (Daphne), classic werewolf legends (shifting by the full moon), or any other voluntary shifting that only happens once and the result is permanent. Because I also set as a goal that I would be looking for human (or half-human) heroes first and foremost, I also ruled out tales about legendary creatures that have a dual nature such as selkies (seal maidens), bird brides, and the pink dolphins of the Amazon that tend to show up in human form and charm mortal maidens — unless people discover the air hole on the top of their head, which is considered a major turnoff.

Suddenly the research just got a whole lot more intriguing.

Shape-shifting stories (with the exception of human-to-human) are very close to nature, and remind us of times when our wishes and dreams revolved around the powers and abilities of animals that our human bodies could not match. We were not born on top of the food chain, we had to climb it (and in many parts of the world we are still climbing it). As we will see in the stories that follow, shifter tales largely depend on the local flora and fauna, and many times they represent the most dangerous predators of the land.

Shape-shifting is still alive and well in popular media today, although there has been a significant increase in the number and efficiency of the human-to-human variety. Of the animal type wolves are an all-time favorite (with a lot more control over their changes), and plants ... also occur sometimes.

I could have chosen a lot more stories than what is included here, but I did not want to tip the scale too much in the favor of one specific ability. Feel free to browse the sources for more.

# Human Shifting

Human shifting is the ability to change into another person's form. This might include taking on someone else's exact features in order to trick people (or, in the case of King Arthur's father Uther Pendragon: to get the lady), or simply covering up one's true self with a generic new look, the way Greek gods often disguise themselves as old men, beggars, and other inconspicuous individuals. Human shifting, in fact, is often the privilege of the gods, who put on their "mortal guise" to walk among us unnoticed.

*Human shifters:* James Martin (NBC's *Heroes*), Jaquen H'ghar (*Song of Ice and Fire*), Mystique (Marvel)

## Pomona and Vertumnus

*Ability:* Human shape-shifting
*Source of power:* Divine
*Origin:* Ancient Rome
*Teachings:* Perseverance and the importance of shared interests in a relationship. Be yourself.
*Age group:* 10+
*Sources:* Ovid, *Metamorphoses*, Book XIV, 623–771.
*Variants:* Not many variants of this story are known; in fact, this is one of the few tales in Ovid's *Metamorphoses* that does not have Greek origins. It seems like it is thoroughly Roman, and if one takes a closer look at the story's message about work over frolicking, that is not all that surprising in the end.
*Text:* Pomona was a dork before dorks were invented. She was a nymph, every bit as beautiful as all the other nymphs ... and the similarities ended right at this point. For, instead of running around all day dressed in spider webs and sunshine, Pomona preferred something much less graceful and nymph-like:

gardening. She had a garden full of trees that bore fruit so ripe and heavy they made the branches bow down; she grew olives, and grapes, and made her own wine. She had cherries, brought in from a faraway land, and pears, and peaches, and pomegranates full of ruby seeds. Her garden was an island of sweetness and color in the wild hills of Italy, and many mortals were jealous of its treasures. Pomona loved her garden — the way she had never loved anything, or anyone else in the world.

She was, however, still a beautiful young nymph, even though the sun painted freckles on her tan skin, and she always had dirt under her fingernails. She caught the eyes of quite a few young fauns, silens, and mortals, and even greater gods like the unruly Pan and the age-old Silvanus, god of the forest. The creatures of the wild had no taste for gardening, but all of them wanted a piece of the gardener.

Pomona was a young girl, living alone, and she did not feel quite safe. She had heard enough tales about other nymphs who were careless, and suffered for their mistake — and she decided to take some precautions. She built a wall around her garden, a strong, sturdy stone wall with a huge wooden gate, and locked herself in with her beloved trees and vines, and never opened the door for anyone. She was alone, safe, and quite happy.

Now, there was a young god who lived nearby; his name was Vertumnus. He was a foreigner, an Etruscan who decided to move to Roman lands and expand the circle of his worshippers. He was the god of change by profession, responsible for the change of seasons, the change of colors on the leaves, the eternal circle of nature. He was a cheerful young man who loved the countryside, and the first time he took a long walk, the neat little garden caught his eyes. At first he only saw the stone walls and the branches heavy with fruit arching over them; and then he caught a glimpse of Pomona sitting on a tree, eating a peach with the juice dripping down her chin, and Vertumnus was in love for the first time in his eternal life.

But the gates were closed, and Pomona refused to open them for anyone. Vertumnus spent countless hours walking up and down the road in front of the garden in different shapes. He believed that every woman has her weak point; if he could only find the right face, the right shape, the right hair color, maybe she would notice him too. And he was determined to try as many of them as he needed.

One day, he was a reaper, carrying a basket full of barley from the fields, his skin tanned by the scorching Italian sun. The next, he was a farmer, freshly cut hay stuck in his unruly dark hair. Once he was an ox-driver leading his animals down the road, then he returned, carrying a ladder and a basket, ready to pick some fruit — in case *someone* asked him to help. But she didn't. Vertumnus kept trying; he was a fisherman with a rich catch, then a wealthy merchant with a purse full of gold, and then a soldier with bulging muscles and a nice square chin. But no matter how many shapes he took on, how many professions he faked, Pomona did not even throw him a look from behind the walls. Vertumnus, god of eternal change, was running out of ideas.

Then, one late afternoon, an old woman walked up to the garden, and knocked on the gate. Pomona peeked out and saw her, looking tired and pitiful, and opened the gates to let her in. The old woman, leaning on a staff, her head wrapped in a ragged scarf, admired the garden and the fruits, and found herself a spot in the shadows to sit down and rest. Opposite of her, in the middle of the garden, there was an elm tree, tall and grand. Pomona used the tree to support the vines she had been planting, and heavy, sweet grapes hung from all the branches. The old woman pointed at them with her staff and said: "See that, young lady? You should learn from the elm and the vine. If there was no vine, the tree would be fruitless and useless alone; if there was no tree, the vine would be crawling on the ground, bearing no fruit at all."

Strange as that was, Pomona did not answer. The old woman kept talking.

"You have this tree right in the middle of the garden, yet you do not heed its example. You have more suitors than the fair Helen of Troy and Penelope combined, great gods and strong young men among them, and you still do not wish to marry! You are young, Pomona, you should not be alone. Let me tell you a story."

And so she did. She told Pomona the sad tale of Iphis and Anaxarete. The young man Iphis was desperately in love with the beautiful Anaxarete, but she shunned him and mocked him for his passion. Iphis lost his will to live without her, and hanged himself in his sadness. When his funeral procession moved past the house of his beloved, Anaxarete looked out the window to see it; as soon as she saw Iphis dead the coldness of her heart spread out all over her body, and she turned to stone in that spot, as a warning sign from Venus, the goddess of love to all of those who reject her blessings.

Pomona listened to the gloomy story, and she was still not convinced. The old woman shook her head.

"You are wary, my daughter, and I cannot blame you. Many young men would just toy with your heart, and they would not make good husbands. The fauns and silens and wild men out there all just want you for one thing, and you should not take any of them as your companion. They cannot be trusted. But if you would listen to the advice of an old woman who has seen a lot, listen to mine: there is a young man out there, his name is Vertumnus, and *him* you can trust. He is the god of change, and loves everything you love in this garden. He does not give his heart easily; you are his first love, and you will be his last flame as well."

With those last words, the old woman started to change; she stood up, growing taller, cast off the scarf to reveal dark hair, and in a few moments, Vertumnus stood in the middle of the garden, with a smile that was half hope, and half apology.

"I will go if you want," he said.

Pomona looked at him for a long moment, and then she smiled. "Stay."

And from that day on, two people worked in the garden instead of one.

*Comments:* Yes, I am aware that I am breaking the "no divinity" rule.

To my defense, Pomona and Vertumnus are both minor deities with very limited powers in this tale, and as for their behavior, they are quite human. I believe a lot of women and men can relate to their parts in this story, and I also enjoy the fact that this is one of the few mythical love stories that does not end in tragedy.

This story has been with me for a very long time, and was one of the first tales I ever told in English. I fell in love with mythology way before I fell in love with any guy, and I was intrigued by Ovid's colorful stories of shapeshifting men and women (I also love fruit). When I went on to college to study Roman archaeology, I ran into the familiar couple once again, and did some research into the story behind the story.

One major thing that is different in my version from the original is the ending. In Ovid's telling when Vertumnus casts off the disguise of an old woman he is "ready to force" Pomona in case she does not return his feelings. Now, being a female storyteller, and the child of our day and age, I prefer my characters to fall in love rather than rape. Also, I believe that Vertumnus could have broken into the garden any time he wanted to if he was *that* kind of a guy. But he wasn't: he tried to seduce her again and again by changing himself, until he realized talking is the best way to go. So, yes, I changed the ending, and I do not even feel bad about it.

# Animal Shifting

Animal shifting (also known as therianthropy) is the ability to turn into animals. For the sake of this story collection, I selected tales where the ability only pertains to one (or three...) specific animal — turning into multiple animals by choice is classified under multi-shifting.

Animal shifting is one of the most common supernatural abilities in folklore. The closer a culture is to nature, the hazier the line between human and animal, and the easier to cross it.

The most common form of animal shifting is that of turning into large mammals, usually predators. Depending on the culture's natural flora and fauna, these animals can be bears, wolves, lions and other big felines, or aquatic mammals such as seals or dolphins. Birds are also quite common, especially birds of prey: eagles, hawks, and sometimes crows or ravens. Fish feature in quite a few stories, and in the insect kingdom, spiders are by far the most popular.

But let's start with the wolves.

*Some Animal shifters:* Animorphs (*Animorphs*), Beast Boy (DC), Wolfsbane (Marvel)

## Sigmund and Sinfjötli

*Ability:* Skin-changing (wolf)

*Source of power:* Enchanted object (wolf skin)

*Origin:* Medieval Norse (Icelandic)

*Teachings:* Family, bravery, self-sacrifice, making the right choices, the darkness of war.

*Age group:* 12+

*Sources:* Colum, P., and W. Pogány (1920). *The Children of Odin.* New York: Macmillan.

*The Völsunga Saga* (13th century Icelandic).

*Variants:* The original story comes from one source, the *Völsunga Saga.* It has been re-told in books like the one listed under sources. There are countless other tales about people turning into wolves, either by the full moon's curse, by will, or magic items such as a ring or a belt.

*Text:* The winter was cold, bitter, and endless. It was always dark outside, and as people huddled around their fires in the villages, wolves roamed the forest and the land. Not all the wolves had four legs: many of them walked on two, burning, pillaging and robbing as they went. They were free to do so: their freedom came from King Siggeir, and there was no one to stop them.

The king's heart was just as cold as the winter winds — but the queen's heart bled warm blood every time she saw the suffering of her people. She did not marry Siggeir for love. She was forced into the marriage after Siggeir killed her father and threw her ten brothers into the dungeon. Every night, they said, a starving she-wolf would go into their prison and devour one of the brothers, until there was only one left, the youngest, Queen Signy's twin, Sigmund. Finally, the terror was too much to take; the queen bribed the servants to cover Sigmund's face in honey, and as the wolf started licking him, the young warrior bit her tongue out of her mouth, and the wolf bled to death at his feet. Sigmund escaped the prison and the woods swallowed him up. But the queen knew in her heart that he was still alive out there, the last of the noble bloodline of the Völsungs, and that was what kept her hope alive.

The queen had three sons, and although she hated her husband with a passion, she did not hate the children. She decided that she was going to send them out into the woods to find Sigmund, because he was the only one who could teach them to become great warriors, strong enough to one day defeat the king. When her eldest son grew old enough to go out on his own, Queen Signy sent him away. After a long time wandering, the boy finally found Sigmund's cottage in the woods. When Sigmund heard the knock and opened the door, he only needed to take one look at the boy and he knew whose son he was.

"There is a sack of flour, boy," he pointed to the corner. "I am going out to hunt. Bake bread by the time I get back home."

Hours later, when Sigmund returned from the hunt, he found the sack of flour untouched in one corner, and the boy shivering in the other.

"That flour, there is something moving in it!" the boy cried.

"Go home, boy. You are not fit to be a Völsung."

The boy went home, and in time, Signy sent out her second son. The exact same thing happened to this one too: scared of what was hiding in the flour, he was deemed unworthy of becoming a warrior, and Sigmund sent him home.

Now it was time for the youngest son to try his bravery in the woods. His name was Sinfjötli, and there has always been something odd about him; a light in his eyes made him different from his brothers. He set out and found the cottage in the woods; and when Sigmund opened the door, he recognized the light in the boy's sky-blue eyes. As he invited him in, he noticed that Sinfjötli's hands were bleeding.

"What happened to your hands?"

"My gloves were soaked with water and they froze to my hands, so when I took them off the skin came with them," the boy answered.

"Does it not hurt?"

"It hurts."

"Then why are you not crying?"

"A Völsung never cries."

Sigmund smiled, just a bit, and pointed at the sack of flour in the corner. "Make bread by the time I'm home."

When Sigmund returned from the hunt, the smell of freshly baked bread greeted him in the door. "Boy! What did you make that bread from?"

"From the flour in the sack."

"Wasn't there something odd about that flour?"

"Oh yes, there was a poisonous snake in it."

"What did you do with the snake?"

"I baked it in the bread."

Sigmund laughed, and nodded. "I can teach you."

And he did. Day after day, he trained Sinfjötli in the art of fighting, and the boy became a strong young warrior. Sigmund started taking him out on raids, hunting and killing the king's soldiers and keeping the villages safe. Rumors started to spread that someone was standing up to the soldiers; but Sigmund and his nephew were always careful not to give themselves away.

One day as they were walking through the woods, they came across another cottage. As they peered in through the door they saw the shapes of two men lying on the floor, and above them, on the wall, they saw the skins of two wolves hanging down. That was all they needed to see to know exactly what those men were: they were skin-changers. Sigmund and Sinfjötli quietly sneaked into the room and stole the skins. The first time they put them on, a strange transformation happened: the skins tightened around them, their hands turned into paws, their teeth grew into fangs, their hair turned into fur, and they became real wolves, ready to hunt.

And then the real hunt began.

Tales spread like wildfire among the villagers about the two great wolves that were stalking the king's men. They were strong enough on their own to fight, so they often split up and went their own way. Every time they parted, Sigmund warned his nephew to call for him if he had to face more than seven men.

But Sinfjötli was young and proud, and he felt invincible in his wolf skin. He hunted alone, and fought with the strength of a Völsung. One day, Sigmund heard the sound of fighting in the woods. His ears perked up, but he heard no call for help, even though he could tell several men were fighting. He followed the sounds, and soon came across the corpses of the king's soldiers — one, two, three, four, five, six, seven, eight ... eleven corpses, mauled and torn, until finally he found the tracks of Sinfjötli.

The boy had killed too much. The lust for blood was on him, and now he had turned into a real wolf, hunting for the kill wherever he could smell it, and he was going straight for the nearby village, and the people inside. Sigmund chased him, and the villagers hiding in their houses could hear the howl of two wolves as the older one dragged the younger one down into the snow, and then the fight began. They were howling, snapping, snarling and growling as they rolled around and around, biting into each other and tearing out chunks of fur. Blood colored the snow red, until the young wolf's strength ran out, and he lay dying at his uncle's feet.

Sigmund realized what he had done. He ran out into the forest, looking for a way to save his nephew's life. As he searched and wandered, he saw two weasels fighting over a scrap of food in the snow; one weasel bit the other and killed it, but then it ran away and returned with leaves in his mouth, and as soon as he put the leaves on the dead creature, it sprang back to life. Sigmund followed the tracks of the weasel, and found the plant with the magical leaves; he gathered a mouthful of them, and ran back to Sinfjötli as fast as his four legs could carry him. He put the leaves on his wounds, and healed them; and then he peeled off the wolf skin, and carried the boy home to nurse him back to health.

When Sinfjötli was well again, the two warriors built a fire, and burned the wolf skins to ash. I will not tell you how they went on to finally defeat King Siggeir and take revenge for their family, but I will tell you this: they did it without wearing the skin of a wolf.

*Comments:* This story is part of a much longer epic that starts with Sigmund's father and goes on for several generations, including Sigmund's son, Sigurd (who became known as Siegfried of the famous *Niebelungenlied*). In this lineage of heroes, Sigmund and Signy stand shoulder to shoulder, fighting for family, honor, and vengeance.

The truth is, the story gets much darker and more complicated than the version I wrote here. For one, Sinfjötli is actually the son of Sigmund. Signy, seeing that her children from the king are not strong and brave enough, disguises herself with a wise woman's help and sleeps with her twin brother to produce an heir that is a full-blooded Völsung. Sigmund does not find out until much later. For another matter, Signy is quite the cold mother: she orders her brother to kill her children that were not fit to become warriors (and *sews* the gloves to the boy's hands). Later on, when Sigmund and Sinfjötli are sneaking into the castle to kill the king, the two younger children of Signy notice them, so the queen orders them to be murdered too, lest they tell their father. Sigmund refuses to kill children, but Sinfjötli, who apparently still has some instincts left over from the bloodthirsty wolf, carries out the order with no qualms. Incest, infanticide and plain murder follow along the way of this story, just like in many Icelandic sagas. My personal opinion is, use as many of the original ingredients as your stomach can handle. It largely depends on you, and your audiences.

Shape-shifting is an important part of this story in many ways. Apart from the wolf-skins, there is Signy's illusion to seduce her brother (very much like Morgause in Arthurian legends, or Merlin's spell to disguise Uther Pendragon). There is also the fact that the wolf that devours the prisoners and is killed by Sigmund in such a heroic and gory way, was rumored to have been King Siggeir's mother, another shape-shifter.

---

## Boots and the Beasts

*Ability:* Shape-shifting (lion, falcon, ant)
*Source of power:* Natural (helpful animals)

*Origin:* Norway

*Teachings:* Ingenuity.

*Age group:* 6+

*Sources:* Asbjørnsen, P.C. (1908). *Tales from the Fjeld.* London: Gibbings & Co.

Lunge-Larsen, L. (1999). *The Troll with No Heart in His Body, and Other Tales of Trolls from Norway.* Boston: Houghton Mifflin.

Taggart, J.M. (1990). *Enchanted Maidens: Gender Relations in Spanish Folktales of Courtship and Marriage.* Princeton, NJ: Princeton University Press.

*Variants:* This tale belongs to the type AaTh 554, the Grateful Animals, although it is different from many other versions of this type (see comments). Taggart lists a series of examples from Spain.

*Text:* Once upon a time there was a young man named Boots (at least that was what everybody called him). When his old father died, he was left in the world with nothing but a few morsels of food, a piece of torn linen, and a sword. Without having any hope of settling down and starting a life with those, he set out on a journey to find his luck elsewhere.

He walked and he walked, and as he climbed a hill he stumbled upon a dead horse and three creatures fighting over it: a lion, a falcon, and an ant (well, actually, he only saw the lion and the falcon at first, but the ant was very loud in voicing his opinions). He was about to turn around and sneak away before the lion looked up, but he was not fast enough.

"Hey! You!" said the lion. "Come over here and help us settle this. Who should have which part of this prime fresh carcass?"

Boots looked at the dead horse for a moment, thinking, and then drew his sword and divided it between the three animals. The lion got the biggest share, the falcon got the intestines, and the ant got the head.

"There," he smiled, wiping his sword. "The lion is the biggest of you three, so he should have the most meat. The falcon likes the soft parts, so he shall have the intestines. And the ant should have the head, because he likes crawling around in nooks and crannies."

The animals were all very pleased with Boots's judgment.

"We would have never come to a decision without you," they admitted. "What would you ask for in exchange?"

"It is enough that I could help," Boots shrugged, but the animals insisted that he should have three wishes, if not as payment, then as a gift of friendship.

"I could not possibly think of anything worthy of wishing..." Boots mused. The animals looked at each other and tried to think of the greatest gift they could grant to the young man ... and they all decided it would be best if they taught him how to turn himself into a lion, a falcon, and an ant.

Boots was quite happy with their gifts. Putting down the old sword and his bag, he turned himself into a falcon, and soon he figured out how to use his wings to fly. He set out once again, over mountains and forests, and finally a lake so big he could not see the far shore until he was in the middle. He took a short rest on a rock that jutted out of the waves then flew until he reached the main land.

On the main land there happened to be a castle, and in the castle a princess. As falcon–Boots settled down on a branch in the garden and started ruffling his feathers, she looked outside and wished the magnificent bird could be hers. She lured the falcon into her room with food and a kind smile (two things that would always catch a man, even when he is a falcon), and before Boots realized what was happening, he was locked in a cage.

Boots, however, was only a part-time falcon. As soon as the princess went to sleep he turned into an ant, crept out of the cage, turned back into his human form, and sat down on the edge of the bed. The princess woke and screamed bloody murder, and the king came running to her room.

"There is someone here!" the princess yelled, but when the king looked around, there was no other creature in the room but a very sleepy-looking falcon in a cage.

"You were dreaming," he concluded, patting his daughter on the head. "Go back to sleep."

As soon as everything quieted down, and the princess was breathing evenly in her bed, Boots crept out of the cage one again, and sat down next to her. The next moment there was more screaming, and more running, and the king burst into the room, sword in hand, looking for an intruder. The falcon blinked at him from the cage, and there was no mysterious man to be found.

"He was right here! I saw him!" the princess whimpered, but the king told her once again that she was dreaming, and went back to bed.

The third time Boots sat down on the edge of the bed, the princess did not scream.

"You do not need to be afraid of me," he said with a friendly smile. "I did not mean to scare you."

The princess sighed in relief, and told Boots she thought he was the evil troll her father happened to promise her to. The first time she set foot outside her castle the troll was bound to take her. Also, every Thursday the troll sent his messenger, a flying dragon, to take nine fat pigs as tax from the king. The king, who seemed to be in the royal habit of promising his daughter to people, announced that whoever could rid the kingdom of the dragon and the pig tax would have his blessing to marry the princess.

When morning came Boots told the princess to announce him to her father as a champion. The king was very pleased; the kingdom was running out of pigs.

Boots went to the place where the pigs were awaiting their fiery fate, and waited for the dragon to come.

He did not have to wait long. The dragon appeared in the sky, growing fast as it drew closer, and soon turned out to be a nine-headed, fire-and-venom spitting monstrosity that made everyone who dared to look cower in fear. It was about to eat up Boots together with the pigs, but the young man turned himself into a lion ... and the real battle began. The lion was strong, but the dragon was stronger; flames and venom rained down on Boots as he jumped and slashed, tearing head after head off the dragon until only one was left. The dragon roared and snapped at the lion, but Boots was quicker. The dragon collapsed to the ground, leaving its last head in the jaws of the lion.

The kingdom rejoiced in their sudden bounty of swine. Boots was quite happy with the princess as well, and the first chance he had he took her for a walk in the gardens ... forgetting about the prophecy entirely. The princess had not been in the sun for more than an hour when a terrible troll came flying from the sky, snatched her up, and carried her away.

The king, who witnessed all of this, begged Boots to stay behind, since now he was the only person the kingdom could rely on. But Boots was not a champion for nothing. He turned down the king's request, and, shifting into a falcon, flew off after the troll.

He landed on the same rock in the middle of the lake he had visited before, and looked around, searching in vain for the troll and the princess. He turned and shuffled, and suddenly something felt strange under his bird-feet: there was a crack in the smooth rock. Boots turned himself into an ant and crawled in, searching in the darkness until he came to a door. Slipping through the keyhole he found himself in a great underground room where a three-headed troll sat peacefully on a chair, his hair being combed by a princess. She looked so much like the princess Boots knew that she could have been no one else but her older sister. Scurrying across the room ant–Boots slipped under a door at the far end, and found another chamber, with a six-headed troll and a younger princess. Sensing a pattern, he moved on to yet another door, and the keyhole soon revealed the inner chamber where his own beloved princess was tasked with combing the hair on the chief troll's nine ugly heads.

Ant-Boots crept up the princess's leg and stung her, letting her know he was there. The princess (who was smart enough not to slap at the bite) asked the troll if she could step outside the room for a moment. Once she was outside Boots turned back into his human form and told her his plan. All she needed to do was convince the troll to let her visit her father and mother. Once the plan was clear, he turned back into an ant and traveled back to the room on the princess's shoe.

"I wish I could return home," she sighed as she sat back down. "I miss my father and my mother! I am afraid I will never see them again...."

"You never will," agreed the troll, who became quite talkative from getting his hair brushed. "Under the tongue of the ninth head of the dragon that your father's champion killed there is a grain of sand. That one grain could kill me and my brothers in an instant if someone brought it to this rock. Because of that, you will never go home."

That was all Boots needed to hear. He crawled outside through the keyholes and the cracks, flew back to the castle, and then rooted around in the dead dragon's mouths until he found the grain of sand under the tongue of the ninth head. Shifting back into a falcon he carried the grain in his beak, but by this time he was so exhausted that he dropped it ... right onto the sand by the lake.

It took ant–Boots three days to find that particular grain of sand on the lake shore, and it was more exhausting than the fight against the dragon had been. He was about to give up hope when he finally found the one special grain among millions. Picking it up very carefully falcon–Boots flew back to the rock in the lake, and dropped the grain of magic sand down into the crack.

The ground started to shake and the rock split in half. Water shimmered then disappeared, giving way to green meadows. Out of the ground rose a splendid palace, gold and silver, fresh and clean, and completely troll-free. The three princesses had been rescued.

Boots married the youngest princess, and moved into the palace on the lake. Both he and his wife, together with the king, the sisters, and the rest of the kingdom, lived happily ever after.

*Comments:* While in most versions of this folktale type the animals show up when the hero needs help, in this particular story they grant the gift of shape-shifting to Boots himself instead. Using the special abilities that come with the three animal forms — strength, flight, stealth — Boots completes his heroic tasks and sets the princess (and the kingdom) free from the trolls.

In Asbjørnsen's version the villain was translated as "ogre" which is a general term used in many books translated into English around the turn of the century, and it can designate a whole range of different mythical creatures, from Arabian ghouls to Scandinavian trolls. In this case I thought it more authentic to call the villain a troll, and retain the folktale's Norwegian flavor.

---

## The Weretiger

*Ability:* Shape-shifting (tiger)
*Source of power:* Unknown
*Origin:* Malaysia
*Teachings:* Sometimes people label you for what you are even if you do not harm them. Hate, peace, preconceptions, and other important issues.

*Age group:* 12+

*Sources:* Abbott, G., and Khin Thant Han. (2000). *The Folk-Tales of Burma.* Boston: Brill.

Clifford, H. (1897). *In Court and Kampong: Being Tales and Sketches of Native Life in the Malay Peninsula.* London: Grant Richards.

Hutton, J.H. (1921). *Leopard-Men in the Naga Hills.* Report of the Board of Regents of the Smithsonian Institution, pp. 529–540.

Newman, P. (2012). *Tracking the Weretiger: Supernatural Man-Eaters of India, China and Southeast Asia.* Jefferson, NC: McFarland.

*Variants:* There are many different kinds of weretigers in the folklore of Southeast Asia. Some of them are originally tigers who disguise themselves as humans. Others are human sorcerers who learn the art of shape-shifting to satisfy their hunger for blood. There are many fascinating stories about them (see sources). This one has motifs that are common in tales about other were-creatures (such as the wound that marks the shifter, or the changing tracks).

*Text:* Not so long ago, in the valley of the Slim River in Malaysia, there was a tradesman called Haji Ali. He traveled with his two sons, Abdulrahman and Abas, selling sarongs and other pieces of clothing in the villages along the river. They haggled and bargained, and walked long miles in single file with their heavy bundles balanced on their shoulders. One day they came across a village that was so friendly and lovely that even when all their goods had been traded, Haji Ali could not find it in his heart to leave. He bought a compound and planted coconut palms, cut out a piece of land for a rice swamp, and settled down with his sons for a quiet life of farm work.

Haji Ali was wealthy, from his past trading as well as from his farm. It was not long before the local families started offering their daughters as his wife. He was well past the middle of his life, yet, like so many rich men, he had his pick of the best eligible maidens of the neighborhood. His choice fell on a girl named Patimah, who was plump, cheerful and hard-working. The dowry was paid, the wedding was celebrated, and the bride was escorted to her new home in the palm grove.

According to tradition, Haji Ali should have spent the first months of his marriage at his in-laws' house, but they were too poor and he was too wealthy to do that — and Patimah was too eager to move away from home. She was happy to be a rich man's wife and the caretaker of a great household.

Yet, three days later, before dawn, she was found on her father's doorstep, crying, torn, and begging to come home.

At first, her parents thought her new husband had beaten her — but they soon found out that was not the case. The story she told was far, far more terrifying. It took them a long time to coax it out of her between sobs and chattering teeth, but finally the truth emerged, and it went something like this:

The first evening Patimah spent in her new home, she overcooked the rice. She could have expected blows from her husband for her clumsiness, yet he did not beat her (even though the two sons ate their meal with a frown). In fact, he was a very gentle, caring husband, and the young wife was happy in her new home. There was only one strange thing she noticed: Haji Ali disappeared from her side every night after the hour of the evening prayer, and did not return until an hour before dawn. The first two nights she fell asleep and only woke up when he lay down on the sleeping mat beside her. The third night, however, she could not fall asleep. Just before dawn she heard a noise below the house. Unbolting the door that she had barred after the sons had gone to sleep she crept outside.

Malaysian houses are built on poles above the ground, and a ladder leads up to the entrance. The moon was hidden behind clouds and the dawn was still some time away, but there was enough light outside for Patimah to see the head of a large tiger resting on the top of the ladder.

The beast stretched its striped body along the ladder, and placed its giant paws on the edge of the floor. Slowly, as the ripple of wind passes over the surface of calm water, the tiger's features changed and melted, until before the horrified girl's eyes, the face of Haji Ali emerged like the face of a diver coming up for air.

Something in Patimah finally snapped. Leaping over the body of her husband she plunged into the nearby jungle and ran as fast as she could, never looking back. No one ever goes into the jungle alone, especially not at night — yet she did, running for her life, even though her dress was torn and her feet bloody, and she knew that anything that lurked out in the shadows could not be as horrible as the beast waiting for her in her own home.

News traveled fast in the village. Haji Ali never claimed his wife back. All the families whose daughters were not chosen as his wife were not-so-secretly relieved. Everyone avoided Haji Ali and his compound, and people barely ever saw any of the three men after that day.

But the story was not yet over.

Some time later, a fine young water buffalo that belonged to the headman Mat Saleh was savaged and killed by a tiger. Since it was not eaten by the beast, Mat Saleh constructed a trap with a wire and a gun, hoping the tiger would return at night, trigger the trap, and get wounded or killed.

He did not have to wait long. In the middle of the night a shot rang out and a roar echoed across the village. Everyone woke up, but they knew all too well that a wounded tiger is very, *very* dangerous, especially in the dark, so no one opened a door till dawn. By then, everything was quiet. People finished their morning prayers and gathered at the carcass of the buffalo. It was clear from the tracks that a tiger had been there, and a fresh splatter of blood proved that the trap had been successful. Mat Saleh gathered his men armed with guns and spears, and they set out through the jungle.

The wounded tiger was easy to track. It had been dragging one of its hind legs, breaking a wide path in the underbrush, leaving drops of blood behind. The hunters could tell from the signs that the tiger could still be dangerous if cornered, so they kept a sharp eye out as they tracked it farther upriver. The jungle grew thicker before it started to ease away ... and suddenly they found themselves at the bamboo fence of a compound.

They all knew who lived there.

The tracks crossed the fence and ended in a mop of tall *lalang* grass. And while it was clearly the heavy paw of a tiger that left the tracks all the way there ... it was the feet of a human that led from the patch of blood and trampled grass all the way to the house of Haji Ali.

Mat Saleh and his men climbed the ladder and entered the house. In the main room they found the younger son, Abas, preparing betel-nuts.

"We have come to talk to your father," the headman announced.

"My father is lying sick," Abas answered, not even looking up. "You cannot talk to him today."

"Why is there a patch of blood in the *lalang* grass?"

"We slaughtered a goat yesterday."

"Do you have the skin? I want to buy it from you. I am making a new drum."

"It was mangy. We tossed it away."

"What ails your father?"

"He is ill," came the voice of the older brother, Abdulrahman, who was standing in the doorway of the inner room, with a sword in his hand. "And your voice disturbs his rest. You should leave. He cannot see you today."

Mat Saleh was a careful and wise man, and did not want to end the day in bloodshed. He knew all too well that claiming the victim was a sorcerer would not be an excuse in the face of the white man's government. He and his people backed out of the house, and descended the ladder. But as they walked around the compound they noticed something unusual: in a spot right under the inner room of the house there was a pool of red water, seeping down through the cracks of the bamboo floor.

They did not have a chance to examine it any closer and decide if it was blood, or the juice of the betel nuts. The two brothers ushered them off the compound and barred the bamboo fence behind them.

Mat Saleh went to the district officer to report his suspicions. Unfortunately the officer was European, which meant he did not really believe in the "superstitions" of the local people. It took the headman several days to convince him to at least visit Haji Ali's compound and start an investigation.

By that time, it was already too late. Haji Ali and his sons had disappeared, stealing away in the night, and no one had seen them leave. Their crops and fruits were ripening unharvested, and they left most of their possessions behind.

For a long time, the district officer suspected that the locals had killed the tradesmen for their wealth, and covered up the murder with the unlikely tale of the were-tiger. But a few months later, news came that Haji Ali and his sons were alive and well, living in a town a few days' travel away, and they were as quiet and calm and human as they had ever been.

Except Haji Ali was now lame on one of his legs.

*Comments:* This story was written down by Sir Hugh Charles Clifford, a British colonial officer who spent almost twenty years in Malaysia around the turn of the last century. He collected stories, curiosities and information, and published them in books. His writing style is entertaining and eloquent — the original text of this story is a very captivating read. He knew Mat Saleh personally, and claimed that the events described in the tale had only happened a couple of years before his time.

He also makes a very interesting observation about weretigers, werewolves and other were-creatures. Belief in them, he writes, "seeks to account for the extraordinary rapacity of an animal by tracing its origin to a human being." In other words, he thinks the beasts in these tales all around the world are not dangerous because of their animal nature — they are dangerous because they are part human. How is that for thought provoking?

## *Nanaue, the Shark-Man*

*Ability:* Shape-shifting (shark), shark jaws, superhuman strength
*Source of power:* Divine parentage
*Origin:* Hawaii
*Teachings:* Community and family. Your origins do not define you — your actions do.
*Age group:* 12+
*Sources:* Allen, B. (1944). *Legends of Old Hawaii as Told by Tutu to Her Grand-Children.* Honolulu: Tongg Publishing Company.

*The First Annual Report of the Hawaiian Historical Society.* (1893). Honolulu: The Hawaiian Gazette Company.

Nakuina, E.M., and D. Kawaharada (1994). *Nanaue the Shark-Man and Other Hawaiian Shark Stories.* Honolulu: Kalamaku Press.

Thrum, T.G. (1907). *Hawaiian Folk Tales.* Chicago: A.C. McClurg & Co.

Westervelt, W.D. (1915). *Hawaiian Legends of Ghosts and Ghost-Gods.* Boston: Ellis.

*Variants:* See sources for different variants of this tale. For a storyteller's version, listen to Alton Chung's telling on his CD, "Tales from the Lanai: Legends and Stories from Hawaii." There are two main versions I found, one more elaborate (the one my version is based on) and one shorter (included in Westervelt) which lacks the final epic battle and most of King Umi's role in the events.

*Text:* Kamohoalii, the king of the sharks, had an eye for human beauty. Not in the predatory carnivorous fish way either—he strictly forbade all his shark subjects to eat human flesh—but in a much more intimate one: he admired human women. There was one beautiful girl in particular that had caught his eye.

Her name was Kalei. She was slender and graceful, and a very strong swimmer. Even when her friends stayed out of the water on stormy days she would still dive and swim alone, and collect shellfish, which was her favorite delicacy. She lived in Waipio Valley, a lush green place surrounded by steep mountainsides. The Waipio River came down from the heights as a waterfall and ended in an inland pool, clear and deep, then flowed on into another pool that was open to the ocean. All the people in Waipio loved swimming in those two pools—and so did the shark king.

One night he turned himself into the form of a human chief, and went to visit the village. Everyone was charmed by his politeness, and Kalei soon noticed the handsome stranger. A courtship started, and it quickly turned into betrothal, and then marriage.

Kalei was pregnant when Kamohoalii told her that he had to leave. He was the king of the sharks, after all, and he had to return to his own dominion. But before he did, he warned Kalei to keep their child safe and hidden from human eyes, because he was going to bear the mark of the shark. He also warned her never to feed him any flesh. Revealing to her who he really was, he said goodbye and left.

In due time Kalei gave birth to a baby boy. He was strong and healthy, but, just like his father said, there was something strange about him. On his back, between his shoulder blades, there was a thin opening. As the baby grew, the opening grew, and soon it turned into a shark's mouth, full of razor sharp teeth.

Kalei took good care of her child. She made him wear a kapa, a cloak, to cover the mouth on his back, and did not allow him to play or swim with other children. She named him Nanaue. Nobody knew what he really was, except for Kalei and the immediate family.

Every once in a while Kalei took her son to the pools on the Waipio River, and watched from the shore while he dove into the water and turned himself into a shark. She held the kapa on her lap and kept an eye out for people, making sure no one ever saw Nanaue's back uncovered.

Nanaue grew strong and handsome. His grandfather was very proud of him and he secretly hoped that one day the boy would turn into a great and powerful warrior. When Nanaue was old enough to eat in the men's lodge, his grandfather took him there himself, and fed him the best pieces of choice meat.

He should not have.

From the first moment he tasted meat, Nanaue grew hungrier by the day. Soon pork and dog meat were not enough for him. His grandfather grew old and died, and there was no one left to feed the shark boy. He had to turn to another source of fresh meat.

People started to disappear. They would walk down to the sea to swim or fish, and pass Nanaue's house on the way. He was usually working on his mother's taro and potato patch, but he would stop and talk to people, asking them where they were headed. If they said "to the pools" he would warn them to be careful.

"You might get bit or eaten by a shark!" he joked, and they laughed, and went down to the pools, and never came back.

Nanaue never played with the other young men, even though they all admired him for his strength and posture, and invited him to all their pastimes. He grew up to be a fine young warrior — who was also a fearsome, man-eating shark.

One day King Umi ordered all the people to go and pay their dues to him by working on the royal fields. Nanaue was no exception from this order, and he had to join all the other young men. As they worked in the fields, one by one they started taking off their capes and cloaks, until they were all bare-chested except for Nanaue. No matter how hot the day grew — and it grew very hot — he refused to take the kapa off. People joked about it for a while, but they grew more and more curious, and their curiosity soon turned into annoyance. "Does he think he is better than us? He is behaving like royalty!" Finally a few young warriors crept up behind him, and tore off his cloak.

The secret was out.

Nanaue snapped his shark-teeth and mauled several men before they managed to subdue him. News traveled like lightning, and suddenly everything made sense: the kapa, the disappearances, the shark sightings in the pools. King Umi, although he was sad that his best young warrior turned out to be a cannibal, ordered a great fire to be lit to kill Nanaue. His priests told him that a man-shark could only be killed by fire, otherwise his spirit would just jump into a fish-shark and keep terrorizing the fishermen and swimmers.

While the fire was being built up, no one paid attention to Nanaue. Lying on the ground he gathered his strength, turned himself into his shark form, and as the ropes fell off him he rolled into the river. People noticed too late. They ran along the river throwing rocks and spears at the shark, but he was faster. He swam out into the ocean and disappeared.

Because they did not have the shark anymore, people looked for a scape-goat, and found it in Kalei, Nanaue's mother. They dragged her and all her relatives in front of King Umi, asking permission to execute them for raising such a monster. But the king was wiser than that: he knew he could not blame the family for the sins of the child, and he also knew that the king of sharks would disapprove if they murdered his wife and relatives. Instead he ordered a ritual to be held and told the priest to call upon Kamohoalii. The king of sharks manifested himself through a medium, and held a meeting with King Umi.

"I am deeply saddened by the actions of my son," he said. "If he was not my child I would order my own shark soldiers to kill him right away. But he is, so I will allow him to live, if he never comes close to the shores of Hawaii again. If he kills a human, I will judge him for his sins."

King Umi promised to set Kalei and her family free, and a deal was made.

In the meantime, Nanaue swam over to the island of Maui, and because he could not spend all his time as a shark, he became a man once again. He was greeted by the people of Maui; everyone instantly liked the handsome young warrior. After he spent some time on the island the chief offered his own sister to him in marriage. For a while, no one was attacked by a shark.

But happy as he was, Nanaue could not fight his hunger for long. Soon he started hunting again. He got bolder every day until finally he grew careless, and one day a group of fishermen witnessed him as he pushed a girl into the water, jumped after her, turned into a shark, and dragged her down.

Nanaue had to flee again. This time he swam to Molokai where no one knew him, and started a new life. He worked on his field and gave his usual warning to swimmers and fishermen on their way to the sea ... then killed every single one. The shark attacks grew so frequent and deadly that people turned to a shark *kahuna*, a priest, to tell them what to do. No one was safe anymore, not in shallow water, not in inland pools.

The *kahuna* told people to lie in ambush after Nanaue had given one of them his warning, and pull the kapa off his shoulders. Even though they were not sure what that would accomplish, the men obeyed, and grabbed Nanaue on his way to the sea. The kapa was torn off, the shark mouth revealed — everything had fallen into place.

Nanaue fought for his life with the strength of a great shark, snapping and tearing at the men around him. More than once he almost got away, but they always dragged him back from the edge of the water. They started building a fire to put and end to him once and for all. This time, the captors were smarter: they put down nets in the water, blocking the shark's way to freedom.

Still, Nanaue snapped and struggled against the ropes. Finally he managed to roll into the sea, tangling himself with the nets, trying to break free and make his way into the deeper waters. Seeing how wild he was the *kahunas* called upon a local demigod, another child of Kamohoalii, for help. His name was Unauna. He was half god just like the shark-man, but a lot younger, and inexperienced. If it had not been for the ropes and the nets, and the loss of blood from spears and clubs, Nanaue might have gotten the better of him. A mighty struggle started, and it seemed to last forever, and Unauna hooked a rope around a great rock and slowly, inch by inch, dragged his thrashing half-brother onto the shore. The shark was so heavy his body cut a groove into the ground that can still be seen to this very day at a place called Puumano, Shark Hill.

People built up the fire and threw Nanaue on it. But the great shark's body leaked so much water and blood that it put out the fire more than once. Finally Unauna told them to cut the shark up and burn him piece by piece. By the time they were finished they had cut down an entire bamboo grove for firewood.

This is the story of how Nanaue the shark-man perished at the hands of Unauna, and the people of Molokai.

*Comments:* King Umi-a-Liloa was ruler of Hawaii between 1470 and 1525. Waipio Valley is one of the most spectacular places on the island of Hawaii.

Once again (just like in the case of the weretigers) it is suggested that the thirst for human blood is a characteristic of the shape-shifter, not the original animal. The king of sharks himself condemns this behavior and forbids his subjects to eat human flesh. This alone shows a great deal of respect on the Hawaiian people's part toward sharks, seeing them as noble creatures, contrasted with Nanaue's cannibalistic rampage.

In Westervelt's version the people simply beat Nanaue to death in the end. However, as a storyteller I find the final battle between brothers very intriguing, especially because it shows that evil was not in the nature inherited by the king of sharks (and because it is a great scene). Thrum implies in his telling that Nanaue needed to be in contact with water in order to shape-shift, but this indication is completely missing from the other versions.

# Plant Shifting

Plant shifting is the ability to turn into a plant (tree, flower, blade of grass, etc.). Although not as common in folklore as animal shape-shifters, some examples can be found. In Greek mythology, wood nymphs (hamadryads) can often turn into the trees and plants they represent.

This category could be a lot wider if I included people who had been turned into plants, but I have promised before I was not going to do that. I also decided to exclude some Eastern tales where flowers and trees appear in human form. In the folklore of many East Asian cultures plants and even inanimate objects can have spirits that appear in human form. One famous example is the tale of the Willow Wife in which a mortal man marries the female spirit of a willow tree.

*Plant shifters (or as close as we can get in vegetation-related powers):* Klara Prast (Marvel), Poison Ivy (DC), Swamp Thing (DC)

## The Elder Tree Witch

*Ability:* Plant shifting
*Source of power:* Magical
*Origin:* England (North Somerset)
*Teachings:* Family cooperation.
*Age group:* 8+
*Sources:* Briggs, K.M. (1977). *British Folk Tales.* New York: Pantheon.
Keding, D., and A. Douglas (2005). *English Folktales.* Westport, CT: Libraries Unlimited.
Tongue, R. (1965). *Somerset Folklore.* London: Folk-lore Society.
Tongue, R. (1970). *Forgotten Folk Tales of the English Counties.* London: Routledge & K. Paul.
*Variants:* This might be the only version I know of the folktale, but witches shape-shifting into other creatures — cats, owls, etc.— is very common in European folklore.
*Text:* People have long been saying that the elder tree is the witches' tree. Others claim it belongs to the fairies, but witch or fairy, doesn't matter, the point is, elders have magic in them, and one should be very careful about cutting them down. People also used to say that if you cut an elder tree, it bleeds, just like a human being.

Well, our story starts with a farmer who might or might not have heard these tales, but he sure did not pay much attention to them. He lived on his own farm with his wife, his daughter, and his old mother (and not an elder tree around). When he bought the farm, his neighbors told him to be careful about the elders, and he shrugged and did not pay attention (since there was not a single elder around the farm).

One day, the farmer noticed that someone had been milking his cows. They gave less and less milk even though they were well fed and well cared for, and the farmer could not afford to lose all that milk. He was so nervous about it that he got up in the middle of the night and went out to make sure his cows were grazing safely. As he walked across the pasture in the moonlight, he noticed the shadow of a tree by the hedge. A tree that had not been there the day before.

This scared the farmer so much that he drove the cows home to their little pasture, and closed the gate, but he did not have the iron chains to lock it, so he just pushed a big stone against them to keep them shut. With that done, he walked back to his house.

In the morning he told the women of the house what he had seen at night. His wife looked alarmed.

"Did you draw a cross in the mud in front of the gate?" she asked him. He just shook his head.

The daughter went to the window and looked out. As soon as she did, her face turned pale white as a sheet and she ran around shutting the windows.

"It's inside the gate! The tree! It's in the pasture with the cows!"

"Lord save us!" cried the wife. "What kind of a tree is it?"

"It's an elder!"

While all that yelling and running was going on, the old grandmother quietly got up, walked over to the fireplace, and placed a shovel in the embers. Then she sat down, waiting.

The farmer was even more scared than the night before. An elder tree! And it was among his cows, and the cows were all his fortune! He gathered all his courage and turned to his wife. "Go fetch the silver buttons that came off my Sunday coat."

The wife ran and got the coat. Of course, she had mended the buttons long ago (her husband never noticed), but she pulled out her scissors and started snipping all of them off right away, without even asking. The farmer loaded his gun with the silver buttons, while his daughter bolted the doors.

Once the gun was loaded, the farmer took a peek out the window.

"It's right in the middle of the pasture. I can't take a shot from here, I am afraid I'd hit one of the cows." He turned to his wife: "Open the door for me, and close it behind me; but make sure you are right here to open it again if I have to make a run for it."

The wife stood by the door; the farmer took a deep breath, and ran outside. He was trembling all over from fright, but he was determined to save the cows, so he ran as close as he dared, aimed ... and missed.

His hands were shaking so badly he could not hold the gun steady, and the silver button flew past the tree. A terrible, screeching scream was heard, and the tree started moving towards him. The farmer yelled too, in fear, turned on his heels and ran back to the house as fast as he could. His wife opened the door and shut it right behind him, so fast that his coattail was caught in the door!

The wife was screaming, the daughter was screaming, the tree was screaming and rattling on the door. In the midst of all the noise, the grandmother stood up, and she said, calmly, to the daughter: "Open the back door."

The girl did as she was told, but as soon as the door was open she ran back screaming to her mother. But Granny, she just stood in the doorway, staring down the elder tree as it was leaping toward her ... and when it was almost in the doorway, she flung the shovelful of burning embers right into its branches!

There was a terrible scream and the crackling of fire, and the elder tree went up in blue flame, until nothing was left of it but ashes. When it was all done, the grandmother picked up an ashen stick and drew the sign of the cross in the ashes. Only then did they open the doors and the windows again, and went to make sure the cows were safe.

The neighbors came over and rejoiced, because they knew that a witch was dead. But then came days and days of guessing who it had been — at first they thought it must have been Madam Widecombe who changed herself into a tree, but no, she was still around, mean as ever. It wasn't the old witch in the next town over either, the travelers said. Finally news came that Raggy Liddy the next town over had been found burnt to a crisp in her bed — so that is who the elder tree really was.

*Comments:* I do not tell a lot of witch stories, but this one intrigued me because of the tree. The almost modern day horror movie setting of the situation escalating from eerie to surreal, and the actions of the family members who, although afraid, know exactly what to do to fight back, make this story a lot of fun to tell. Grandma is especially a favorite of mine. Someone should turn this into an episode of *Supernatural.*

# Inorganic Shifting

Yet another ability that has become a lot more popular in modern times is inorganic shifting. While animal shifters abound in folklore and legends, turning into inorganic materials is not that easy to come by. Once again I had to rule out many a tale where people get turned into statues of stone or iron, since they don't normally do it voluntarily (go figure). After running quite a few futile rounds of research, I finally settled on a Hungarian folktale that seemed intriguing for many a reason.

*Heroes with similar shifting abilities:* Colossus (Marvel), Dust (Marvel), Emma Frost (Marvel), Iceman (Marvel), Mercury (Marvel, sensing a pattern here)

## Kampó Táltos

*Ability:* Ice body, iron body, superhuman strength, fire-breathing
*Source of power:* Natural (possibly shamanistic)

*Origin:* Hungary

*Teachings:* Don't judge a person by his looks.

*Age group:* 10+

*Sources:* Balint, S. (1978). "A szögedi nemzet. A szegedi nagytáj népélete. Harmadik rész." *A Móra Ferenc Múzeum Évkönyve.*

Ipolyi, A. (1854). *Magyar Mythologia.* Pest: Heckenast Gusztav.

Ipolyi, A., and K. Benedek (2006). *A Tengeri Kisasszony: Ipolyi Arnold kéziratos folklórgyűjteménye egész Magyarországról 1846–1858.* Budapest: Balassi Kiadó.

*Variants:* Ipolyi lists a long and elaborate fairy tale in which Kampó volunteers to retrieve King Mátyás's magic horse from the Turks. He is aided by a court of fairies that grant him various extraordinary abilities. Though the tale is very entertaining, it is also very long and complicated.

*Text:* It happened during the reign of King Mátyás I, more than five hundred years ago. The Hungarian Kingdom was at war with the Ottoman Empire. The sultan sent his armies to expand into Europe, marching across the Balkans toward Hungary and, ultimately, Vienna. King Mátyás needed all the help he could find to protect his kingdom and his people.

There was a man in the king's court known as Kampó. He was a stout, short-legged fellow, not too easy on the eyes, but King Mátyás held him in such high respect that no one dared to make fun of him. In fact, he sat on the king's right at the dining table, which annoyed the queen more and more until she could not hold her tongue anymore.

"Why do I have to share a table with that man every night?" she demanded to know, stomping her gilded slipper. "What can he possibly know or do that makes him worthy of our respect? What does he have that a king doesn't?"

King Mátyás was called wise for a reason: he did not argue with the queen. Instead, he invited Kampó to demonstrate his abilities.

The next day, Kampó came to dinner at the king's court. When he arrived, he stopped on the threshold of the dining hall, opened his mouth until it was wide enough to swallow the door frame, and breathed fire into the room.

The queen fainted.

Before she could have collapsed to the floor, however, Kampó was by her side, lifting her gently into her seat. The queen never questioned his worth again.

Some time later news came from the south that the Turkish army had crossed the border, killing and pillaging. Kampó stood immediately from his seat, and only asked one thing from the younger táltos who brought the news: "Where?"

The town of Szeged was under attack. Kampó rode out with his mighty sword, and as soon as the Turkish army heard he was approaching they started to retreat. He reached the River Tisza at Szőreg, but did not have patience for the ferry. Instead he jumped over the water, landed on the ferry that was halfway across, then took another jump to the other side.

An old woman was standing on the riverbank, watching in quiet amusement.

"Point me to the Turks," Kampó said shortly, and the crone pointed.

"There is one with a body of iron," she added. "If you defeat him, the rest will surrender. He only has one weak spot. The rest of his body is invulnerable."

"So is my body of ice," Kampó shrugged, and marched into battle.

It did not take long before he came face to face with the Turkish warrior with the iron body. They fought for a long time, ice against iron, until finally Kampó stabbed the Turk through his navel, the only vulnerable spot on his body. As their champion collapsed, the rest of the army started to run, and Kampó chased them, slashing with his sword, until they could run no more. Then he raised a white flag himself, not to surrender but to let the Turks know that he was giving them mercy.

When the battle was over, Kampó crossed the river again, and lay down to sleep. While he slept a Turkish soldier crept up on him, cut his head off, and carried it home to the sultan. This is how life ended for Kampó Táltos of the ice body.

*Comments:* Kampó Táltos is quite a mysterious figure in Hungarian folklore. He appears in the southern parts of Hungary around Szeged in various different tales. "Táltos" in Hungarian stands for wise man or seer — it is also the word for shaman.

As for the supernatural powers, the original text glazes over them without commenting. Kampó is merely called "of the ice body" without any explanation, and it is a description that does not occur elsewhere in Hungarian folklore, to my current knowledge. Similarly the Turkish champion is called "of the iron body" and his vulnerable spot is merely implied. It is interesting to note that fire breathing and ice body go together in Kampó's repertoire.

# Multi-Shifting

I use the term multi-shifting for the ability to change shape at will into all the categories mentioned before — human, animal, plant, even inanimate things like flame or stone. This is the most powerful form of shifting since it allows the user an array of abilities depending on the form they take on.

There are at least two famous stories worth mentioning here, even though they did not fit the criteria. One is the Scottish ballad of Tam Lin, in which a man is kidnapped by the fairy queen and his (pregnant) lover can only get him back if she manages to hold on to him while he goes through a series of transformations including lion and snake, and ending as a burning ember. The other example would he Proteus, Greek "Old Man of the Sea," who gives advice to people who manage to keep him in a similar hold. His daughter, Thetis, inherited his shape-shifting ability, and only married Peleus, Achilles's father, after she put him to the test.

The 2nd century Syrian/Greek/Roman writer Lucian of Samosata suggested that these tales could be a metaphor for legendary dancers who could shape and move their bodies to act out the role of many creatures and characters. Not necessarily accurate, but very imaginative.

*Multi-shifting heroes:* Chameleon Boy (DC), Martian Manhunter (DC), Miss Martian (DC), Morph (Marvel), Odo (*Star Trek: Deep Space Nine*), Plastic Man (DC), Sam Merlotte (HBO's *True Blood*, animals and humans only), Skrulls (Marvel)

## Mestra

*Ability:* Multi-shifting
*Source of power:* Divine
*Origin:* Ancient Greece
*Teachings:* Importance of nature, warning against greed.
*Age group:* 12+
*Sources:* Ovid, *Metamorphoses*, Book VIII, 777–884.
*Variants:* Although it is possibly a literary construction, I found a very similar Irish tale about Fionn MacCool in *The Green Hero* by Bernard Evslin.
*Text:* King Erysichthon had no respect for the gods. He was a cruel, bitter man, who burned no incense at the altars, and even though people warned him to change his ways before it was too late, he never listened to anyone.

One day he went too far. He turned his axe against the sacred grove of Demeter, goddess of nature and fertility. In the middle of the grove there was an oak tree, hundreds, maybe thousands of years old; the servants of the king could not bring themselves to cut it down, even under orders. The king, however, was caught up in his greed, and he snatched up an axe himself. As he swung it again and again, the leaves on the tree grew pale, and blood gushed from the trunk, but even then he did not stop until the tree had fallen to the ground.

The Dryads, the tree-nymphs who lived in the grove, brought the news to Demeter, and begged her to punish the king. The goddess was angered, and decided to bring Hunger upon the sinner. But since Demeter and Hunger can never meet, she sent one of her maids, an oread, to the faraway barren land of the Caucasus to bring her orders to Hunger herself. The oread took Demeter's chariot drawn by dragons and flew across the air, until she looked down and found Hunger, digging around for bones in the dirt. She was a terrifying vision, with her pale face, sunken eyes, brittle skin, and mouth green with mold. The oread gave her the message from her mistress and left in a hurry.

Hunger herself obeyed the order with pleasure and went to seek King Erysichthon. She flew into his bedroom as he was asleep, and breathed herself into him, filling up his lungs and his chest and his whole body until he was completely ... empty inside. Then she left, flying back to the lands she came from.

King Erysichthon woke up feeling famished. He called for breakfast at once, but even when he devoured every morsel of it, he was still hungry. He asked for more. And more. The servants and the cooks worked all day and all night, making course after course of the most delicious food, emptying the storage rooms to the last scrap, but no matter how much he ate, King Erysichthon felt hungrier and hungrier with every bite he took. He sent out his servants in a hurry to buy more food, and his famine soon started to burn through his treasure chests, until there was not a morsel of food, not a copper coin left in the palace, and the servants had all run away.

There was only one person left, still looking after the king: his kind-hearted daughter, Mestra. But the king was so hungry, so *famished*, that he did not see her kindness; he only saw her as one more thing to sell for food. He found someone willing to buy his only daughter, the princess, and pay in food instead of gold. Mestra was terrified of the prospect of being sold as a slave, so she ran away, but the buyer, feeling that now she was his possession, followed her, chasing the scared girl all the way down to the beach. Mestra fell to her knees in the sand and, stretching he hands toward the sea, she called for Poseidon. The Lord of the Ocean was quite fond of the girl, since he had been her first lover not long before, and he heard her desperate prayer, and granted her wish.

By the time the buyer got to the beach, there was no princess to be seen. Instead, there was an old fisherman, standing in the water. The merchant asked him if he had seen a young girl running that way, and the fisherman, after some hesitation, pointed him in one direction. As soon as the merchant was out of sight, the fisherman transformed back into Mestra herself, and the girl, with her newfound powers, made her way back home.

When King Erysichthon found out how his daughter freed herself from the buyer, he was too intrigued to be upset. He saw a prospect in her new ability. After that day, he sold her time and time again, every time he got hungry — and he was *always* hungry. Mestra was sold to merchants, princes, sea captains, slave traders and noble families; and every time her price was paid and she was taken away, she would find a moment to change her shape, and return home. Sometimes she changed into a bird, or a mare, or a hind, or an old woman, or any other being, and only return to her true form when she arrived safely back home.

King Erysichthon's hunger was never satisfied. Even if he sold his daughter every single day, he could not eat enough to fill the emptiness inside him. In the end, to ease his suffering, he started gnawing at his own flesh, chewing off finger after finger, tearing limb after limb, until he completely ate himself up, and there was nothing left.

Mestra was finally free from her father's suffering. She lived a long and happy life, and married one of the most intriguing heroes of ancient Hellas: Autolycus, the Lone Wolf. He was a thief by profession, and the son of Hermes. He taught wrestling to none other than Heracles himself, and joined the legendary voyage of Jason and the Argonauts. He was a man every bit as crafty and shifty as Mestra was. They had a daughter whom they named Antikleia; later on, she became the mother of the famous hero Odysseus. With grandparents like that, no wonder Odysseus became famous for his wit and cunning!

*Comments:* This story is not only about superpowers. It is also about a hero, a girl none the less, who uses her gift to overcome the darkness in her past, and achieve happiness on her own. She meets her match in Autolycus, and becomes a part (and the origin) of a much greater legend.

The story also talks about our relationship with nature. The story of chopping down trees and paying no respect to nature until we die of hunger is a very powerful message that has never been truer than in our modern times.

---

## The Mad Pranks of Robin Goodfellow

*Ability:* Multi-shifting
*Source of power:* Fairy
*Origin:* England
*Teachings:* Mischief. Kids love tricksters.
*Age group:* 6+
*Sources: The Merry Pranks of Robin Goodfellow*, a ballad printed in 1628.
Moore, J.S. (1853). *The Pictorial Book of Ancient Ballad Poetry of Great Britain, Historical, Traditional, and Romantic: Together with a Selection of Modern Imitations, and Some Translations.* London: Washbourne & Co.

*Variants:* See the sources above. Puck himself does not need to be introduced. Keep reading.

*Text:* I bet you have heard about a fellow named Puck before. He is a trickster and a troublemaker, and he became quite famous for his role in Shakespeare's *A Midsummer Night's Dream.* With all the pranks and the mischief, he was still responsible and made sure things worked out in the end.

But Puck, as we know him today, has not always been a spirit of the night. No sir. Once upon a time, a long, long time ago, Puck was human, like you and me.... Well, not *quite* human. But close enough. And this is the story of how he became something *else*.

In the old days, hundreds of years ago, fairies used to wander in the night dancing and singing and making mischief; they wiggled through keyholes into houses and played pranks on the people while they slept. If your milk was curdled, if your yarn was tangled, if your cat was frightened in the morning, you knew you had visitors during the night. And, sometimes, even stranger things happened.

There was one house in particular that fairies liked to visit. A beautiful young maiden lived there, so kind, so graceful that the king of the fairies himself, Oberon, noticed her and fell in love. He used to visit her at night, and leave before the morning; she never found out who her secret lover was. Not until her belly started to grow, and she gave birth to a bouncing baby boy, and as soon as the midwife looked at him, she said: "This is a fairy child for sure, it can be nothing else."

Even though the fairy folk are famous for their fleeting fancy, Oberon really took care of his son. He left gifts in and around the cradle and on the doorstep; chores got done around the house at night, and even though she lived alone, the young mother was treated like a lady by the invisible folk. When the day came to baptize the baby, rumors started to spread, and all the town gossips gathered to take a good look. The priest named the boy Robin Goodfellow, hoping the name would be a good omen for the child. He was wrong.

Nobody ever made the mistake of calling young Robin "good." He started playing pranks on people as soon as he could walk, and angered so many of them his mother could not even leave the house without someone complaining to her. She stopped taking Robin to the market, because he pulled faces at people they met, and she got into the habit of answering "Good morning!" with "What has he done now?!"

Well, one day she decided she had had enough, and told Robin if he did not stop all the mischief, she was going to whip him into shape. Robin, who did not like the sound of that at all, turned around, left the house, and never looked back. He lived as a runaway for a few days, until he grew so hungry he could barely walk. A tailor found him by the side of the road, took pity on him, and took him in as an apprentice. But Robin never had a taste for hard work. One night his master went to bed leaving to him to finish a new dress that someone was expecting the next morning. "Just whip the sleeves on, and it will be done," he said, and that was exactly what Robin did: whipped the dress to shreds. In the morning, when the lady came for her dress, there were only strips of cloth; Robin and the tailor's gold were both long gone.

Robin wandered on until one day he came to a forest. He grew tired and lay down to sleep ... and as soon as he closed his eyes, Oberon appeared with all his elves and fairies, and smiled at the young lad. They danced and they sang around him, and their music filled his dreams.

When Robin woke up, the fairies were gone, but he found a scroll, written in golden letters, lying next to him in the grass. It was a message from his father, King Oberon, telling him who he was and that he had been given the power to change his shape into any form that pleased him. "If you prove yourself," wrote the king, "one day, I will bring you home to my kingdom."

Robin wanted to test his new powers right away. First he changed himself into a dog, then a pig, then a horse, then a bird. He enjoyed his newfound freedom to be whatever he wanted to be; but, being the troublemaker he had always been, he instantly started thinking of all the pranks he could pull on people!

He wandered into town, and found out there was a wedding nearby. He had no trouble sneaking in and mingling with all the guests — then, at just the right moment, he changed into a gush of wind, and blew out all the candles. There was a lot of confusion in the sudden darkness, especially because Robin was going around, pinching people, stealing kisses and stepping on toes, and everyone started blaming their neighbor everywhere he went. When the candles were finally lit again, some spiced wine was brought in to calm the nerves ... and suddenly, out of nowhere, a huge bear appeared in the room! People screamed and ran, and did not come back until much later. By then, the bear was gone, and so was most of the wedding feast. The cheerful laughter of a young lad echoed somewhere in the night.

Robin kept wandering, in so many shapes and forms that people he had tricked never caught up with him. Sometimes he was an owl and flew at night; sometimes he was a beggar, or a soldier, or a fox. He would change his voice and call out to travelers, luring them into the woods and making them get lost; other times he turned into flames and wandered the marshes, lighting people's way. He became known by many names: Puck, Hob, Will o' the Wisp, and sometimes even Robin Goodfellow, although, as we already know, he was rarely good. Then again, he was never evil either.

Then, one midsummer night, Robin was out wandering over the hills when he heard the sound of music. He knew he had heard it before; it had been haunting his dreams ever since he found that message from his father, the king. Truly, he had never stopped looking for signs of the fairy folk, so when he heard the songs echoing over the hills, he stopped ... and listened ... and broke into a run over hill and heather until he found the circle of fairies dancing merrily together. Robin joined the circle, and sang, and laughed with his newfound family ... and when the sun came up in the morning, the fairies were gone, and "Puck" had gone with them.

*Comments:* I played Puck in *A Midsummer Night's Dream* in my high school drama group. Best part ever. The little creature full of mischief and sass was a lot of fun to play. He is kind of in-between: definitely not human, but not really fae either, barely controlled by Oberon and Titania, mostly playing his own game, but shifty enough to get away with it.

When I found the ballad that is the source of this story, I was overly excited about it. Not every day do we get to hear an origin story for a trickster, even one as famous as Puck. And what is even more intriguing, Puck is half human, half fae, and has to prove himself through mischief in order to be accepted into the realm of his royal father. And he does a splendid job of it!

I especially like telling this tale to children because they relate to Robin on so many levels. There is not a single child who has not gotten into trouble at some point or another, and parents being angry with them is also a common experience. Every time I tell this story I feel like children, besides enjoying the tale, also become more comfortable with the mischief they get themselves into. Robin, after all, is not a villain; he is just curious, cheerful and as easily distracted as any real life child.

# HONORABLE MENTIONS

The list of superpowers in this book is very far from complete. Supernatural and magical abilities are as diverse and colorful as human imagination. Everyone has a different dream, and everyone has a different idea of what makes someone special.

The fact that a power was not included here does not mean it doesn't exist in folklore or mythology. If one opens up the search criteria just a little bit wider (or burrows deeper into research), a whole new world would open up with them, inviting in deities, magicians, fairies, and supernatural creatures of all kinds. The scope of this book has merely been limited for the sake of holding it all together.

While I was working on this book I kept asking people what were the first ten superpowers that came to their mind when they heard the term. Among the ones that I did not include were psychometry (seeing an object's past by touching it), magnetism, immortality, empathy, time travel, electricity manipulation, light projection, power mimicry, power boosting, power nullification, luck manipulation, and "turning into an enormous green rage monster."

Maybe next time.

# Appendix: Tales by Powers
## *with Page Numbers*

# Further Readings

Some of the books listed below I might not have directly quoted anywhere, but they have nonetheless been very useful to my research on superheroes and superpowers. I also included my sources on folktale types and motifs.

Aarne, A., and S. Thompson (1961). *The Types of the Folktale: A Classification and Bibliography* (2nd revision.). Helsinki: Suomalainen Tiedeakatemia.

Beatty, S., D. Wallace, et al. (2008). *The DC Comics Encyclopedia: The Definitive Guide to the Characters of the DC Universe.* New York: DK Publishing.

Garry, J., and H. El-Shamy (2005). *Archetypes and Motifs in Folklore and Literature: A Handbook.* Armonk, NY: M.E. Sharpe.

Gresh, L.H., and R. Weinberg (2002). *The Science of Superheroes.* Hoboken, NJ: Wiley.

Gresh, L.H., and R. Weinberg (2004). *The Science of Supervillains.* Hoboken, NJ: Wiley.

Irwin, W. (2011). *Superheroes: The Best of Philosophy and Pop Culture.* Hoboken, NJ: Wiley.

Kakalios, J. (2005). *The Physics of Superheroes.* New York: Gotham Books.

Knight, G.L. (2010). *Female Action Heroes: A Guide to Women in Comics, Video Games, Film, and Television.* Santa Barbara, CA: Greenwood.

Marvel (2009). *The Marvel Encyclopedia.* London: DK Publishing.

Misiroglu, G. (2012). *The Superhero Book: The Ultimate Encyclopedia of Comic-Book Icons and Hollywood Heroes.* Detroit: Visible Ink Press.

Thompson, S. (1955). *Motif-Index of Folk-Literature: A Classification of Narrative Elements in Folktales, Ballads, Myths, Fables, Mediaeval Romances, Exempla, Fabliaux, Jest-Books, and Local Legends* (Rev. and enl. ed.). Bloomington: Indiana University Press.

# Index

Milton Keynes UK
Ingram Content Group UK Ltd.
UKHW041828121124
451104UK00011B/44